DEMOCRACY and DISTRUST

DEMOCRACY
and DISTRUST

A Theory of Judicial Review

John Hart Ely

HARVARD UNIVERSITY PRESS
Cambridge, Massachusetts
and London, England
1980

Library of Congress Cataloging in Publication Data

Ely, John Hart, 1938-
    Democracy and distrust.

    Includes bibliographical references and index.
    1.   Judicial-review—United States.   I.   Title.
KF4575.E4   347'.73'12   79-19859
ISBN 0-674-19636-8

For Earl Warren.
You don't need many heroes
if you choose carefully.

Preface

Contemporary constitutional debate is dominated by a false dichotomy. Either, it runs, we must stick close to the thoughts of those who wrote our Constitution's critical phrases and outlaw only those practices they thought they were outlawing, or there is simply no way for courts to review legislation other than by second-guessing the legislature's value choices. Each side has an interest in maintaining the idea that these are the only choices. One racks up rhetorical points by exposing the unacceptability of the only alternative to one's view; if the debate is defined thus, that is quite an easy task — for both sides, and for much the same reason. For neither of the proffered theories — neither that which would grant our appointed judiciary ultimate sovereignty over society's substantive value choices nor that which would refer such choices to the beliefs of people who have been dead for over a century — is ultimately reconcilable with the underlying democratic assumptions of our system. In this book I shall elaborate a third theory of judicial review, one that I shall argue *is* consistent with those underlying assumptions, in fact constructed so as to enlist the courts in helping to make them a reality.

A number of persons and institutions helped me with this book. They include the Ford Program for Basic Research at Harvard Law School, which provided support during 1976-1978, and the Woodrow Wilson International Center for Scholars at the Smithsonian Institution, where I spent the academic year 1978-1979. (The views expressed in the book, of course, are my own and not necessarily those of the Wilson Center.) I am also grateful to the Indiana, Duke, and Maryland Law Schools for inviting me to lecture and thereby inducing me to refine some of the ideas that follow. An early and abbreviated version of Chapters 1 and 2 was presented as the Addison C. Harris Lecture at Indiana University Law School at

Bloomington on February 7, 1978. Chapter 3 was given in earlier form as the Brainerd Currie Lecture at Duke University Law School on March 20, 1978; Chapter 4 as the Morris Ames Soper Lecture at the University of Maryland Law School on April 24, 1978. Five good lawyers and good friends — Nancy Ely, Gerry Gunther, Henry Monaghan, Al Sacks, and Avi Soifer — were very generous with their intellectual and moral support throughout. My research assistants, including Michael Chertoff, David Strauss, and Tom Balliett, were also helpful critics, and my editor, Camille Smith, and my secretary, Betty Lamacchia, not only did their respective jobs superbly but provided support far beyond the call of duty as well.

Contents

DEMOCRACY and DISTRUST

1 The Allure
of Interpretivism

A LONG-STANDING dispute in constitutional theory has gone under different names at different times, but today's terminology seems as helpful as any.* Today we are likely to call the contending sides "interpretivism" and "noninterpretivism"—the former indicating that judges deciding constitutional issues should confine themselves to enforcing norms that are stated or clearly implicit in the written Constitution, the latter the contrary view that courts should go beyond that set of references and enforce norms that cannot be discovered within the four corners of the document.[1]

It would be a mistake to suppose that there is any necessary correlation between an interpretivist approach to constitutional adjudication and political conservatism or even what is commonly called judicial self-restraint. The language and legislative history of our Constitution seldom suggest an intent to invalidate only a small set of historically understood practices. (If that had been the point the practices could simply have been listed.) More often the Constitution proceeds by briefly indicating certain fundamental principles whose specific implications for each age must be determined in contemporary context. What distinguishes interpretivism from its op-

---

*As shall become clear soon enough, "activism" and "self-restraint" are categories that cut across interpretivism and noninterpretivism, virtually at right angles. "Strict constructionism" is a term that certainly might be used to designate something like interpretivism; unfortunately it has been used more often, perhaps most notably in recent years by President Nixon, to signal a quite different thing, a proclivity to reach constitutional judgments that will please political conservatives. The interpretivism-noninterpretivism dichotomy stirs a long-standing debate that pervades all of law, that between "positivism" and "natural law." Interpretivism *is* about the same thing as positivism, and natural law approaches are surely one form of noninterpretivism. But these older terms are just as well omitted here, since they have acquired baggage that can mislead.

1

posite is its insistence that the work of the political branches is to be invalidated only in accord with an inference whose starting point, whose underlying premise, is fairly discoverable in the Constitution. That the complete inference will not be found there — because the situation is not likely to have been foreseen — is generally common ground.[2]

Surely no one who watched the late Justice Hugo Black stand almost alone against the variety of novel threats to freedom of expression the legislators and executives of the 1940s and 1950s were able to devise could suppose that a historically straitjacketed literalism was any part of his constitutional philosophy. Yet Black is recognized, correctly, as the quintessential interpretivist.[3] Some have suggested that this interpretivism came late in Black's life and is best understood as the conservatism of an old man. It is true that it was most dramatic in his dissent in *Griswold v. Connecticut*,[4] decided in 1965 — in which the Court, speaking through Justice Douglas and under no particular constitutional provision, invalidated Connecticut's birth control statute — but it was unmistakably there all along.[5] For example, Black's career-long battle to make the Fourteenth Amendment's Due Process and Privileges or Immunities Clauses mean not that state officials are precluded from acting in any way a majority of the justices regard as uncivilized, but rather that the prohibitions of the Bill of Rights should limit state as well as federal action, was a battle for an interpretivist approach. There were those who wanted those clauses to incorporate the Bill of Rights *and* outlaw other (unlisted) forms of uncivilized behavior as well, but Black made clear from the beginning that he was not among them: the clauses incorporated principles expressed elsewhere in the Constitution *and that was it*.[6] It happened that in enforcing the principles stated in the Constitution, Black was generally in the position of enforcing liberal principles, and there is every reason to suppose that that suited him fine. But when his constitutional philosophy (interpretivism) and his political philosophy (liberalism) diverged, as they did in *Griswold*, "the Judge" went with his constitutional philosophy.

There are signs that interpretivism may be entering a period of comparative popularity.[7] Several reasons seem apparent. The first is that the controversial abortion decision of 1973, *Roe v. Wade*,[8] was the clearest example of noninterpretivist "reasoning" on the part of the Court in four decades: it forced all of us who work in the area to think about which camp we fall into, with the result that a number of persons would today label themselves interpretivists who had not previously given the choice much notice. The second may be that, *Roe* notwithstanding, the Burger Court is by and large a politically conservative Court—or at least more conservative than its predecessor. This means that observers who might earlier have been content to let the justices enforce their own values (or their rendition of society's values) are now somewhat uneasy about doing so and are more likely to pursue an interpretivist line, casting their lot with the values of the framers. Still another reason is more ad hominem: that Justice Black, who died in 1971, is himself enjoying something of a renaissance. His softspoken charm was always apparent to those who were not his rivals, and that he stood where a person had to stand when it counted has been apparent for some time. But there seems to be something new, a growing intellectual appreciation of Hugo Black: people are discovering what to the perceptive was obvious all along, that behind his "backward country fellow" philosophy, with its obviously overstated faith that the language of the Constitution would show the way, there lay a fully elaborated (though surely debatable) theory of the limits of legitimate judicial discretion and the hortatory use of principle. The afterglow of longtime antagonist Felix Frankfurter's pyrotechnics having faded, people can see Black in natural light and are discovering that he was only posing as a rustic.

Interpretivism is no mere passing fad, however; in fact the Court has always, when plausible, tended to talk an interpretivist line.[9] And indeed two significant (and interrelated) comparative attractions of an interpretivist approach can be identified.[10] The first is that it better fits our usual conceptions of what law is and the way it works. In interpreting a statute, in order to decide whether certain private behavior is authorized or whether (and this is closer to the constitutional review situation) it conflicts with another statute, a court obviously will limit itself to a determination of the purposes and prohibitions expressed by or implicit in its language. Were a judge to announce in such a situation that he was not content with those references and intended additionally to enforce, in the name of the statute in question, those fundamental values he believed America had always stood for, we would conclude that he was not doing his job, and might even consider a call to the lunacy commission.[11]

The second comparative attraction of an interpretivist approach, one that is more fundamental, derives from the obvious difficulties its opposite number encounters in trying to reconcile itself with the underlying democratic theory of our government. It is true that the United States is not run town meeting style. (Few towns are either, for that matter.) But most of the important policy decisions are made by our elected representatives (or by people accountable to them).* Judges, at least federal judges — while they obviously are not entirely oblivious to popular opinion — are not elected or reelected. "[N]othing can finally depreciate the central function that is assigned in democratic theory and practice to the electoral process; nor can it be denied that the policy-making power of representative institutions, born of the electoral process, is the distinguishing characteristic of the system. Judicial review works counter to this characteristic."[12] Of course courts make law all the time, and in doing so they may purport to be drawing on the standard sources of the noninterpretivist — society's "fundamental principles" or whatever — but outside the area of constitutional adjudication, they are either filling in gaps the legislature has left in the laws it has passed or, perhaps, taking charge of an entire area the legislature has left to judicial development. There is obviously a critical difference: in nonconstitutional contexts, the court's decisions are subject to overrule or alteration by ordinary statute. The court is standing in for the legislature, and if it has done so in a way the legislature does not approve, it can soon be corrected. When a court invalidates an act of the political branches on constitutional grounds, however, it is overruling their judgment, and normally doing so in a way that is not subject to "correction" by the ordinary lawmaking process.[13] Thus the central function, and it is at the same time the central problem, of judicial review: a body that is not elected or otherwise

---

*See also note 9 to Chapter 3. In general this book is written against the paradigm of judicial review of a decision ultimately traceable to legislative action. To the extent that a case involves the decision of a government employee who is not effectively subject to the direction or control of elected officials, the mantle of "democratic decision" is correspondingly less appropriate, and at least some of this book's arguments are correspondingly attenuated. See generally C. Black, *Structure and Relationship in Constitutional Law* 78, 89-90 (1969). I shall be suggesting in Chapter 5, however, that such failures of accountability are properly regarded as constitutional defects in their own right and thus number among the things courts should be actively engaged in correcting.

politically responsible in any significant way is telling the people's elected representatives that they cannot govern as they'd like. That may be desirable or it may not, depending on the principles on the basis of which it is done. We will want to ask whether anything else is any better, but the usual brand of noninterpretivism, with its appeal to some notion to be found neither in the Constitution nor, obviously, in the judgment of the political branches, seems especially vulnerable to a charge of inconsistency with democratic theory.

This, in America, is a charge that matters. We have as a society from the beginning, and now almost instinctively, accepted the notion that a representative democracy must be our form of government.[14] The very process of adopting the Constitution was designed to be, and in some respects it was, more democratic than any that had preceded it. The Declaration of Independence had not been ratified at all, and the Articles of Confederation had been ratified by the various state legislatures. The Constitution, however, was submitted for ratification to "the people themselves,"[15] actually to "popular ratifying conventions" elected in each state. A few spoilsports pointed out that this was not significantly more "democratic" than submitting the document to the legislatures (since the conventions themselves would necessarily be representative bodies and much the same cast would likely be chosen as the people's representatives).[16] But the symbolism was important nonetheless.[17] The document itself, providing for congressional elections and prescribing a republican form of government for the states, expresses its clear commitment to a system of representative democracy at both the federal and state levels. Indeed, and this surely is remarkable, no other form of government was given more than passing consideration.[18] A passage from *Federalist* 39 — and remember, *The Federalist* was propaganda, designed to assure ratification — testifies eloquently to the day's assumed necessities of effective argument:

> The first question that offers itself is, whether the general form and aspect of the government be strictly republican? It is evident that no other form would be reconcilable with the genius of the people of America; with the fundamental principles of the Revolution; or with that honorable determination which animates every votary of freedom, to rest all our political experiments on the capacity of mankind for self-government. If

the plan of the convention, therefore, be found to depart from the republican character, its advocates must abandon it as no longer defensible.[19]

The passage goes on to indicate that it is "*essential* to such a government that it be derived from the great body of the society, not from an inconsiderable proportion, or a favored class of it . . . "[20] *Federalist* 57 elaborates:

> Who are to be the electors of the federal representatives? Not the rich, more than the poor; not the learned, more than the ignorant; not the haughty heirs of distinguished names, more than the humble sons of obscurity and unpropitious fortune. The electors are to be the great body of the people of the United States. They are to be the same who exercise the right in every State of electing the corresponding branch of the legislature of the State.[21]

It is also instructive that once the Constitution was ratified virtually everyone in America accepted it immediately as the document controlling his destiny.[22] Why should that be? Those who had opposed ratification certainly hadn't agreed to such an arrangement.[23] It's quite remarkable if you think about it, and the explanation has to be that they too accepted the legitimacy of the majority's verdict.[24]

Populist critics like to stress the Constitution's provisions for the election of Senators by the State legislatures and the election of the President by an Electoral College.[25] The former was never all that exciting, given that the legislatures themselves were elected,[26] and in any event the Seventeenth Amendment has provided for the direct election of Senators. Presidential electors also were originally selected by the state legislatures. As early as 1832, however, only South Carolina persisted in this practice, and since 1860 the electors have been directly elected by the people in all states.[27] Although it hasn't happened since 1888, however, the very existence of the Electoral College does create the possibility of a President's being elected without a popular majority or plurality nationwide. There have also existed throughout our history limits on the extent of the franchise and thus on government by majority. But the development again, and again it has been a *constitutional* development, has been continuously, even relentlessly, away from that state of affairs: as Tocqueville observed in 1848, "[o]nce a people begins to interfere with the voting qualification, one can be sure that sooner or later it will abolish it altogether."[28] He was as much a captive of his time's sense of what is natural as anyone, and thus was wrong about where he was—he thought he was seeing the end of the road, that we had achieved "universal suffrage"—but his sense of our manifest destiny was sound. The trend continues to the present day. Excluding the Eighteenth and Twenty-First Amendments—the latter repealed the former—six of our last ten constitutional amendments have been concerned precisely with increasing popular control of our government. And five of those six—the exception being the aforementioned Seventeenth—have extended the franchise to persons who had previously been denied it.

Our constitutional development over the past century has therefore substantially strengthened the original commitment to control by a majority of the governed. Neither has there existed among theorists or among Americans generally any serious challenge to the general notion of majoritarian control. "[R]ule by an aristocracy, even in modern dress, is not what Americans have ever wanted."[29] Moral absolutists and moral relativists alike have embraced and defended democracy on their own terms—the former on the ground that it is a tenet of natural law, the latter as the most natural institutional reaction to the realization that there is no moral certainty. Indeed, much of the history of the struggle between the two schools has been marked precisely by charges that the other side's philosophy is undemocratic.[30] Thus the recurring embarrassment of the noninterpretivists: majoritarian democracy is, they know, the core of our entire system, and they hear in the charge that there is in their philosophy a fundamental inconsistency therewith something they are not sure they can deny.

All this belabors the obvious part: whatever the explanation, and granting the qualifications, rule in accord with the consent of a majority of those governed is the core of the American governmental system. Just as obviously, however, that cannot be the whole story, since a majority with untrammeled power to set governmental policy is in a position to deal itself benefits at the expense of the remaining minority even when there is no relevant difference between the two groups. This too has been understood from the beginning, and indeed the Constitution contains several sorts of devices, which I shall be looking at in some detail later, to combat it. The tricky task has been and remains that of devising a way or ways of protecting minorities from majority tyranny that is not a flagrant contradiction of the principle of majority rule: in law as in logical theory, anything can be inferred from a contradiction, and it will not do simply to say "the majority rules but the majority does not rule." The problem for a noninterpretivist approach has been convincingly to distinguish itself from just this sort of bald contradiction. There have been attempts to do so, and I shall look at them carefully in Chapter 3, but they have generally been halting and apologetic, with no one quite willing to accept anyone else's account of why democratic principles are not offended and indeed with the same commentator often hopping from one account to another. An untrammeled majority is indeed a dangerous thing, but it will require a heroic inference to get from that realization to the conclusion that the enforcement by unelected officials of an "unwritten constitution" is an appropriate response in a democratic republic.

Justice Black and the interpretivist school have an inference, one that seems to find acceptance with friend and foe alike. Of course, they would answer, the majority can tyrannize the minority, and that is precisely the reason that in the Bill of Rights and elsewhere the Constitution designates certain rights for protection. Of course side constraints on majority rule are necessary, but as the framers wisely decided, it is saner and safer to set them down in advance of particular controversies than to develop them as we go along, in the context of the particular political problem and its accompanying passion and paranoia. It is also, the argument continues, more democratic, since the side constraints the interpretivist would enforce have been imposed by the people themselves. The noninterpretivist would have politically unaccountable judges select and define the values to be placed beyond majority control, but the interpretivist takes his values from the Constitution, which means, since the Constitution itself was submitted for and received popular ratification, that they ultimately come from the people. Thus the judges do not check the people, the Constitution does, which means the people are ultimately checking themselves.

This argument's lineage stretches back to Hamilton's *Federalist* 78 and Chief Justice Marshall's opinion in *Marbury v. Madison.* And it seems to enjoy virtually universal contemporary acceptance —not simply by those whose views display an interpretivist cast,[31] but also, grudgingly, by interpretivism's most explicit critics. Thus Professor Thomas Grey, an articulate spokesman for a noninterpretivist approach, has written:

> The truth is that the view of constitutional adjudication [of] Mr. Justice Black is one of great power and compelling simplicity . . . [Its] chief virtue . . . is that it supports judicial review while answering the charge that the practice is undemocratic. Under the pure interpretive model . . . when a court strikes down a popular statute or practice as unconstitutional, it may also reply to the resulting public outcry: "We didn't do it—you did." The people have chosen the principle that the statute or practice violated, have designated it as fundamental, and have written it down in the text of the Constitution for the judges to interpret and apply.[32]

2 The Impossibility of a Clause-Bound Interpretivism

O UR legal culture is right in finding the general idea of interpretivism alluring, but some crucial reservations and refinements are necessary. In the first place, hoary lineage and virtually universal acceptance notwithstanding, the argument that closed Chapter 1 is largely a fake. Given what it takes to amend the Constitution, it is likely that a recent amendment will represent, if not necessarily a consensus, at least the sentiment of a contemporary majority.[1] The amendments most frequently in issue in court, however — to the extent that they ever represented the "voice of the people" — represent the voice of people who have been dead for a century or two.[2] There were those who worried about this even at the beginning. Noah Webster opined that "the very attempt to make perpetual constitutions, is the assumption of a right to control the opinions of future generations; and to legislate for those over whom we have as little authority as we have over a nation in Asia."[3] And Jefferson wrote to Madison " 'that the earth belongs in usufruct to the living'; that the dead have neither powers nor rights over it." His suggestion was that the Constitution expire naturally every nineteen years.[4] Madison and others objected that this would be unworkable and undesirable.[5] (Apparently Jefferson was convinced, since he was President nineteen years into the Republic and didn't suggest the convening of a convention under Article V.) In fact we chose quite the opposite course, ordinarily requiring the concurrence of two-thirds of both Houses of Congress and ratification by the legislatures of three-quarters of the states to get rid of a constitutional provision or to add a new one. I am certainly not saying this is a bad thing, but it does fatally undercut the idea that in applying the Constitution — even the written Constitution of the interpretivist — judges are simply applying the people's will. Incompatibility with democratic theory is a problem that seems to confront interpretivist and non-interpretivist alike.[6]

Interpretivism does seem to retain the substantial virtue of fitting better our ordinary notion of how law works: if your job is to enforce the Constitution then the Constitution is what you should be enforcing, not whatever may happen to strike you as a good idea at the time. Thus stated, the conclusion possesses the unassailability of a truism, and if acceptance of *that* were all it took to make someone an interpretivist, no sane person could be anything else. But the debate over interpretivism is not an argument about the truth of a tautology, for interpretivism involves a further claim, that "enforcing the Constitution" necessarily means proceeding from premises that are explicit or clearly implicit in the document itself.

At this point it is helpful to clarify the concept in a way the literature to date has not, in particular to distinguish two possible versions of interpretivism. One might admit that a number of constitutional phrases cannot intelligibly be given content solely on the basis of their language and surrounding legislative history, indeed that certain of them seem on their face to call for an injection of content from some source beyond the provision, but hold nonetheless that the theory one employs to supply that content should be derived from the general themes of the entire constitutional document and not from some source entirely beyond its four corners. It might even be hoped that this broad form of interpretivism is capable of avoiding the pitfalls of a narrower (or "clause-bound") interpretivism and at the same time preserving those comparative advantages of an interpretivist approach that we canvassed in Chapter 1. In fact, two chapters hence I shall be arriving at much that position and making much that claim. (Whether the view there recommended is properly regarded as a form of interpretivism or instead is more comfortably described as sitting somewhere between an interpretivist and a non-interpretivist approach is a question that seems neither answerable nor important—though the question whether it can in fact avoid a narrower interpretivism's pitfalls without sacrificing its strengths is both.) That position, however, will take some time to develop, and it is not what is generally recommended under the interpretivist flag.[7] The suggestion instead is usually that the various provisions of the Constitution be approached essentially as self-contained units and interpreted on the basis of their language, with whatever interpretive help the legislative history can provide, without significant injection of content from outside the provision. We shall see, however, that this standard form of interpretivism runs into trouble — trouble precisely on its own terms, and so serious as to be dispositive. For the constitutional document itself, the interpretivist's Bible, contains several provisions whose invitation to look beyond their four corners — whose invitation, if you will, to become at least to that extent a noninterpretivist — cannot be construed away.

Constitutional provisions exist on a spectrum ranging from the relatively specific to the extremely open-textured. At one extreme — for example the requirement that the President "have attained to the Age of thirty five years" — the language is so clear that a conscious reference to purpose seems unnecessary. Other provisions, such as the one requiring that the President be a "natural born Citizen," may need a reference to historical usage so as to exclude certain alternative constructions — conceivably if improbably here, a requirement of legitimacy (or illegitimacy!) or non-Caesarian birth[8] — but once that "dictionary function" is served, the provision becomes relatively easy to apply. Others, such as the First Amendment's prohibition of congressional laws "abridging the freedom of speech," seem to need more. For one thing, a phrase as terse as the others I have mentioned is here expected to govern a broader and more important range of problems. For another, and this may have something to do with the first, we somehow sense that a line of growth was intended, that the language was not intended to be restricted to its 1791 meaning. This realization would not faze Justice Black or most other interpretivists: the job of the person interpreting the provision, they would respond, is to identify the *sorts of evils* against which the provision was directed and to move against their contemporary counterparts. Obviously this will be difficult, but it will remain interpretivism — a determination of "the present scope and meaning of a decision that the nation, at an earlier time, articulated and enacted into the constitutional text."[9]

Still other provisions, such as the Eighth Amendment's prohibition of "cruel and unusual punishments," seem even more insistently to call for a reference to sources beyond the document itself and a "framers' dictionary." It is possible to construe this prohibition as covering only those punishments that would have been regarded as "cruel and unusual" in 1791, but that construction seems untrue to the open-ended quality of the language. The interpretivist can respond as he did to the First Amendment, that even though it is true that the clause shouldn't be restricted to its 1791 meaning, it should be restricted to the general categories of evils at which the provision was aimed. If you pursue this mode of "interpretation" with regard to the Eighth Amendment, however—and the First Amendment case will come down to much the same thing—you'll soon find yourself, at worst, begging a lot of questions or, at best, attributing to the framers a theory that may be *consistent* with what they said but is hardly discoverable in their discussions or their dictionaries. But even admitting this, the disaster for the interpretivist remains less than complete. The Cruel and Unusual Punishment Clause does invite the person interpreting it to freelance to a degree, but the freelancing is bounded. The subject is punishments, not the entire range of government action, and even in that limited area the delegation to the interpreter is not entirely unguided: only those punishments that are in some way serious ("cruel") and susceptible to sporadic imposition ("unusual") are to be disallowed.

. The Eighth Amendment does not mark the end of the spectrum, however. The Fourteenth Amendment—and I shall argue later that the Ninth Amendment is similar—contains provisions that are difficult to read responsibly as anything other than quite broad invitations to import into the constitutional decision process considerations that will not be found in the language of the amendment or the debates that led up to it.

Due Process

The provision most often cited in this connection is the Fourteenth Amendment's Due Process Clause, which provides that no state shall "deprive any person of life, liberty, or property, without due process of law." This is the clause to which the Court has tended to refer to "support" its sporadic ventures into across-the-board substantive review of legislative action. Its frequent invalidations of various sorts of worker protection provisions during the first third of this century cited the Due Process Clause as the basis of the Court's review authority. These cases are conventionally referred to under the head of *Lochner v. New York*,[10] one of the earlier ones, and are now universally acknowledged to have been constitutionally improper—for obvious reasons by interpretivists, for somewhat less obvious ones by noninterpretivists. The Court's 1973 invalidation of the antiabortion laws of all fifty states in *Roe v. Wade*[11] also relied on this clause. This "substantive due process" notion is widely accepted by commentators. For example Archibald Cox, who rejects *Roe* on other grounds, is not troubled by the interpretivist critique that nothing in the Constitution seems to address itself even remotely to the question of abortion. "I find sufficient connection in the Due Process Clause . . . The Court's persistent resort to notions of substantive due process for almost a century attests the strength of our natural law inheritance in constitutional adjudication, and I think it unwise as well as hopeless to resist it."[12]

In fact this interpretation of the clause — as incorporating a general mandate to review the substantive merits of legislative and other governmental action — not only was not inevitable, it was probably wrong. The Fourteenth Amendment's Due Process Clause was taken from the identical provision, save that the earlier one applied to the federal government, of the Fifth Amendment. There is general agreement that the earlier clause had been understood at the time of its inclusion to refer only to lawful *procedures*.[13] What recorded comment there was at the time of replication in the Fourteenth Amendment is devoid of any reference that gives the provision more than a procedural connotation.[14] So far it all sounds quite straightforward, and more than a few commentators have concluded that it is crystal clear that the framers of the Fourteenth Amendment intended their Due Process Clause to reach only procedural questions. Thus Professor Stanley Morrison, in the course of what is otherwise a strident attack on Justice Black's views on the Fourteenth Amendment, agrees with him on one thing: "When he thus seeks to abolish substantive due process, he is on solid ground historically. If the clause is to be interpreted in accordance with the meaning it had to the framers and others in 1868, the doctrine cannot be justified. It is . . . a later excrescence derived from natural-law sources."[15]

Things are seldom so simple, however, particularly where the intent of the framers of the Fourteenth Amendment is concerned. Despite the procedural intendment of the original Due Process Clause, a couple of pre-Civil War decisions had construed the concept more broadly, as precluding certain substantive outcomes. One was *Wynehamer v. People* (1856), in which the New York Court of Appeals invalidated a prohibition law under a state due process guarantee identical in wording to that of the Fifth Amendment.[16] Probably more notorious was *Dred Scott v. Sandford*, decided a year later, in which the Supreme Court voided the Missouri Compromise, Chief Justice Taney delivering an "Opinion of the Court" (in whose theory only two of his brethren actually seem to have concurred) indicating in a passing reference that slaveholders had been denied due process.[17] I am by no means suggesting that with these decisions the path of the law had been altered, that by the time of the Fourteenth Amendment due process had come generally to be understood as possessing a substantive component. Quite the contrary: *Wynehamer* and the *Dred Scott* reference were aberrations, neither precedented nor destined to become precedents themselves. (Other courts on which they were urged were quite acid in the judgment that they had misused the constitutional language by giving it a substantive reading.[18]) I *am* suggesting that given these decisions—of at least one of which the framers of the Fourteenth Amendment were certainly well aware[19]—one cannot absolutely exclude the possibility that some of them, had the question been put, would have agreed that the Due Process Clause they were including could be given an occasional substantive interpretation.[20]

To put the question thus, however, is to lose the forest in the trees. It would be a mistake—albeit an understandable one in light of the excesses one witnesses at the other extreme—to dismiss "the intent of the framers" as beside any relevant point. Something that wasn't ratified can't be part of our Constitution, and sometimes in order to know what was ratified we need to know what was intended. (Unless we know whether "natural born" meant born to American parents on the one hand or born to married parents on the other, we don't know what the ratifiers thought they were ratifying and thus what we should recognize as the constitutional command.) Neither am I endorsing for an instant the nihilist view that it is impossible ever responsibly to infer from a past act and its surrounding circumstances the intentions of those who performed it.[21] To frame the issue thus, however, is to bring to the fore what seems invariably to get lost in excursions into the intent of the framers, namely that *the most important datum bearing on what was intended is the constitutional language itself*. This is especially true where the legislative history is in unusual disarray—as is certainly the case with the Fourteenth Amendment[22] — but the validity of the point extends further. In the first place, and this is also true of statutes and other group products, not everyone will feel called upon to place in the "legislative history" his precise understanding, assuming he has one, of the meaning of the provision for which he is voting or to rise to correct every interpretation that does not agree with his. One of the reasons the debate culminates in a vote on an authoritative text is to generate a record of just what there was sufficient agreement on to gain majority consent. Beyond that, however, the constitutional situation is special in a way that makes poring over the statements of members of Congress in an effort to amend or qualify the constitutional language doubly ill-advised. Congress's role in the process of constitutional amendment is solely, to use the Constitution's word, one of "proposing" provisions to the states: to become law such a provision must be ratified by three-quarters of the state legislatures. Now obviously there is no principled basis on which the intent of those voting to ratify can be counted less crucial in determining the "true meaning" of a constitutional provision than the intent of those in Congress who proposed it. That gets to include so many different people in so many different circumstances, however, that one cannot hope to gather a reliable picture of their intentions from any perusal of the legislative history. To complicate matters further, many of the records of the Fourteenth Amendment's ratification debates have not survived.[23] Thus the only reliable evidence of what "the ratifiers" thought they were ratifying is the language of the provision they approved. The debates (or other contemporary sources) can serve the "dictionary function" of resolving ambiguities, as in the natural born citizen case, but that function fulfilled, the critical record of what was meant to be proposed and ratified is what was proposed and ratified.

> Every member of [a constitutional] convention acts upon such motives and reasons as influence him personally, and the motions and debates do not necessarily indicate the purpose of a majority of a convention in adopting a particular clause . . . And even if we were certain we had attained to the meaning of the convention, it is by no means to be allowed a controlling force, especially if that meaning appears not to be the one which the words would most naturally and obviously convey. For as the constitution does not derive its force from the con-

vention which framed, but from the people who ratified it, the intent to be arrived at is that of the people, and it is not to be supposed that they have looked for any dark or abstruse meaning in the words employed, but rather that they have accepted them in the sense most obvious to the common understanding, and ratified the instrument in the belief that that was the sense designed to be conveyed. These proceedings therefore are less conclusive of the proper construction of the instrument than are legislative proceedings of the proper construction of a statute; since in the latter case it is the intent of the legislature we seek, while in the former we are endeavoring to arrive at the intent of the people through the discussions and deliberations of their representatives.[24]

These words were written, by Thomas Cooley, over one hundred years ago, but as today's self-consciously "historical" discussions of the Fourteenth Amendment continue to illustrate, their lesson has yet to be learned.[25]

Let us then turn, surely we are long overdue, to the language of the Due Process Clause. It *is* a bit embarrassing to suggest that a text is informative "when so many, for so long, have found it to be only evocative,"[26] but there is simply no avoiding the fact that the word that follows "due" is "process." No evidence exists that "process" meant something different a century ago from what it does now — in fact as I've indicated the historical record runs somewhat the other way — and it should take more than occasional aberrational use to establish that those who ratified the Fourteenth Amendment had an eccentric definition in mind.[27] Familiarity breeds inattention, and we apparently need periodic reminding that "substantive due process" is a contradiction in terms — sort of like "green pastel redness."*

One might assume that this doesn't matter, that it is revisionism for the sheer hell of it, since I've advertised that the Fourteenth Amendment *does* contain provisions — notably the Privileges or Immunities Clause, which I shall consider presently — that contain the sort of invitation to substantive oversight that the Due Process Clause turns out to lack. Why should we care whether such oversight is called "substantive due process" or something else? The question

---

*By the same token, "procedural due process" is redundant.

is a fair one, but it turns out it may matter, because of the negative feedback effect the notion of substantive due process seems to be having on the proper function of the Due Process Clause, that of guaranteeing fair procedures. Until recently, the general outlines of the law of procedural due process were pretty clear and uncontroversial. The phrase "life, liberty or property" was read as a unit and given an open-ended, functional interpretation,[28] which meant that the government couldn't seriously hurt you without due process of law. What process was "due" varied, naturally enough, with context, in particular with how seriously you were being hurt and what procedures would be useful and feasible under the circumstances. But if you were seriously hurt by the state you were entitled to due process.[29] Over the past few years, however, the Court has changed all that, holding that henceforth, before it can be determined that you are entitled to "due process" at all, and thus necessarily before it can be decided what process is "due," you must show that what you have been deprived of amounts to a "liberty interest" or perhaps a "property interest."[30] What has ensued has been a disaster, in both practical and theoretical terms. Not only has the number of occasions on which one is entitled to any procedural protection at all been steadily constricted, but the Court has made itself look quite silly in the process—drawing distinctions it is flattering to call attenuated[31] and engaging in ill-disguised premature judgments on the merits of the case before it. (It turns out, you see, that whether it's a property interest is a function of whether you're entitled to it, which means the Court has to decide whether you're entitled to it before it can decide whether you get a hearing on the question whether you're entitled to it.[32]) The line of decisions has been subjected to widespread scholarly condemnation, which suggests that sometime within the next thirty years we may be rid of it.

It is interesting to speculate on how it got started, though. As I indicated, the law of procedural due process was not in serious disarray, and the proposition that the government should be able seriously to hurt you without due process of law is hardly one that cries out for affirmation.[33] Part of the explanation may lie in the recent resurrection of substantive due process. So long as *Lochner* lay in disrepute, and substantive due process was therefore as good as dead —that is, nonexistent or reduced to an essentially meaningless requirement that the government behave "rationally"—there was little risk in the premise that any serious governmental hurt should proceed by due process of law. That just meant people were typically entitled to fair procedures. But once "due process" is reinvested with serious *substantive* content, things get pretty scary and judges will naturally begin to look for ways to narrow the scope of their authority. The reaction is one that might have suggested that the error was in resurrecting substantive due process, but instead it seems to have meant that due process, properly so called, has been constricted.

Even if the Due Process Clause were restricted to its proper role of guaranteeing fair procedures, that would not make it unimportant. For even if it lacks authority to second-guess the substantive policy being pursued, the Court can still render the implementation of that policy difficult by making the procedural requirements comparatively stringent. What's more, its judgment here is also somewhat untethered: asking what process is due will get the Court into some questions to which the Constitution does not begin to provide answers. This bothered Justice Black, perhaps most conspicuously in his 1970 dissent in *In re Winship*, where he refused to go along with the majority's holding that the Constitution required proof "beyond a reasonable doubt" in state criminal cases. The reasonable doubt standard does not appear anywhere in the Bill of Rights, so Justice Black, pursuing his "incorporation" theory, refused to read it into the Fourteenth Amendment.

> The Bill of Rights, which in my view is made fully applicable to the States by the Fourteenth Amendment . . . does by express language provide for, among other things, a right to counsel in criminal trials, a right to indictment, and the right of a defendant to be informed of the nature of the charges against him. And in two places the Constitution provides for trial by jury, but nowhere in that document is there any statement that conviction of crime requires proof of guilt beyond a reasonable doubt. The Constitution thus goes into some detail to spell out what kind of trial a defendant charged with crime should have, and I believe that Court has no power to add to or subtract from the procedures set forth by the Founders. I realize that it is far easier to substitute individual judges' ideas of "fairness" for the fairness prescribed by the Constitution, but I shall not at any time surrender my belief that that document itself should be our guide, not our own concept of what is fair, de-

cent, and right . . . As I have said time and time again, I prefer to put my faith in the words of the written Constitution itself rather than to rely on the shifting, day-to-day standards of fairness of individual judges.[34]

Indeed he had said it "time and time again," and it is a valuable speech, but it rings less true in a procedural context. It is true that in deciding what process is due the Court will have to take into account various costs, principally in money and time, that the Constitution will not help us assess. But that is hardly unique to due process. And the questions that are relevant here — how seriously the complainant is being hurt and how much it will cost to give him a more effective hearing — are importantly different from the question the Court makes relevant in "substantive due process" decisions like *Lochner* and *Roe*, namely how desirable or important the substantive policy the legislature has decided to follow is. Moreover, and here the parallel to the Cruel and Unusual Punishment Clause is extended, the decisions here are made in limited compass. The question is what procedures are required to treat the complainant this way, not whether the complainant can be treated this way at all: it's an important and difficult question, but a more limited one. Finally, what procedures are needed fairly to make what decisions are the sorts of questions lawyers and judges are good at. (Observe a lawyer on a committee with nonlawyers and see what role he or she ends up playing.) Thus the delegation, though assuredly it is that, is a limited and not terribly frightening one.

It is no surprise, therefore, that even Justice Black was moved to exercise it from time to time, holding that convictions by biased tribunals, under vague statutes, or based on evidence known to be false violate due process, even though none of those defects is mentioned anywhere in the Constitution. He even once joined a dissenting opinion arguing that due process requires a reasonable doubt standard![35] Instead of carrying his speech on subjectivity, so convincing as to "substantive due process," over to the area of due process properly so called, he would have done well to stick with the earlier inclination he expressed in a note to Justice Murphy in 1947: "I have not attempted to tie procedural due process exclusively to the Bill of Rights. In fact there are other constitutional prohibitions relating to procedure which I think due process requires to be observed."[36]

Privileges or Immunities

The Fourteenth Amendment's Privileges or Immunities Clause—
"No State shall make or enforce any law which shall abridge the
privileges or immunities of citizens of the United States"—seems on
its face to convey the sort of substantive review authority that has
erroneously been attributed to the Due Process Clause. Yet although
it was probably the clause from which the framers of the Fourteenth
Amendment expected most, it has to all intents and purposes been
dead for a hundred years. In the *Slaughter-House Cases*,[37] decided
in 1873, a majority of the Court, or at least this is the received reading,[38] limited the clause to those rights that are otherwise guaranteed by the Constitution or clearly implicit in the citizen's relation to
the federal government. But as Justice Field observed in dissent, and
it is not really possible to deny: "If this inhibition . . . only refers, as
held by the majority of the court in their opinion, to such privileges
and immunities as were before its adoption specially designated in
the Constitution or necessarily implied as belonging to citizens of the
United States, it was a vain and idle enactment, which accomplished nothing, and most unnecessarily excited Congress and the
people on its passage."[39] Needless to say, there is not a bit of legislative history that supports the view that the Privileges or Immunities
Clause was intended to be meaningless. Yet the *Slaughter-House*
interpretation persists to the present day.

    Slaughter-House was a strange case to form the occasion for the
Supreme Court's first interpretation of the Reconstruction Amendments. It involved a challenge brought by white plaintiffs assailing
as violative of every provision of the Thirteenth and Fourteenth
Amendments a butchers' monopoly established by Louisiana's Reconstruction government, and the distorting effect of the situation is
obvious. The complaining would-be butchers were forced to make
extravagant claims about the amendments, since nothing else would
serve them. Thus Justice Miller "and his four assenting Brothers saw
only two alternatives: to restrict the Privileges or Immunities Clause
to nearly nothing, or to interpret it as the self-executing source of a
full panoply of legal rights (including business freedoms) to be enforced by the Court. The Court split five to four on this choice. No
one spoke for a third view, probably for the understandable (if
inadequate) reason that neither of the opposing sets of litigants

would have been aided by it . . ."[40] Later Courts, correctly diagnosing a case of overreaction, have backed away, with a vengeance, from *Slaughter-House*'s comparably narrow interpretation of the Equal Protection Clause. Yet the Court hasn't moved an inch on Privileges or Immunities.[41]

The reason has to be that the invitation extended by the language of the clause is frightening,[42] so the question is in order whether there is any apparent middle ground between the chaos the *Slaughter-House* complainants were inviting and the tautology to which the Court seems to have ended up lashing itself. One possibility, which deserves some attention in light of the historical setting of the Reconstruction Amendments, is that the Privileges or Immunities Clause (and for that matter the whole of the Fourteenth Amendment) should be construed entirely in the light of the amendment's overall animating purpose, the cause of equality for blacks. The phrase was taken from Article IV, Section 2 of the original Constitution, which provides that "The Citizens of each State shall be entitled to all Privileges and Immunities of Citizens in the several States." This was an equality provision, intended to keep states from treating outsiders worse than their own citizens. Might it not be, then, that just as the Article IV clause had been directed to equality between locals and out-of-staters, so the similar clause inserted in the Fourteenth Amendment was intended to ensure equality among locals? This interpretation was suggested by Justice Field in his *Slaughter-House* dissent: "What the clause in question did for the protection of the citizens of one State against hostile and discriminating legislation of other States, the fourteenth amendment does for the protection of every citizen of the United States against hostile and discriminating legislation against him in favor of others, whether they reside in the same or in different States."[43]

The Fourteenth Amendment's Privileges or Immunities Clause can surely be conceived as contributing to the goal of equality for blacks: one way of ensuring substantial equality is by designating a set of goods that no one can be denied. But that equality for blacks, or even equality more broadly conceived, was the *only* relevant purpose of the entire Fourteenth Amendment is a proposition much more difficult to defend. Abolitionist concerns had broadened over time—partly because of the kinship of the impulses, partly because of the persecution of abolitionists—from a narrow focus on the rights of blacks to a broader occupation with the civil rights and liberties of everyone.[44] The various clauses of the Fourteenth Amendment reflect that development. The Due Process Clause addresses itself to procedural fairness. The Equal Protection Clause is directly concerned with equality (and it is no small problem for the suggested interpretation of the Privileges or Immunities Clause that it would render the Equal Protection Clause superfluous). The Privileges or Immunities Clause adds yet another dimension: it seems to announce rather plainly that there is a set of entitlements that no state is to take away (at least not from a United States citizen[45]).

Thus Justice Field did not stick with his equality thesis, but went on to rhapsodize about fundamental and inalienable rights, thereby attempting to give the clause a substantive content as well.[46] This apparent schizophrenia is hardly censurable: before, during, and after the framing of the Reconstruction Amendments notions of equality and substantive entitlement tended to merge, and understandably so. One can guarantee substantive rights directly (by pointing to them) or, fairly well, by an equality provision commanding that everyone generally get what the best-off are getting. Similarly, one can guarantee equality either by thus commanding it, or, fairly well, by pointing to the things one considers important and saying everyone is to get them. The Fourteenth Amendment takes both approaches, but the slightest attention to language will indicate that it is the Equal Protection Clause that follows the command of equality strategy, while the Privileges or Immunities Clause proceeds by purporting to extend to everyone a set of entitlements. To construe it as simply replicating the Equal Protection Clause would be to lose significant differences of constitutional language in a simplistic conception of the amendment's purpose.

The most serious attempt to give the Privileges or Immunities Clause determinate independent content — the prevailing interpretation, of course, leaves it without any — was that of Justice Black, who finally settled on the view that this was the clause that "incorporated" the Bill of Rights and made it applicable to the states. Early in the debate Black had been somewhat elusive about what provision accomplished the incorporation, indicating that it was the Fourteenth Amendment "as a whole."[47] The reason for this may be that the Privileges or Immunities Clause, unlike the Due Process and Equal Protection Clauses, can be read to limit its protection to

United States citizens, and the justice wanted to protect noncitizens as well. Whether or not this explains Black's behavior, the point has surely bothered others. It seems to be generally agreed that no conscious intention to limit the protection of the clause to citizens appears in the historical records.[48] Most commentators conclude, however, that the language is clear to this effect and we are thus stuck with the conclusion that only citizens are protected.[49] I certainly agree that we should defer to clear constitutional language: for one thing it is the best possible evidence of purpose. But when the usual reading is out of accord with what we are quite certain was the purpose, we owe it to the framers and ourselves at least to take a second look at the language. "No State shall make or enforce any law which shall abridge the privileges or immunities of citizens of the United States" *could* mean that only citizens are protected in their privileges or immunities, but it surely doesn't have to. It could just as easily mean there is a set of entitlements, "the privileges and immunities of citizens of the United States," which states are not to deny to anyone. In other words, the reference to citizens may define the class of rights rather than limit the class of beneficiaries.[50] Since everyone seems to agree that such a construction would better reflect what we know of the purpose, and since it is one the language will bear comfortably, it is hard to imagine why it shouldn't be followed.[51]

For whatever reason—probably the fact that no other clause could plausibly serve as the vehicle for incorporating the entire Bill of Rights[52]—Black had settled, by the time of his 1968 concurrence in *Duncan v. Louisiana*, on the Privileges or Immunities Clause as the incorporating provision.[53] However, his historical argument for the proposition that the Fourteenth Amendment generally had been intended to make the Bill of Rights applicable to the states had been made in 1947, in a lengthy appendix to his dissent in *Adamson v. California*.[54] For a time it was voguish to assert that Black's argument had been decisively refuted by Professor Charles Fairman in a critical article published two years later.[55] It isn't so voguish any more: people are coming to realize that this is an argument no one can win.[56]

Black's argument relied heavily on the statements of the floor leaders, Congressman Bingham and Senator Howard, who between them wrote the whole of Section 1 of the amendment. In these terms he was able to mount a powerful case. Howard's statements alone must give serious pause to anyone who would deny an intention to incorporate. It was he, acting as temporary cochairman of the Joint Committee, who presented the Fourteenth Amendment to the Senate. Purporting to present "the views and the motives which influenced that committee" so far as he understood him, he stated:

> Such is the character of the privileges and immunities spoken of in the second section of the fourth article of the Constitution. [Howard had just read from the opinion in *Corfield v. Coryell*, which I shall consider presently.] To these privileges and immunities, whatever they may be — for they are not and cannot be fully defined in their entire extent and precise nature — to these should be added the personal rights guarantied and secured by the first eight amendments of the Constitution; such as the freedom of speech and of the press; the right of the people peaceably to assemble and petition the Government for a redress of grievances, a right appertaining to each and all the people; the right to keep and to bear arms; the right to be exempted from the quartering of soldiers in a house without the consent of the owner; the right to be exempt from unreasonable searches and seizures, and from any search or seizure except by virtue of a warrant issued upon a formal oath or affidavit; the right of an accused person to be informed of the nature of the accusation against him, and his right to be tried by an impartial jury of the vicinage; and also the right to be secure against excessive bail and against cruel and unusual punishments.
>
> Now, sir, here is a mass of privileges, immunities, and rights, some of them secured by the second section of the fourth article of the Constitution, which I have recited, some by the first eight amendments of the Constitution; and it is a fact well worthy of attention that the course of decision of our courts and the present settled doctrine is, that all these immunities, privileges, rights, thus guarantied by the Constitution or recognized by it, are secured to the citizen solely as a citizen of the United States and as a party in their courts. They do not operate in the slightest degree as a restraint or prohibition upon State legislation . . .
>
>   . . . The great object of the first section of this amendment is, therefore, to restrain the power of the States and compel them at all times to respect these great fundamental guarantees.[57]

There's no ambiguity here, so Fairman took the tack of arguing that statements like this are few and far between, that most of the framers and ratifiers of the Fourteenth Amendment gave no indication of believing they were applying the commands of the Bill of Rights to the states.[58] Black admitted that that was so, but argued that the statements of the floor leaders are precisely where we should look to determine the purpose, since that is where those who were voting would have sought it.

As I said, the legislative history argument is one neither side can win.[59] It really shouldn't be critical, however. What is most important here, as it has to be everywhere, is the actual language of the provision that was proposed and ratified. On that score Justice Black argued that "No State shall make or enforce any law which shall abridge the privileges or immunities of citizens of the United States" was an "eminently reasonable way of expressing the idea that henceforth the Bill of Rights shall apply to the States."[60] But there's a point that seems equally strong on the other side — that if the Fourteenth Amendment's Privileges or Immunities Clause had been meant to incorporate the entire Bill of Rights, the incorporation would include the Fifth Amendment's Due Process Clause, and the Fourteenth Amendment's Due Process Clause would be superfluous. This observation does great damage to the incorporation thesis in the strong form in which it was put by Justice Black, that the Fourteenth Amendment meant that "henceforth the Bill of Rights shall apply to the States." It does not, however, greatly damage what by now should have emerged as the more sensible formulation, that although the ratified language does not compel the conclusion that the provisions of the Bill of Rights were "henceforth" to be counted among the privileges and immunities of citizens, there is at the same time nothing in the language (or what we know of its surrounding intentions) that should preclude our arriving at that result.

[T]o seek in historical materials relevant to the framing of the Constitution . . . specific answers to specific present problems is to ask the wrong questions. With adequate scholarship, the answer that must emerge in the vast majority of cases is no answer . . . It is not true that the Framers intended the Fourteenth Amendment to outlaw segregation or to make applicable to the states all restrictions on government that may be evolved under the Bill of Rights; but they did not foreclose them and may indeed have invited them.[61]

There is another edge to this, that nothing in the material that has been discussed supports Justice Black's *limitation* of the Fourteenth Amendment's Privileges or Immunities Clause to the function of incorporating the Bill of Rights. There is some legislative history suggesting an intention to incorporate the Bill of Rights: there is none at all suggesting that was *all* the Privileges or Immunities Clause was designed to do, and indeed Howard's speech, which is Black's strongest proof of incorporation, is quite explicitly against him on the limitation point. The words of the clause *are* an "eminently reasonable" way of applying the Bill of Rights to the states, but apter language could have been found had that been the *only* content intended. Thus Black's argument for the limitation half of his position cannot rely on the text or its intended purpose, but must instead depend on his discomfort with the discretion the clause on its face gave judges. I certainly understand that discomfort. But once Black rejected the counsel of text and historical purpose and turned to his own vision of what is right, he began to engage in his own brand of noninterpretivism.

Thus the most plausible interpretation of the Privileges or Immunities Clause is, as it must be, the one suggested by its language — that it was a delegation to future constitutional decision-makers to protect certain rights that the document neither lists, at least not exhaustively, nor even in any specific way gives directions for finding. This fits the language and also fits a significant chunk of legislative history I have not yet discussed, namely that in discussing the meaning of the phrase "privileges or immunities" the framers of the Fourteenth Amendment adverted repeatedly to an interpretation given its Article IV counterpart by Justice Washington, sitting alone on Circuit, in the 1823 case of *Corfield v. Coryell.*[62] Discussing the question of which "privileges and immunities" Article IV guaranteed out-of-staters presumptively equal enjoyment, Washington purported to place limits but ended up with a virtually infinite reference:

> The inquiry is, what are the privileges and immunities of citizens in the several States? We feel no hesitation in confining this expression to those privileges and immunities which are, in

their nature, fundamental; which belong, of right, to the citizens of all free governments; and which have, at all times, been enjoyed by the citizens of the several states which compose this Union, from the time of their becoming free, independent, and sovereign. *What these fundamental privileges are, it would perhaps be more tedious than difficult to enumerate. They may, however, be all comprehended under the following general heads:* Protection by the government; the enjoyment of life and liberty, with the right to acquire and possess property of every kind, *and to pursue and obtain happiness and safety;* subject nevertheless to such restraints as the government may justly prescribe for the general good of the whole. The right of a citizen of one state to pass through, or to reside in any other state for purposes of trade, agriculture, professional pursuits, or otherwise; to claim the benefit of the writ of habeas corpus; to institute and maintain actions of any kind in the courts of the state; to take, hold and dispose of property, either real or personal; and an exemption from higher taxes or impositions than are paid by the other citizens of the state; *may be mentioned as some of the particular privileges and immunities of citizens, which are clearly embraced by the general description of privileges deemed to be fundamental;* to which may be added, the elective franchise, as regulated and established by the laws or constitution of the state in which it is to be exercised . . .[63]

This was the opinion of a single justice, it was *dictum*, and it is at least strongly arguable that Washington was mistaken in even purporting to limit to the "fundamental"—though obviously that wasn't much of a limitation[64]—those privileges and immunities to which the Article IV clause guarantees out-of-staters presumptively equal access.[65] All this must tempt one so inclined to discount the discussion's relevance. That would be unfair, however. The fact that Washington's purported methodology respecting Article IV may have been mistaken suggests that perhaps it should not be followed with respect to that article, but it cannot erase the significance for a responsible interpretation of the Fourteenth Amendment of the fact that *that* amendment's framers repeatedly adverted to the *Corfield* discussion as the key to what they were writing.

I am not suggesting that the *Corfield* list should be some sort of recipe: Washington indicated that it was representative rather than exhaustive, and you'll recall that Senator Howard's allusion to it represented it as only part of the story. I bring it up only to underscore the conclusion, which shouldn't need underscoring, that it is no mistake to take the clause at face value, as a delegation to future constitutional decision-makers to protect rights that are not listed either in the Fourteenth Amendment or elsewhere in the document. Rather than using a restrictive enumeration of rights, as they had, for example, in the Civil Rights Act of 1866, the framers opted to protect "the privileges or immunities of United States citizens."[66] In fact, Howard was "frank to say that only the future could tell just what application the privileges and immunities provision might have."[67] "The tradition of a broadly worded organic law not frequently or lightly amended was well-established by 1866, and, despite the somewhat revolutionary fervor with which the Radicals were pressing their changes, it cannot be assumed that they or anyone else expected or wished the future role of the Constitution in the scheme of American government to differ from the past."[68] Thus there were few citations of specific purpose that went beyond the coverage of the Civil Rights Act. But there was at the same time "an awareness on the part of these framers that it was *a constitution* they were writing, which led to a choice of language capable of growth."[69]

Equal Protection

We know from the face of the Equal Protection Clause that it was meant to forbid certain kinds of inequality: "No State shall . . . deny to any person within its jurisdiction the equal protection of the laws." We know from its history that it was meant particularly to combat inequality toward blacks.[70] We also know, however — and would rightly presume it even if we didn't — that the decision to use general language, not tied to race, was a conscious one.[71]

Obviously all unequal treatment by the state cannot be forbidden. Legislation characteristically classifies, distributing certain benefits to, or requiring certain behavior of, some but not others. What's more, such classification typically proceeds on the basis of generalizations that are known to be imperfect. We all order our lives on the basis of such generalizations: without them life would be impossible. Thus a storekeeper may not accept checks drawn on out-of-town banks, even though he or she knows most of them are good, just as an airline may not hire overweight pilots, though it knows most of them will never suffer heart attacks. And so the legislature may allow optometrists but not opticians to replace eyeglass lenses, even though it is aware that many opticians are entirely capable of doing so.[72] Thus unless all legislation that classifies, which is to say virtually all legislation, is to fall, the baseline equal protection requirement must be close to that the Court in fact has developed, the so-called "rational basis" test.[73] The meaning of these words is not as clear as we sometimes pretend, but the meaning of the test that is important at the moment is that counterexamples, even a large number of counterexamples, do not void a classification so long as a reasonable person could find sufficient correlation between the evil combated and the trait used as the basis of classification.

That can't be the whole story, however. In particular, the core case of racial discrimination cannot adequately be handled by a rational basis test. As Professor Cox has observed, "Honest men not only could, but many do, conclude after serious study that the academic progress of children is greater when the races are segregated."[74] Indeed, apartheid generally is a *rational*, if misguided, means of avoiding racial strife, and one might *rationally* distribute jobs on the basis of color — giving what we generally think of as the better ones to whites — in light of the statistical reality, however invidious its historical roots, that blacks by and large are not as well educated in our society as whites.[75] Something stronger than the usual rational basis test must therefore be invoked (and in fact has been) if the amendment's core purpose is to be vindicated and racial classifications held unconstitutional. The upshot of all this is that we need at least two standards under the Equal Protection Clause, maybe more. The constitutional text doesn't give us a clue as to what they might be, and we are left with a provision whose general concern — equality — is clear enough but whose content beyond that cannot be derived from anything within its four corners or the known intentions of its framers.[76]

It is tempting to conclude that this is an observation of limited range, akin to my earlier observation that the Cruel and Unusual Punishment Clause seems to call for some reference to outside sources. The idea would be that just as the Eighth Amendment deals only with punishments, so the Equal Protection Clause deals only with discriminations among classes of persons. Some "freelancing" is inevitable, but it too is bounded, "limited" to the subject of equality. The problem with that viewpoint is that any case, indeed any challenge, can be put in an equal protection framework by competent counsel. If you wish to challenge the fact that you're not getting good X (or are getting deprivation Y) it is extremely probable that you will be able to identify someone who *is* getting good X (or is not getting deprivation Y). What's more, though the argument doesn't need this step, the odds are good that the reasons adduced for giving X to the other person but not to you are much the same as would be produced if you simply, without reference to the other person, challenged the fact that you weren't getting X. This adds up to something important, that it doesn't matter greatly whether you accepted my revisionist reading of the Privileges or Immunities Clause. Because the limitation to cases involving differential treatment turns out to be no significant limitation at all, the Equal Protection Clause has to amount to what I claimed the Privileges or Immunities Clause amounts to, a rather sweeping mandate to judge of the validity of governmental choices. And the content of the Equal Protection Clause — the answer to the question of what inequalities are tolerable under what circumstances — will not be found anywhere in its terms or in the ruminations of its writers.

Equal Protection and the Federal Government

The Equal Protection Clause does not apply to the federal government. Nonetheless, in *Bolling v. Sharpe* — striking down segregated schooling in the District of Columbia the same day that *Brown v. Board of Education* struck it down in the states — the Court held, in essence, that the Due Process Clause of the Fifth Amendment incorporates the Equal Protection Clause of the Fourteenth Amendment. This is gibberish both syntactically and historically, and was explained by Chief Justice Warren in terms of a judicial unwillingness to hold the states to a higher constitutional standard than the federal government. "In view of our decision that the Constitution prohibits the states from maintaining racially segregated public schools, it would be unthinkable that the same Constitution would impose a lesser duty on the Federal Government."[77]

But unthinkable in what sense? Not in terms of the historical intent: the members of the Reconstruction Congress might well have trusted themselves and their successors in a way they didn't trust the existing and future legislatures of Southern states. They knew how to bind their successors when they wanted to: the Fifteenth Amendment provides that the right to vote shall not be denied or abridged "by the United States or by any State" on account of race. The evidence of the document is thus strong that the decision not to bind Congress by the Equal Protection Clause was at least conscious. In an oft-quoted phrase Justice Holmes announced, "I do not think the United States would come to an end if we lost our power to declare an Act of Congress void. I do think the Union would be imperiled if we could not make that declaration as to the laws of the several States."[78] Holmes had been wounded at Antietam.[79]

Unthinkable in 1954, then? This one is closer, though Justice Linde has argued that Congress would have had no choice but to bring the District into line with *Brown:* "With serious congressional work on civil rights legislation having been foreclosed for years only by Southern filibusters, the ultimate outcome could not have been seriously in doubt."[80] Maybe not, but such an optimistic account devalues the costs of the likely delay and the likely ways that delay would have been achieved, not to mention what those two together would have cost in terms of *state* compliance. I therefore confess I would have strained sorely to side with the Chief Justice had the language of the Fifth Amendment been able to bear his construction.

It's hard to see how it can, however. What is more, the fact that "due process," read responsibly, means due *process* is something we may be able to shrug off in the context of the Fourteenth Amendment, which contains other phrases that do seem to mean what "due process" has wrongly been read to mean.[81] In the Fifth Amendment, however, the Due Process Clause stands alone. Hope for responsible application of an equal protection concept to the federal government may therefore lie, if anywhere, in that old constitutional jester, the Ninth Amendment — in particular in the conclusions, first, that it is no mistake to take that amendment for what it purports to be, and second, that as informed by the concept of representation that has been at the Constitution's core from the outset, such an open-ended provision is appropriately read to include an "equal protection" component.[82]

The Ninth Amendment

The Ninth Amendment, which applies to the federal government, provides that "[t]he enumeration in the Constitution, of certain rights, shall not be construed to deny or disparage others retained by the people." Occasionally a commentator will express a willingness to read it for what it seems to say, but this has been, and remains, a distinctly minority impulse. In sophisticated legal circles mentioning the Ninth Amendment is a surefire way to get a laugh. ("What are you planning to rely on to support that argument, Lester, the Ninth Amendment?") The joke is somewhat elusive. It's true that read for what it says the Ninth Amendment seems open-textured enough to support almost anything one might wish to argue, and that thought can get pretty scary. But this is equally true of the "substantive due process" concept, which *is* generally accepted, albeit with some misgivings, in the selfsame sophisticated circles. That puts the world exactly upside down, however, for whereas the Due Process Clause speaks of process, the Ninth Amendment refers to unenumerated rights.

The received account of the Ninth Amendment, which Justice Black once went so far as to say "every student of history knows,"[83] goes like this. There was fear that the inclusion of a bill of rights in the Constitution would be taken to imply that federal power was not in fact limited to the authorities enumerated in Article I, Section 8, that instead it extended all the way up to the edge of the rights stated in the first eight amendments. (As in "Obviously the federal government has authority to do everything *except* abridge freedom of speech and so forth.") The Ninth Amendment, the received version goes, was attached to the Bill of Rights simply to negate that inference, to reiterate that ours was a government of "few and defined powers."

Every student of history does not know this. It is true that there was fear, no matter how strained it may seem to a contemporary observer, that the addition of a bill of rights might be taken to imply the existence of congressional powers beyond those stated in the body of the Constitution. It is also true that the alleviation of this fear was one reason Madison gave for adding the Ninth Amendment to the Bill of Rights. The conclusion that that was the *only* reason for its inclusion does not follow, however, and in fact it seems wrong. The Tenth Amendment, submitted and ratified at the same time, completely fulfills the function that is here being proffered as all the Ninth Amendment was about. That amendment provides that "The powers not delegated to the United States by the Constitution, nor prohibited by it to the States, are reserved to the States respectively, or to the people." This says—in language as clearly to the point as the language of the Ninth Amendment is not—that the addition of the Bill of Rights is not to be taken to have changed the fact that powers not delegated are not delegated. It does seem that a similar thought was part of what animated the Ninth Amendment, but if that were *all* that amendment had been calculated to say, it would have been redundant.

There isn't much legislative history bearing on the Ninth Amendment, but what there is unsurprisingly confirms that one of the thoughts behind it was the thought that its terms convey. A letter Madison wrote to Jefferson in October 1788 gave the reasons why the writer, though in favor of a Bill of Rights, had not yet pressed for the inclusion of one:

> My own opinion has always been in favor of a bill of rights; provided it be so framed as not to imply powers not meant to be included in the enumeration . . . I have not viewed it in an important light—1. because I conceive that in a certain degree . . . the rights in question are reserved by the manner in which the federal powers are granted. 2. because there is great reason to fear that a positive declaration of some of the most essential rights could not be obtained in the requisite latitude. I am sure that the rights of conscience in particular, if submitted to public definition would be narrowed much more than they are likely ever to be by an assumed power.[84]

When it came to Madison's explanation of the Ninth Amendment on the floor of Congress the following June, however, the clarity of the letter to Jefferson—separating the question of unenumerated powers from the question of unenumerated rights—gave way to some confusion:

> It has been objected also against a bill of rights, that, by enumerating particular exceptions to the grant of power, it would disparage those rights which were not placed in that enumeration; and it might follow by implication, that those rights that were not placed in that enumeration, that those rights which were not singled out, were intended to be assigned into the

hands of the General Government, and were consequently inse-
cure. This is one of the most plausible arguments I have ever
heard urged against the admission of a bill of rights into this
system; but, I conceive, that it may be guarded against. I have
attempted it, as gentlemen may see by turning to the last clause
of the fourth resolution.[85]

Here the points are telescoped, and the possibility that unenumerated rights will be disparaged is seemingly made to do service as an
intermediate premise in an argument that unenumerated powers
will be implied (though at the very end of the first sentence it seems
to flip again and the possibility that unenumerated powers will be
inferred now seems threatening because of what that would mean to
unenumerated rights). The confusion is understandable in context:
a good deal of the debate over a bill of rights was marked by what
we would today regard as a category mistake, a failure to recognize
that rights and powers are not simply the absence of one another but
that rights can cut across or "trump" powers.[86] (As in "A law prohibiting the interstate shipment of books may be a regulation of
commerce, but it violates the First Amendment and thus must
fall.") What is important is that even here Madison, though he may
have linked them in a way that seems unnatural today, made both
the points he had made more clearly earlier — that he wished to forestall *both* the implication of unexpressed powers *and* the disparage-
ment of unenumerated rights. What is more important is that just
as the Tenth Amendment clearly expresses the former point, the
Ninth Amendment clearly expresses the latter. And it is, of course,
that language on which the Congress and the state legislatures were
asked to vote. Thus the Ninth Amendment speaks clearly of unenumerated rights and in addition there is evidence, though I'd
argue it's unnecessary, that its author understood what he had written.[87]

That doesn't mean we're home free, though. For once the received "federalism" account has been discarded, a further choice
comes into focus. It still might be the case that the Ninth Amendment was intended to indicate not that there were other federal constitutional rights, but rather that the enumeration of certain rights
in the first eight amendments was not to be taken to deny or disparage the existence of *other sorts of rights* — rights that do not rise
to the constitutional, at least not to the federal constitutional, level.

That is, it might have been intended to make clear that despite the Bill of Rights Congress could create further rights, or that state legislatures (or common law courts) could do so, or that a state could do so in its own constitution.

This is a possibility that seems more plausible than the received "federalism" construction, since it is vastly more consistent with the amendment's language. It seems pretty clear, however, that it too must be rejected. One thing we know to a certainty from the historical context is that the Ninth Amendment was not designed to grant Congress authority to create additional rights, to amend Article I, Section 8 by adding a general power to protect rights. That power did not come, if it ever did, until Section 5 of the Fourteenth Amendment was ratified seventy-seven years later. (Nor is "others retained by the people" an apt way of saying "others Congress may create.") Thus unless the reference was to other, unstated federal constitutional rights, it must have been to other rights protected by state law —statutory, common, or constitutional. That interpretation seems to make just as little sense, however. It is quite clear that the original framers and ratifying conventions intended the Bill of Rights to control only the actions of the federal government. It is just as clear, and was then too, that state law, even state constitutional law, is incompetent to do so and must therefore content itself with controlling the actions of the state government. We thus run up against an inference that seems so silly it would not have needed rebutting. What felt need could there have been to rebut the inference that the Bill of Rights, controlling only federal action, had somehow preempted the efforts of the people of various states to control the actions of their state governments?*

Apropos of the incorporation debate, Dean Wellington has argued that "[c]ontemporary technology, a population moving frequently across state lines, and the expanding role of the federal government in law enforcement have made America too much one country for considerations of federalism to sustain at a constitutional level" the idea that the states are subject to significantly less stringent restrictions than those the Bill of Rights imposes on the

---

*The "need" to rebut the inference that the Bill of Rights meant that state legislatures and courts could no longer order relations among their citizens by the creation of nonconstitutional "rights" would have been, if anything, still more attenuated.

federal government.[88] Maybe that's right, but the argument is at least as strong the other way around: in terms of respect for the judgments of federal courts and the success of enforcement efforts it seems important that the states not be bound by a set of textually unstated constitutional rights that do not restrain the actions of the federal government. Of course this is essentially the argument that prevailed in *Bolling v. Sharpe*, but with one critical difference: the Ninth Amendment, unlike the Due Process Clause on which the Court attempted to balance its *Bolling* result, will bear the meaning tendered. In fact, the conclusion that the Ninth Amendment was intended to signal the existence of federal constitutional rights beyond those specifically enumerated in the Constitution is the only conclusion its language seems comfortably able to support.

Justice Black's response to the Ninth Amendment was essentially to ignore it.[89] Usually more than willing to return to the original understanding when intervening precedent stood in his way, he displayed a curious contentment with the crabbed interpretations of his predecessors on this point. Of course it really isn't curious at all — he didn't like the jurisprudential implications of such an open-ended provision: "I discuss the due process and Ninth Amendment arguments together because on analysis they turn out to be the same thing — merely using different words to claim for this Court and the federal judiciary power to invalidate any legislative act which the judges find irrational, unreasonable or offensive."[90] But Black most of all shouldn't behave this way. He urged us, correctly, to behave like lawyers rather than dictators or philosopher kings and thus to heed the directions of the various constitutional clauses. On candid analysis, though, the Constitution turns out to contain provisions instructing us to look beyond their four corners. That instruction troubled him, but he was a man who spent his life railing against people who ignored the language and purpose of constitutional clauses because they didn't like where they led. There is a difference between ignoring a provision, such as the First Amendment, because you don't like its specific substantive implications and ignoring a provision, such as the Ninth Amendment, because you don't like its institutional implications. But it's hard to make it a difference that should count.

An interpretivist like Black has two possible answers left. The first, which I've never heard, would go something like this. Suppose there were in the Constitution one or more provisions providing for the protection of ghosts. Can there be any doubt, now that we no longer believe there is any such thing, that we would be behaving properly in ignoring the provisions? The "ghost" here is natural law, and the argument would be that because natural law is the source from which the open-ended clauses of the Ninth and Fourteenth Amendments were expected to derive their content, we are justified, now that our society no longer believes in natural law, in ignoring the clauses altogether.

This argument is too slick. Although there were during both relevant eras people who expected the Constitution to be informed by natural law, this theme was far from universally accepted and probably was not even the majority view among those "framers" we would be likely to think of first.

> Some of the intellectual stalwarts of rebellion, like James Otis, actually came to associate principles of natural law and natural equity with positive law — to assert that what is right is therefore law. But those giants who managed the awesome transition from revolutionaries to "constitutionaries" — men like Adams and Jefferson; Dickinson and Wilson; Jay, Madison, Hamilton, and, in a sense, Mason and Henry — were seldom, if ever, guilty of confusing law with natural right. These men, before 1776, used nature to take the measure of law and to judge their own obligations of obedience, but not as a source for rules of decision.[91]

These people — needless to say they have their Reconstruction counterparts — certainly didn't have natural law in mind when the Constitution's various open-ended delegations to the future were inserted and approved, which undoubtedly is one reason the Constitution at no point refers to natural law. If it did, *then* we'd have our ghosts case.

The second answer is that even granting that clauses like those under consideration established constitutional rights, they do not readily lend themselves to principled *judicial* enforcement and should therefore be treated as if they were directed exclusively to the political branches. (This suggestion I *have* seen — from the pen, surprisingly, of Felix Frankfurter, who indicated in correspondence in the late 1950s that he wished the Due Process Clause, his idea of an

open-ended provision, had been so treated.[92]) It would be a cheap
shot to note that there is no legislative history specifically indicating
an intention that the Ninth Amendment was to receive judicial enforcement. There was at the time of the original Constitution little
legislative history indicating that *any* particular provision was to receive judicial enforcement: the Ninth Amendment was not singled
out one way or the other. What is mildly instructive, and it cuts
the other way, is that the precursor decisions typically cited as
"proof" that judicial review was intended — though they are too few
and unclear really to amount to that — were often "noninterpretivist" decisions, drawing their mandates not from any documentary
prohibition but rather from some principle derived externally.[93] As
far as the Fourteenth Amendment is concerned, it is true that the
(misplaced) anticipation seems to have been that it would receive
its most meaningful enforcement by Congress, acting under Section
5, rather than by the courts. It is also true that at the time of its
ratification only three Acts of Congress had been declared unconstitutional by the Supreme Court. That doesn't mean the authority
went unnoticed, however. *Dred Scott* drew heavy fire, and even
prior to that time,

> [W]e may draw two conclusions concerning the criticism of the
> Supreme Court: first, the court was criticized quite as much for
> not declaring congressional acts unconstitutional as for doing
> so; second, it seems clear that both Federalist and Republican
> criticism during these years was directed not so much at the
> possession of the power of the court to pass on the validity of
> acts of Congress as at the effect of its exercise in supporting or
> invalidating some particular party measure.[94]

It is also relevant that a number of *state* statutes had been struck
down in the first half of the nineteenth century. The Reconstruction
Amendments were, after all, primarily directed at the states. The
Republican criticism of *Dred Scott*, and of *Barron v. Baltimore*[95] as
well, continued throughout the drafting and ratification processes.
Naturally this sometimes spilled over into a general distrust of the
institution of judicial review,[96] but in general the institution was
assumed and the attack was limited to the specific offending instances. Surely there was nothing remotely resembling a consensus
that judicial authority to review was generally to be curtailed: if
anything, the consensus ran the other way.[97] More important for

present purposes, there was no indication that the Fourteenth Amendment was to be treated any differently in this respect from other provisions.*

This, however, is a question on which history cannot have the last word, at least not the last affirmative word. If a principled approach to judicial enforcement of the Constitution's open-ended provisions cannot be developed, one that is not hopelessly inconsistent with our nation's commitment to representative democracy, responsible commentators must consider seriously the possibility that courts simply should stay away from them. Given the transparent failure of the dominant mode of "noninterpretivist" review, Justice Black's instinct to decline the delegation was healthy. But the dominant mode can be improved upon, or at least that is the burden of the rest of this book.

---

*One taking the view under discussion would also have to face the question of which phrases are on which side of the line. As we have seen, the Constitution is not divided into two sets of provisions, precise and open-ended. What, for example, would the view in question make of the Cruel and Unusual Punishment and Just Compensation Clauses? Would they be judicially enforceable? One has to assume so. But although the compass of each is limited, each surely requires the injection of content not to be found in the document.

3   Discovering
Fundamental
Values

[I]t remains to ask the hardest questions. Which values . . . qualify as sufficiently important or fundamental or whathaveyou to be vindicated by the Court against other values affirmed by legistive acts? And how is the Court to evolve and apply them?
—*Alexander Bickel* [1]

No answer is what the wrong question begets . . .
—*Alexander Bickel* [2]

SINCE interpretivism — at least a clause-bound version of interpretivism — is hoist by its own petard, we should look again, and more closely, at its traditional competitor. The prevailing academic line has held for some time that the Supreme Court should give content to the Constitution's open-ended provisions by identifying and enforcing upon the political branches those values that are, by one formula or another, truly important or fundamental. Indeed we are told this is inevitable: "there is simply no way for courts to review legislation in terms of the Constitution without repeatedly making difficult substantive choices among competing values, and indeed among inevitably controverted political, social, and moral conceptions."[3] "[C]onstitutional law must now be understood as the means by which effect is given to those ideas that from time to time are held to be fundamental . . ."[4] The Court is "an institution charged with the evolution and application of society's fundamental principles," and its "constitutional function," accordingly, is "to define values and proclaim principles."[5]

The Judge's Own Values

> *The ultimate test of the Justices' work, I suggest, must be good-ness . . .*
>
> —*J. Skelly Wright*[6]

The view that the judge, in enforcing the Constitution, should use his or her *own values* to measure the judgment of the political branches is a methodology that is seldom endorsed in so many words.[7] As we proceed through the various methodologies that are, however, I think we shall sense in many cases that although the judge or commentator in question may be talking in terms of some "objective," nonpersonal method of identification, what he is really likely to be "discovering," whether or not he is fully aware of it, are his own values. It is thus important at the outset to understand just why a "judge's own values" approach is unacceptable: that under-standing will illumine the unacceptability of the entire enterprise.

How might one arrive at such a view? Much of the explanation seems to involve what might be called the fallacy of transformed realism. About forty years ago people "discovered" that judges were human and therefore were likely in a variety of legal contexts con-sciously or unconsciously to slip their personal values into their legal reasonings. From that earth-shattering insight it has seemed to some an easy inference that that is what judges *ought* to be doing. Two observations are in order, both obvious. The first is that such a "real-ist" theory of adjudication is not a theory of adjudication at all, in that it does not tell us *which* values should be imposed.[8] The second is that the theory's "inference" does not even remotely follow: that people have always been tempted to steal does not mean that steal-ing is what they should be doing. This is all plain as a pikestaff, which means something else has to be going on. People who tend to this extreme realist view must consciously or unconsciously be en-visioning a Court staffed by justices who think as they do. That assumption takes care of both the problems I've mentioned. It tells you what values are to be imposed (the commentator's own) and also explains (at least to the satisfaction of the commentator) why such a Court would be desirable. But it's a heroic assumption, and the argument that seems to score most heavily against such a "realist" outlook is one that is genuinely realistic — that there is absolutely no assurance that the Supreme Court's life-tenured members (or the other federal judges) will be persons who share your values.

But let that pass and grant the realists their strange assumption. There remains the immense and obvious problem of reconciling the attitude under discussion with the basic democratic theory of our government. At this point a distinction is drawn. In America it would not be an acceptable position that appointed judges should run the country, and that is not the position of the commentators under discussion. Saying the judges should run the country is different, however, and many have argued that it is significantly different, from saying the judges should use their own values to give content to the Constitution's open texture. Consistency with democratic theory will supposedly be found in the idea that the judiciary isn't really in a position to make much of a difference to the way the country is run.[9] This assumption has impressive historical roots, running back to Hamilton's *Federalist* 78:

> Whoever attentively considers the different departments of power must perceive, that, in a government in which they are separated from each other, the judiciary, from the nature of its functions, will always be the least dangerous to the political rights of the Constitution; because it will be least in a capacity to annoy or injure them . . . The judiciary . . . has no influence over either the sword or the purse; no direction either of the strength or of the wealth of the society; and can take no active resolution whatever. It may truly be said to have neither FORCE nor WILL, but merely judgment; and must ultimately depend upon the aid of the executive arm even for the efficacy of its judgments.[10]

This must have made a good bit of sense at the outset of our nation: in the absence of precedent, the lack of independent enforcement machinery and the various constitutional checks on the judiciary must have seemed sufficient to ensure that it would play a quite insignificant role. What are harder to justify are the "realist" literature's *contemporary* iterations of Hamilton's assurances, most unrealistically untouched by two hundred years of experience.[11] The Court may be purseless and swordless, but its ability importantly to influence the way the nation functions has proved great, and seems to be growing all the time. It may be true that the Court cannot *permanently* thwart the will of a solid majority,[12] but it can certainly delay its implementation for decades—workmen's compensation, child labor, and unionization are among the more obvious examples[13]—and to the people affected, that's likely to be forever.

The formal checks on the Court have surely not proved to be of much consequence. Congress's control over the budget of the federal courts — note, though, that it cannot constitutionally reduce judicial salaries — has proved an instrument too blunt to be of any real control potential. The country needs functioning and competent federal courts, and everybody knows it does. Despite the two-thirds requirement, impeachment *might* have developed into an effective mode of controlling decision. However, in part precisely because of our allegiance to the idea of an independent judiciary, it didn't, and today it is understood to be a weapon reserved for the grossest of cases. (It is no easier to impeach a justice than a President, as Richard Nixon learned, from both sides.) Congress's theoretical power to withdraw the Court's jurisdiction over certain classes of cases is so fraught with constitutional doubt[14] that although talked about from time to time, it has not been invoked for over one hundred years.[15] Altering the size of, or "packing," the Court was quite popular in the nineteenth century, but only once, during the Grant Administration, is it even arguable that it had its desired effect.[16] And that is the last time it's been done. Franklin Roosevelt tried it, and although he failed, the prevailing mythology for a time was that his effort had pressured the Court into mending its ways. More recently discovered Court records have indicated, however, that the Court's "switch" was independent of (in fact prior to) the announcement of his plan. The message is mixed, but what now seems important about the episode is that an immensely popular President riding an immensely popular cause had his lance badly blunted by his assault on judicial independence.

There is also the possibility of constitutional amendment, but even when this course works it takes time — during which the Court's roadblock stays in place — and in any event it seldom works. Our recent experience with the Equal Rights Amendment, endorsed by both major parties and hardly advancing a radical proposition, corroborates the difficulty of amending the Constitution. In all our history only four decisions of the Supreme Court have been reversed by constitutional amendment.[17] It is also true that often, though by no means always, the cooperation of political officials is required to enforce Supreme Court decisions. But they generally go along, however grudgingly: it is, after all, their perceived legal duty to do so. (One inclined to regard failure to obey as a viable means of controlling the Court would do well to reflect on the fact that the President of the United States — one hardly renowned for his reverence to the rule of law — did surrender those fatal tapes.) What's left is the fact that the President appoints and the Senate confirms the new members of the Court, and certainly there is something there. But it generally takes several successive presidential terms, and the concurrence of several successive Senates, to replace a majority of the justices. It has also proved hard to predict how someone in another line of work will function as a justice and one sometimes wonders whether the appointee who turns out differently from the way the President who appointed him expected is not the rule rather then the exception. (Truman and Eisenhower are both reported to have regarded Supreme Court appointments — Clark and Warren, respectively — as the worst mistakes they had made as President.[18]) Nor is it the least bit unusual for a justice to sit for decades during which the issues are likely to have shifted markedly from those the President had in mind when the appointment was made.

So it can't be the actual invocation of the formal checks the realists mean to rely on in assuring us that the Court is no threat to influence importantly the governance of the country. The point tends to be made more mysteriously, generally in the language of "destruction." Thus we are told that the Court's "essentially anti-democratic character keeps it constantly in jeopardy of destruction":[19] it knows "that frequent judicial intervention in the political process would generate such widespread political reaction that the Court would be destroyed in its wake."[20] Readers who are even passingly familiar with the literature on judicial review of the 1960s and 1970s will recognize the theme: it is incanted as an article of faith and forms the foundation for much conservative "realism."[21] But what is it supposed to mean? What sort of "destruction" is it that lurks around the activist corner? We're never exactly told, but to be coherent the idea has to be that although the formal checks appear to the naive observer to have atrophied, the Court knows better, and understands that if it gets too rambunctious — if it too regularly exercises what the public will understand are properly political functions — those checks will be invoked.

This isn't the way it works, and the justices know it isn't. Throughout its history the Court has been told it had better stick to its knitting or risk destruction,[22] yet somehow "[t]he possibility of judicial emasculation by way of popular reaction against constitutional review by the courts has not in fact materialized in more than a century and a half of American experience."[23] The warnings probably reached their peak during the Warren years; they were not notably heeded; yet nothing resembling destruction materialized.[24] In fact the Court's power continued to grow, and probably has never been greater than it has been over the past two decades.[25] For public persons know that one of the surest ways to acquire power is to assert it. "[J]udicial activism feeds on itself," Professors Karst and Horowitz have written. "The public has come to expect the Court to intervene against gross abuses. And so the Court must intervene."[26] "*Must* intervene"? I'd argue not, at least not as the formula is stated here. But "can get away with intervening"? For sure.[27]

It's because everybody down deep knows this that few come right out and argue for the judge's own values as a source of constitutional judgment. Instead the search purports to be objective and value-neutral; the reference is to something "out there" waiting to be discovered, whether it be natural law or some supposed value consensus of historical America, today's America, or the America that is yet to be.

Natural Law

> *"Well, what may seem like the truth to you," said the seventeen-year-old bus driver and part-time philosopher, "may not, of course, seem like the truth to the other fella, you know."*
> *"THEN THE OTHER FELLOW IS WRONG, IDIOT!"*
> —*Philip Roth*, The Great American Novel [28]

At the time the original Constitution was ratified, and during the period leading up to the Fourteenth Amendment as well, a number of people espoused the existence of a system of natural law principles.[29] "This law of nature being coeval with mankind and dictated by God himself is of course superior in obligation to any other. It is binding over the whole globe, in all countries and at all times. No human laws are of any validity if contrary to this . . ."[30] Some sort of natural law theory (which need not necessarily be deistic) thus seems an obvious candidate in the search for a source of values to give content to the Constitution's open-ended provisions.

The historical record here is not so uncomplicated as it is some-

times made to appear. As noted above, some of our nation's founders did not find the concept intelligible in any context, and even
those who did "were seldom, if ever, guilty of confusing law with
natural right."[31] It therefore seems no oversight that the Constitution at no point adverts to the concept. Of course the Declaration of
Independence *had* spoken in such terms. Part of the explanation for
the difference is undoubtedly that intellectual fashions had changed
somewhat over that eventful decade and a half.[32] But surely that
can't be all there was to it — ideas do not come and go so fast — and a
more important factor seems to have been the critical difference in
function between the two documents. The Declaration of Independence was, to put it bluntly, a brief (with certain features of an in-
dictment). People writing briefs are likely, and often well advised,
to throw in arguments of every hue. People writing briefs for revolution are obviously unlikely to have apparent positive law on their
side, and are therefore well advised to rely on natural law.* This the
argument for our Revolution did, combining natural law concepts
with references to positive law, both English and colonial, to the
genuine "will of the people," to the "rights of Englishmen" — in
short, with references to anything that seemed to help.[33] "It was the
quarrel with Britain that forced Americans to reach upward and
bring natural law down from the skies, to be converted into a political theory for use as a weapon in constitutional argument; in that
capacity it was directed against British policies and was never intended as a method of analysing the rights and wrongs of colonial
life."[34] The Constitution was not a brief, but a frame of government. A broadly accepted natural law philosophy surely could have
found a place within it, presumably in the Bill of Rights. But such
philosophies were not that broadly accepted. Since the earlier im-
petus that had moved the Declaration, the need to "make a case,"
was no longer present, these controversial doctrines were omitted, at
least in anything resembling explicit form, from the later document.[35]

Natural law was also part of the rhetoric of antislavery, but again
it was just one arrow in the quiver. As suited their purposes, the

---

*This is not a new insight. "If the written law tells against our case, clearly we
must appeal to the universal law, and insist on its greater equity and justice." Aristotle, "Rhetoric" 1375a, in *The Basic Works of Aristotle* 1374 (R. McKeon ed.
1941).

abolitionists, like the revolutionaries before them, argued both positive law, now in the form of existing constitutional provisions, and natural law.[36] And for them too, the latter reference was virtually unavoidable, since it took a purity of spirit that transcended judgment not to recognize that the original Constitution, candidly considered, not only did not outlaw slavery, but deliberately protected it.[37] "When it was the fashion to speak and write of 'natural' law very few stopped to consider the exact significance of that commonplace of theological, economic, literary, and scientific, as well as political, thought. Particularly is this true of the use of theories of natural law in the heat of controversies. At such times it is the winning of a cause, not the discussion of problems of ontology, which occupies men's minds."[38] *Justice Accused*, Robert Cover's fine recent book on antislavery and the judicial process,[39] corroborates the conclusion that for early American lawyers, references to natural law and natural rights functioned as little more than signals for one's sense that the law was not as one felt it should be.[40] This is not to say that "natural law" was entirely without perceived legal significance. It was thought to be invocable interstitially, when no aspect of positive law provided an applicable rule for the case at hand. But it was subordinate to applicable statutes and well-settled precedent as well as to constitutional provisions, and not generally perceived as a source of values on whose basis positive law could be constitutionally upset.[41]

We shouldn't make too much of this historical record, though. If there is such a thing as natural law, and if it can be discovered, it would be folly, no matter what our ancestors did or didn't think, to ignore it as a source of constitutional values. It's not nice to fool Mother Nature, and even Congress and the President shouldn't be allowed to do so. The idea is a discredited one in our society, however, and for good reason. "[A]ll theories of natural law have a singular vagueness which is both an advantage and disadvantage in the application of the theories."[42] The advantage, one gathers, is that you can invoke natural law to support anything you want. The disadvantage is that everybody understands that. Thus natural law has been summoned in support of all manner of causes in this country — some worthy, others nefarious — and often on both sides of the same issue. Perhaps the most explicit invocation of natural law in a Supreme Court opinion appears in Justice Bradley's 1872 opinion in

Bradwell v. Illinois, denying Ms. Bradwell's application to become a lawyer:

> [T]he civil law, as well as nature herself, has always recognized a wide difference in the respective spheres and destinies of man and woman . . . The constitution of the family organization, which is founded in the divine ordinance, as well as in the nature of things, indicates the domestic sphere as that which properly belongs to the domain and functions of womanhood . . . The paramount destiny and mission of woman are to fulfill the noble and benign offices of wife and mother. This is the law of the Creator.[43]

But in fact the list of causes natural law has supported is almost infinite.

> [N]atural law has had as its content whatever the individual in question desired to advocate. This has varied from a defence of theocracy to a defence of the complete separation of church and state, from revolutionary rights in 1776 to liberty of contract in recent judicial opinions, from the advocacy of universal adult suffrage to a defence of rigid limitations upon the voting power, from philosophical anarchy in 1849 with Thoreau to strict paternalism five years later with Fitzhugh, from the advocacy of the inalienable right of secession to the assertion of the natural law of national supremacy, from the right of majority rule to the rights of vested interests.[44]

It was, indeed, invoked on both sides of the slavery question.[45] Calhoun cited natural law to "prove" the inferiority of blacks,[46] and the Kentucky Constitution of 1850 and the Kansas Constitution of 1857 declared the right to own slaves "before and higher than any constitutional sanction." Small wonder, then, that abolitionists like Wendell Phillips came to realize that "[b]ecause 'nature' no longer spoke with a single voice, only the judge's conscience ultimately determined the source of right."[47]

It has thus become increasingly evident that the only propositions with a prayer of passing themselves off as "natural law" are those so uselessly vague that no one will notice — something along the "No one should needlessly inflict suffering" line.[48] "[A]ll the many attempts to build a moral and political doctrine upon the conception of a universal human nature have failed. They are repeatedly trapped in a dilemma. Either the allegedly universal ends are too few and abstract to give content to the idea of the good, or they are too numerous and concrete to be truly universal. One has to choose between triviality and implausibility."[49] The concept has consequently all but disappeared in American discourse.[50] The influence of religion has declined, but that isn't the real point: even persons who count themselves religious are unlikely to hold that the Almighty speaks with a sufficiently unambiguous ethical voice to help with today's difficult issues of public policy. Perhaps physical laws will be found "out there," though even that faith is fraying, but in any event moral laws will not. In 1931 Benjamin Wright wrote, in *American Interpretations of Natural Law:* "Since the Civil War the concept has been of importance only in the field of constitutional law. Here certain of the traditional individual rights doctrines have been taken over and woven into the fabric of due process of law and liberty of contract. In systematic theory it has served almost solely as an object of criticism."[51] One thing has changed since 1931: constitutional lawyers have gotten the message, and the concept is no longer respectable in that context either.[52]

This is not to say that the arguments against "moral absolutism" have not been overstated. It is no fairer to cite the dissenting "morality" of Adolf Hitler to prove the nonexistence of moral truth than it would be to invoke the views of the Flat Earth Society to prove there is not a correct position on the shape of the world. There *are* ethical positions so hopelessly at odds with assumptions most of us hold that we would be justified in labeling them (if not with absolute precision) "irrational."[53] But the set of such propositions will turn out to be the mirror image of the set of propositions sufficiently vague and uncontroversial to pass themselves as "natural law": an example here would be the proposition that the infliction of needless suffering is morally acceptable. The existence of such a set of plainly unentertainable ethical propositions will obviously be no more relevant to constitutional disputes than will their plainly undeniable counterparts. Constitutional litigation will involve an action that has been approved by the legislative branch of the government involved or someone ultimately accountable thereto, whose action in addition has seemed sufficiently acceptable to a government lawyers' office to result in governmental defense in court. Such actions will involve a *choice* of evils (or goods). They may involve the infliction of suffering for reasons whose sufficiency on balance is open to argument; they will not involve the infliction of suffering that can fairly be labeled needless.

Another point that is sometimes made in this context is that what appear on the surface to be ethical disputes will often turn out on analysis to be disagreements over what the facts are. This position can be overstated. Some disputes—cruelty to animals and abortion are two—are over the appropriate breadth of the moral universe and not over any factual claim. More often, an apparent ethical dispute will preeminently involve a balancing or comparison of two or more quite well understood costs—abortion again, once fetuses are admitted to the universe of moral concern, is an example—and this is a paradigmatically ethical dispute. It is undoubtedly true, however, that at least some apparent moral disagreements do hide different factual assumptions. What follows for the constitutional context, though? That courts should resolve the disputes, by finding the actual facts and applying to them what all, presumably, would then agree—let's pass *that* problem—was the appropriate moral principle? That can't be right. In the first place, it isn't clear why judges should be the ones to find the facts in such situations. Broad questions of public policy are likely to involve what are called, uncoincidentally, "legislative facts," or broad factual generalizations, as opposed to specific "adjudicative facts." The conventional wisdom here, that courts are markedly worse than legislatures at determining legislative facts, surely can stand significant qualification—but at the same time there isn't any reason to suppose they are better at it. More fundamentally, these are likely to be situations in which the facts are inherently intractable, not susceptible to resolution in any way that would satisfy all observers. The ancient, and recently reheated, controversy over whether the death penalty actually deters homicides is a good example. It shows us what is genuinely likely to be at stake in public policy controversies, namely questions of *how public institutions should behave under conditions of empirical uncertainty*. That factual uncertainty is an element of a problem does not mean the problem is not a profoundly moral one, or that it is one courts have any superior claim to being able or entitled to solve.

When I was a lad studying philosophy in the late 1950s, epistemology and logic were all the rage, and moral and political philosophy were sneered at by knowledgeables: after all, one couldn't really *reason* about ethical issues, could one? That day, happily, has passed: people *do* reason about such issues and some of them number among our most renowned contemporary philosophers. But the kind of reasoning that is involved in the arguments of contemporary moral philosophers proceeds from ethical principles or conclusions it is felt the reader is likely already to accept to other conclusions or principles he or she might not previously have perceived as related in the way the writer suggests.[54] Surely this is reasoning, for reasoning in other areas consists in nothing more. But note the critical appeal at the outset to acceptance of the initial proposition or conclusion: the inference proceeds, as it must, from one "ought" to another. We have learned once again that we *can* reason about moral issues, but reasoning about ethical issues is not the same as discovering absolute ethical truth. So we're where we were: our society does not, rightly does not, accept the notion of a discoverable and objectively valid set of moral principles, at least not a set that could plausibly serve to overturn the decisions of our elected representatives.

Neutral Principles

In 1959 Herbert Wechsler delivered a widely heralded lecture, which became a widely heralded article, entitled "Toward Neutral Principles of Constitutional Law."[55] He argued that the Supreme Court, rather than functioning as a "naked power organ" simply announcing its conclusions ad hoc, should proceed on the basis of principles that transcend the case at bar and treat like cases alike. Having announced such a principle in one case, the Court should then proceed unflinchingly to apply it to all others it controls. Consciousness of this obligation to the future will obviously help shape the principle the Court will formulate, and thus the result it will reach, in the first case. (What he said, in short, is that the Court should act in a principled fashion.)

Even this suggestion has had its detractors. There are those who will wax quite eloquent on the byzantine beauty of what is sometimes called the common law method, one of reaching what instinctively seem the right results in a series of cases, and only later (if at all?) enunciating the principle that explains the pattern—a sort of connect-the-dots exercise.[56] This quarrel is of no concern to us here, though obviously I wouldn't have written this book if I weren't with Wechsler on *that* point. What is relevant here is that as embellished by the subsequent literature, Wechsler's suggestion was given another dimension, one it is not entirely clear he intended. "Neutral principles" became not simply an appropriate *requirement* for judicial behavior but also, in the minds of much of the profession, a *source* of constitutional judgment—a sufficient as well as necessary condition of legitimate constitutional decision-making. The articulation of a neutral principle, the idea seems sometimes to run, is itself sufficient guarantee that the Court is behaving appropriately.[57]

We needn't spend long on this suggestion. Its unambiguous endorsement has been rare, and its fallacy has been pointed out by others. An insistence on "neutral principles" does not by itself tell us anything useful about the appropriate content of those principles or how the Court should derive the values they embody.[58] The requirement means initially—this much is easy in theory, though we all know people who don't abide by it[59]—that a principle, once promulgated, is to be applied to all cases it controls and not just when one is in the mood. But that can't be enough: the principle that "Freedom of speech is guaranteed to Republicans" would not satisfy us as "neutral," no matter how unblinkingly it was applied. Thus some degree of generality must also be required to make a principle count as "neutral" in Wechsler's sense. Even in the unlikely event that we could agree on what degree of generality should be required, however, we still would not have arrived at a formula that would guarantee the *appropriateness* of the principle. The principle that "Legislatures can do whatever they want"—even if (especially if) unblinkingly applied—would obviously be unacceptable, but hardly because of inadequate generality.

"Neutral principles" has often served as a code term for judicial conservatism, probably because Wechsler himself originally used the concept in criticizing *Brown v. Board of Education* as wrongly decided. But it needn't have been so: there are neutral principles of every hue. (How about "No racial segregation, ever"?) In fact the Warren Court probably came as close to the ideal as any of its predecessors: the problem for the commentators may actually have been too much generality, not too little.[60] But however that may be, requirements of generality of principle and neutrality of application do not provide a source of substantive content.

Reason

> *If a society were to design an institution which had the job of finding the society's set of moral principles and determining how they bear in concrete situations, that institution would be sharply different from one charged with proposing policies . . . It would provide an environment conducive to rumination, reflection, and analysis. "Reason, not Power" would be the motto over its door.*
> —*Harry Wellington* [61]

The constitutional literature that has dominated the past thirty years has often insisted that judges, in seeking constitutional value judgments, should employ, in Alexander Bickel's words, "the method of reason familiar to the discourse of moral philosophy."[62] "Judges have, or should have, the leisure, the training, and the insulation to follow the ways of the scholar in pursuing the ends of government."[63] This view, like the others we are considering, seldom appears in unadulterated form. (Indeed, much of the point is that these various value sources, in their understandable confusion, fall all over one another.) It is, however, one of the more important presences.

Technically, of course, reason alone can't tell you anything: it can only connect premises to conclusions. To mean anything, the reference has to be somewhat richer, to implicate the invocation of premises along with the ways in which one reasons from them. The basic idea thus seems to be that moral philosophy is what constitutional law is properly about, that there exists a correct way of doing such philosophy, and that judges are better than others at identifying and engaging in it. Now I know lawyers are a cocky lot: the fact that our profession brings us into contact with many disciplines often generates the delusion that we have mastered them all. But surely the claim here cannot be that lawyers and judges are the best imaginable people to tell good moral philosophy from bad: members of the clergy, novelists, maybe historians, to say nothing of professional moral philosophers, all seem more sensible candidates for this job. I suppose that this isn't the relevant comparison, though, and that all that has to be demonstrated is that of the institutions existing in our government, courts are those best equipped to make moral judgments, in particular that they are better suited to the task than legislatures.

Since judges tend generally to be drawn from roughly the same ranks as legislators, the heart of the argument here is that moral judgments are sounder if made dispassionately, and that because of their comparative insulation judges are more likely so to make them. "[T]he environment in which legislators function makes difficult a bias-free perspective. It is often hard for law-makers to resist pressure from their constituents who react to particular events (a brutal murder, for instance) with a passion that conflicts with common morality."[64] One might begin by questioning the alleged incompatibility between popular input on moral questions and "correct" moral judgment. In fact there are reasons for supposing that our moral sensors function *best* under the pressure of experience. Most of us did not fully wake up to the immorality of our most recent war until we were shown pictures of Vietnamese children being scalded by American napalm. Professor Bickel makes this point in what must have seemed to him an unrelated section of his book:

> There was an unforgettable scene . . . in one CBS newscast from New Orleans, of a white mother fairly foaming at the mouth with the effort to rivet her distracted little boy's attention and teach him how to hate. And repeatedly, the ugly, spitting curse, NIGGER! The effect, achieved on an unprecedented number of people with unprecedented speed, must have been something like what used to happen to individuals (the young Lincoln among them) at the sight of an actual slave auction, or like the slower influence on northern opinion of the fighting in "Bleeding Kansas" in 1854-55.[65]

It is thus no surprise that the case that our "insulated" judiciary has done a better job of speaking for our better moral selves turns out to be historically shaky. "Can we really be sure that it was Marshall or Taney rather than Clay or Webster who did the better job of articulating values? Which of the Civil War Justices excelled Lincoln in voicing the hopes and goals of the republic? . . . Which Justice in the 1920's gave better tongue than Norris or LaFollette to the American dream?"[66]

A more fundamental error underlies the view under consideration, however — an outsider's error, akin to the assumption nonlawyers frequently make that there is something called "the law" whose shape good lawyers will describe identically. (Whatever one's profession, I assume this phenomenon is recognizable.) The error here is one of assuming that something exists called "the method of moral philosophy" whose contours sensitive experts will agree on, that "there are only two kinds of reasoning—one is sound and the other is unsound."[67] That is not the way things are. Some moral philosophers think utilitarianism is the answer; others feel just as strongly it is not. Some regard enforced economic redistribution as a moral imperative; others find it morally censurable. What may be the two most renowned recent works of moral and political philosophy, John Rawls's *A Theory of Justice* and Robert Nozick's *Anarchy, State and Utopia*,[68] reach very different conclusions. There simply does not exist *a* method of moral philosophy.

Ronald Dworkin also succumbs to this error. Writing in 1972 he said:

> Constitutional law can make no genuine advance until it isolates the problem of rights against the state and makes that problem part of its own agenda. That argues for a fusion of constitutional law and moral theory, a connection that, incredibly, has yet to take place. It is perfectly understandable that lawyers dread contamination with moral philosophy, and particularly with those philosophers who talk about rights, because the spooky overtones of that concept threaten the graveyard of reason. But better philosophy is now available than the lawyers may remember. Professor Rawls of Harvard, for example, has published an abstract and complex book about justice which no constitutional lawyer will be able to ignore.[69]

The invitation to judges seems clear: seek constitutional values in— that is, overrule political officials on the basis of—the writings of good contemporary moral philosophers, in particular the writings of Rawls. Rawls's book *is* fine. But how are judges to react to Dworkin's invitation when almost all the commentators on Rawls's work have expressed reservations about his conclusions?[70] The Constitution may follow the flag, but is it really supposed to keep up with the *New York Review of Books?*

One might be tempted to suppose that there will be no systematic bias in the judges' rendition of "correct moral reasoning" aside from whatever derives from the philosophical axioms from which they begin. ("We like Rawls, you like Nozick. We win, 6-3. Statute invalidated.") That would certainly be bad enough, but the actual situation is likely to be somewhat worse. Experience suggests that in fact there will be a systematic bias in judicial choice of fundamental values, unsurprisingly in favor of the values of the upper-middle, professional class from which most lawyers and judges, and for that matter most moral philosophers, are drawn. People understandably think that what is important to them is what is important, and people like us are no exception.* Thus the list of values the Court and the commentators have tended to enshrine as fundamental is a list with which readers of this book will have little trouble identifying: expression, association, education, academic freedom, the privacy of the home, personal autonomy, even the right not to be locked in a stereotypically female sex role and supported by one's husband.[71] But watch most fundamental-rights theorists start edging toward the door when someone mentions jobs, food, or housing: those are important, sure, but they aren't *fundamental*.[72]

Thus the values judges are likely to single out as fundamental, to the extent that the selections do not simply reflect the political and ethical predispositions of the individuals concerned, are likely to have the smell of the lamp about them.[73] They will be — and it would be unreasonable to expect otherwise if the task is so defined — the values of what Henry Hart without irony used to call "first-rate lawyers."[74] The objection to "reason" as a source of fundamental values is therefore best stated in the alternative: either it is an empty source, in the same way "neutral principles" turned out to be an empty source, or, if not empty, it is so flagrantly elitist and undemocratic that it should be dismissed forthwith.** Our society did not make the constitutional decision to move to near-universal suffrage only to turn around and have superimposed on popular decisions the values of first-rate lawyers. As Robert Dahl has observed, "After

---

*"And so we arrive at the result, that the pleasure of the intelligent part of the soul is the pleasantest of the three, and that he of us in whom this is the ruling principle has the pleasantest life.

"Unquestionably, he said, the wise man speaks with authority when he approves of his own life." Plato, *The Republic*, Book IX, in 2 *The Dialogues of Plato* 455 (4th ed. B. Jowett 1953).

**The danger that upper-middle-class judges and commentators will find upper-middle-class values fundamental is obviously present irrespective of methodology. I think it's exacerbated when "reason" is the supposed value source, however, partly because the values we have mentioned are the values of the "reasoning class," and partly because "reason," being inherently an empty source, may lend itself unusually well to being filled in by the values of one's own kind.

nearly twenty-five centuries, almost the only people who seem to be convinced of the advantages of being ruled by philosopher-kings are . . . a few philosophers."[75]

Tradition

> *Running men out of town on a rail is at least as much an American tradition as declaring unalienable rights.*   —*Garry Wills* [76]

Tradition is an obvious place to seek fundamental values,[77] but one whose problems are also obvious. The first is that people have come to understand that "tradition" can be invoked in support of almost any cause.[78] There is obvious room to maneuver, along continua of both space and time, on the subject of which tradition to invoke. Whose traditions count? America's only? Why not the entire world's? (For some reason Justice Frankfurter liked to refer to the "traditions of the English-speaking people."[79]) And what is the relevant time frame? All of history? Anteconstitutional only? Prior to the ratification of the provision whose construction is in issue? Why not, and indeed this seems the more usual reference, extending to the present day? (Once you're there, however, you're verging into a somewhat distinct approach.) And who is to say that the "tradition" must have been one endorsed by a majority? Is Henry David Thoreau an invocable part of American tradition? John Brown? John Calhoun? Jesus Christ? It's hard to see why not. Top all this off with the tremendous uncertainties in ascertaining anything very concrete about the intellectual or moral climates of ages passed, and you're in a position to prove almost anything to those who are predisposed to have it proved[80] or, more candidly, to admit that tradition doesn't really generate an answer, at least not an answer sufficiently unequivocal to justify overturning the contrary judgment of a legislative body.*

---

*A related technique is to discredit a practice by associating it with a disreputable tradition. See, e.g., Shaughnessy v. United States *ex rel.* Mezei, 345 U.S. 206, 217-18 (1953) (Black, J., dissenting). The techniques of association and dissociation can obviously be used in tandem. See, e.g., Poe v. Ullman, 367 U.S. 497, 542 (1961) (Harlan, J., dissenting) (emphasis added): "The balance of which I speak is the balance struck by this country, *having regard to what history teaches are the traditions from which it developed as well as the traditions from which it broke.*" This technique is virtually omnipotent, since there is no litmus that can separate

The indications in *Regents of the University of California v. Bakke*[81] that racial preferences for historically disadvantaged minorities are to be treated as (at least somewhat) constitutionally suspect[82] were quite explicitly rooted in an appeal to tradition. "This perception of racial and ethnic distinctions is rooted in our Nation's constitutional and demographic history."[83] And indeed Justice Powell was able to assemble a collection of historical statements to the effect that a person's legal status should not be affected by his race.[84] Those statements, however, were made in the context of discussing whether whites should be permitted to advantage themselves at the expense of racial minorities: to quote them in the affirmative action context without taking account of that critical fact[85] is to succumb to the understandable temptation to vary the relevant tradition's level of abstraction to make it come out right.[86]

Even with respect to the use of racial discrimination to *dis*favor minorities, our country has two conflicting traditions: the egalitarian one to which most official documents have paid lip service over the past century, and the quite different and malevolent one that in fact has characterized much official and unofficial practice over the same period (and certainly before).[87] Presumably no reader would wish to endorse the latter tradition, but I'd be interested to hear the argument that can make it go away. Assume that by some magic it will, however, and assume therefore a unitary American tradition against the use of racial classification to disadvantage minorities: even that contrivance will not, unless we cheat, generate a unitary tradition on the different question of whether racial minorities can be favored. In recent years there have been numerous official programs that give breaks of one sort or another to persons because of their minority race. It is true that in some earlier periods such programs did not exist, but that may have been because those concerned with improving the lot of minorities had their hands full attempting, generally unsuccessfully, to combat widespread official discrimination *against* minorities. In fact the only prior period during which affirmative action for racial minorities seems even to have

---

prior practices that are properly regarded as part of our tradition from those the framers "must have been rebelling against" (though any commentator is likely almost automatically to assume that those of which he or she disapproves belong in the latter category).

been a realistic possibility was Reconstruction. Some did object, apparently in part on principle—the name of Andrew Johnson is one that comes to mind here—but it surely seems more relevant that the Reconstruction Congress, the same Congress that gave us the amendment under which Bakke brought his challenge, passed over Johnson's veto such explicit preferences for blacks as those contained in the Freedmen's Bureau Act of 1866.[88] In the heat of debate one might attempt to identify Reconstruction as the relevant period from which to draw those traditions that should define our construction of the Fourteenth Amendment, and surely that seems no more disreputable than other appeals to tradition we have seen. The more honest conclusion, however, is that one must look elsewhere to decide what racial and other groups are to be permitted constitutionally to do to and for each other.[89] There does not exist an unambiguous American tradition on the question of whether racial majorities can act to aid minorities, and one can make it seem there is only by quoting out of context.

It is never satisfactory to rest one's whole objection to a constitutional theory on grounds of indeterminacy, if only because the implications of *any* nontrivial theory will be open to debate. There are, however, serious theoretical problems with tradition as a source of constitutional values. Its overtly backward-looking character highlights its undemocratic nature: it is hard to square with the theory of our government the proposition that yesterday's majority, assuming it was a majority, should control today's. Of course part of the point of the Constitution is to check today's majority. This observation simply compounds the problems with making tradition a source of constitutional values, however, since the provisions for which we are seeking a source of values were phrased in open-ended terms to admit the possibility of growth. (If one wanted to freeze a tradition, the sensible course would be to write it down.[90]) Moreover, "[i]f the Constitution protects only interests which comport with traditional values, the persons most likely to be penalized for their way of life will be those least likely to receive judicial protection,"[91] and that flips the point of the provisions exactly upside down. Reliance on tradition therefore seems consistent with neither the basic theory of popular control nor the spirit of the majority-checking provisions to which we are seeking to give content. For these reasons the reference is invariably a passing one, buttressing what turns out to be the most common reference-in-chief, the genuine consensus of contemporary American thought.[92]

Consensus

> *Few of us would march our sons and daughters off to war to preserve the citizen's right to see "Specified Sexual Activities" exhibited in the theaters of our choice.*
>
> *— United States Supreme Court (1976)*[93]

The idea that society's "widely shared values" should give content to the Constitution's open-ended provisions — that "constitutional law must now be understood as expressing contemporary norms"[94] — turns out to be at the core of most "fundamental values" positions.[95] Just as those who talk about tradition usually wind up with something like "today's values viewed in the light of tradition," something like contemporary value consensus almost inevitably ends up giving content to the inherently contentless notions of "reason" and "principle."[96] The reference has received its clearest recent articulation by Harry Wellington, who put it in terms of "conventional" or "common" morality: "The Court's task is to ascertain the weight of the principle in conventional morality and to convert the moral principle into a legal one by connecting it with the body of constitutional law."[97]

In theory this approach solves two problems we have seen with earlier ones. In theory it is not incomplete. Consensus or conventional morality is postulated as something "out there" that can be discovered. And in theory it is not undemocratic. Quite to the contrary, it is billed by Wellington as a "reference to the people."[98] F. A. Hayek elaborates: "Only a demagogue can represent as 'anti-democratic' the limitations which long-term decisions and the general principles held by the people impose upon the power of temporary majorities."[99]

I guess this makes me a demagogue, but I think both claims — that judicial references to popular consensus are not incomplete and that they are not undemocratic — are wrong. As to the first, there is a growing literature that argues that in fact there is no consensus to be discovered (and to the extent that one may seem to exist, that is likely to reflect only the domination of some groups by others). It is sometimes said that the American consensus disintegrated in the 1960s. That would be rebuttal enough, but in fact it may be only the recognition that is recent:

> The lack of common interest between master and slave is obvious. So is the relationship between the military during World War II and the Japanese-Americans who were herded into internment camps in an order whose constitutionality was upheld by the Supreme Court. Latter-day disputes concerning the legitimate role of race in governmental decision-making, whether for purposes of segregation or affirmative action, or the legitimacy of the state's allowing the cessation of the possibility of life, by abortion or euthanasia, also present differences of the greatest magnitude regarding conceptions of justice.[100]

Even if we assume, however — though it's virtually self-contradictory to do so — that there *is* a consensus lurking out there that contradicts the judgment of our elected representatives, there would still remain the point, sufficient in itself, that that consensus is not reliably discoverable, at least not by courts. As Louis Jaffe once inquired:

> How does one isolate and discover a consensus on a question so abstruse as the existence of a fundamental right? The public may value a right and yet not believe it to be fundamental. The public may hold that the rights of parents are fundamental and yet have no view whether they include sending a child to a private school. There may be a profound ambiguity in the public conscience; it may profess to entertain a traditional ideal but be reluctant to act upon it. In such a situation might we not say that the judge will be free to follow either the traditional ideal or the existing practice, depending on the reaction of his own conscience? And in many cases will it not be true that there has been no general thinking on the issue?[101]

Thus when one gets down to cases, one finds much the same mix we found when the reference was to "natural law" — a mix of the uselessly general and the controversially specific. Roberto Unger's observation about references to tradition seems equally applicable here: "To make the doctrine plausible in the absence of divinely revealed moral truth, its proponents rely on references to moral opinions shared by men of many different ages and societies. The more concrete the allusions to this allegedly timeless moral agreement, the less convincing they become. Therefore, to make their case the proponents of objective value must restrict themselves to a few abstract ideals whose vagueness allows almost any interpretation."[102] Express skepticism about the existence of moral consensus to someone who claims it means something, and you're likely to be given some jejune maxim like "No one should profit from his own wrong." Ask for an actual case where a constitutional court could legitimately overrule a legislative judgment on the basis of a moral consensus, and things get a little strange. In *Breithaupt v. Abram*, decided in 1957, the Supreme Court held that the drawing of twenty cubic centimeters of blood from the unconscious body of the obviously unconsenting petitioner, and the subsequent use of that blood to convict him of drunk driving, did not deny him due process. In doing so it rather explicitly employed a consensus methodology: "[D]ue process is not measured by the yardstick of personal reactions . . . but by that whole community sense of 'decency and fairness' that has been woven by common experience into the fabric of acceptable conduct. It is on this bedrock that this Court has established the concept of due process."[103] Bedrock indeed: what the Court fails to note, for all its talk of community sense, is that three of the nine justices dissented. The doubtful attribution of consensus is not, I should hasten to add, a technique reserved for "conservative" causes. In their separate concurring opinions in *Furman v. Georgia* (1972), Justices Brennan and Marshall argued quite directly that the death penalty was unconstitutional because it was out of accord with contemporary community values.[104] The risk in such a claim is obvious, and in this case it was tragically realized. Following *Furman* there was a virtual stampede of state reenactments of the death penalty, and the clarity of that community reaction surely had much to do with the Court's turnaround on the issue.[105]

The commentators' readings of society's values are as questionable as those of the justices. Professor Bickel wrote: "I would assert that the rightness of the Court's decision in the *School Segregation Cases* can be demonstrated [in terms of an appeal to societal values]. I would deny, however, that any similar demonstration can be or was mounted . . . to show that a statute setting maximum hours or minimum wages violates fundamental presuppositions of our society."[106] One can surely understand the goal that is evident here—to find a way of approving *Brown* while disapproving *Lochner*. And I think that combination can responsibly be defended, but not in these terms. I suppose it's possible, though in fact it seems unlikely,[107] that by 1954 the values of most of the country—assuming, despite our federal system, that opinion nationwide is what should count here—had moved to the point of condemning "separate but equal" schooling.[108] And obviously, given the existence of the legislation whose constitutionality was in issue, there were in some quarters serious reservations about laissez-faire capitalism around the time of *Lochner*. Bickel's *comparative* judgment, however, seems indefensible: racism of the sort that supported separate schools was into the 1950s (and remains today) a strong strain in American life, and laissez-faire capitalism was a philosophy that was very widely entertained around the turn of the century.[109] Dean Wellington, developing the implications of his "conventional morality" approach, pronounces, if more hesitantly, the same dubious verdict as Bickel on *Lochner*'s roots in popular opinion.[110] His ability to distinguish propositions that conventional morality supports from those it does not is displayed even more impressively, however, in the area of abortion:

> I take some comfort in the fact that the American Law Institute's Model Penal Code also would permit abortion for rape, to save the life of the mother, or if "the child would be born with grave physical or mental defect." The work of the Institute is a check of sorts. Its conclusions are some evidence of society's moral position on these questions. It is, indeed, better evidence than state legislation, for the Institute, while not free of politics, is not nearly as subject to the pressures of special interest groups as is a legislature.
>
> The Institute, however, would permit abortion in additional situations, most importantly where there was "a substantial risk that continuance of the pregnancy would gravely impair the physical or mental health of the mother." I would like to be able to find support for that position in conventional morality, for it surely coincides with my personal preference. But the Institute's position is here the best evidence there is and that does not seem enough. I do not understand how, by noticing commonly held attitudes, one can conclude that a healthy fetus is less important than a sick mother.[111]

It's quite a slalom, but I doubt that there's room on it for anyone besides Wellington.[112]

Examples could be multiplied, but it should by now be clear that by viewing society's values through one's own spectacles — resolving apparent inconsistencies in popular thinking in the "appropriate" direction by favoring the "emergent over the recessive,"[113] the "general over the particular,"[114] or whatever* — one can convince oneself that some invocable consensus supports almost any position a civilized person might want to see supported. As elsewhere, though, it is hard to claim that this alone adds up to a dispositive argument: there does not exist a nontrivial constitutional theory that will not involve judgment calls. In fact I think this one is worse than most in that regard, but in any event the comparative judgment is devastating: as between courts and legislatures, it is clear that the latter are better situated to reflect consensus. Sophisticated commentary never tires of reminding us that legislatures are only imperfectly democratic.[115] Beyond the fact that the appropriate answer is to make them more democratic,[116] however, the point is one that may on analysis backfire. The existing antimajoritarian influences in Congress and the state legislatures, capable though they may be of *blocking* legislation, are not well situated to get legislation passed in the face of majority opposition.[117] That makes all the more untenable the suggestion under consideration, that courts should invalidate legislation in the name of a supposed contrary consensus.[118] Beyond that, however, we may grant until we're blue in the face that legislatures aren't wholly democratic, but that isn't going to make courts more democratic than legislatures.[119]

An appeal to consensus, or to consensus tempered by the judge's

---

*Such techniques are evident in the work of consensus theorists generally, and are sometimes made explicit. Ronald Dworkin argues that community values must be refined by the judge in a way that removes prejudice, emotional reaction, rationalization, and "parroting," and in addition should be tested for sincerity and consistency. R. Dworkin, *Taking Rights Seriously* 126, 240-58 (1977). See also, e.g., Wellington, "Common Law Rules and Constitutional Double Standards: Some Notes on Adjudication," 83 *Yale L. J.* 221, 251 (1973) (courts "must be reasonably confident that they draw on conventional morality and screen out contemporary bias, passion, and prejudice, or indeed, that they distinguish cultivated taste from moral obligation"); Perry, "Substantive Due Process Revisited: Reflections on (and beyond) Recent Cases," 71 *Nw. U. L. Rev.* 417, 442 (1976) (distinction should be drawn between "the commands to which conventional moral culture subscribes and the commands to which it not only subscribes but believes should have the force of law"). Some such collection of "laundering" devices is plainly needed, lest one be forced to the conclusion that the law the legislature passed is likely to reflect the way contemporary community values bear on the issues in question. Cf. Note, "Legislative Purpose, Rationality, and Equal Protection," 82 *Yale L. J.* 123, 127-32, 135-37 (1972).

own values, may make some sense in a "common law" context, where the court is either filling in the gaps left by the legislature — "legislating interstitially," in Cardozo's phrase — or, perhaps, responding to a broad legislative delegation of decision-making authority. Since they are "standing in" for the legislature, courts presumably should try to behave as (good) legislatures behave, and that may involve combining their best estimate of popular opinion with their own best judgment. All too often commentators accustomed to working in fields other than constitutional law, fields where appeals to this sort of filtered consensus may make sense, seek to transfer their analytical techniques to the constitutional area without dropping a stitch.[120] After all, the inference seems to run, law is law, isn't it, and if it made sense there it should make sense here. The problem is that the constitutional context is worlds away: the legislature has spoken, and the question is whether the court is to overrule it in a way that can be undone only by the cumbersome process of constitutional amendment. That is precisely what constitutional courts must do — quite often, I shall argue. But to do so on the theory that the legislature does not truly speak for the people's values, but the Court does, is ludicrous.[121]

The notion that the genuine values of the people can most reliably be discerned by a nondemocratic elite is sometimes referred to in the literature as "the Führer principle,"[122] and indeed it was Adolf Hitler who said "My pride is that I know no statesman in the world who with greater right than I can say that he is the representative of his people."[123] We know, however, that this is not an attitude limited to right-wing elites. "The Soviet definition" of democracy, as H. B. Mayo has written, also involves the "ancient error" of assuming that "the wishes of the people can be ascertained more accurately by some mysterious methods of intuition open to an elite rather than by allowing people to discuss and vote and decide freely."[124] Apparently moderates are not immune either.

The final problem, the most fundamental of all, comes into perspective when you step back a couple of paces and think about why we're engaging in this entire exercise. There are two possible reasons one might look to consensus to give content to the Constitution's open-ended provisions. One *might* say one was seeking to protect the rights of the majority by ensuring that legislation truly reflect popular values. If that were the purpose, however, the legislative process would plainly be better suited to it than the judicial. This leaves the other possible reason for the reference, to protect the rights of individuals and minority groups against the actions of the majority. That, of course, is what we've been about in this chapter. No one suggests that we look to "natural law" or "tradition" to ensure that the majority's will is in fact being worked; such references are instead calculated to protect minorities from the unchecked exercise of the majority's will. Now think again about consensus as a possible source, and the message will come clear: it makes no sense to employ the value judgments of the majority as the vehicle for protecting minorities from the value judgments of the majority.[125] The consensus approach therefore derives what apparent strength it has from a muddle: its methodology, which people slide into accepting because of its similarity to what courts may do properly in common law contexts, has nothing to do with the tasks they can legitimately set themselves in the area of constitutional adjudication.

Predicting Progress

In his 1969 Holmes Lectures, subsequently published as *The Supreme Court and the Idea of Progress*,[126] the thinking of Alexander Bickel apparently took a new tack. The Warren Court, he claimed, had tried to prefigure the future, to shape its constitutional principles in accord with its best estimate of what tomorrow's observers would be prepared to credit as progress. In this, he argued, it had failed: already the Warren Court's "bets on the future" were coming up political losers. Bickel was somewhat elusive about whether he himself was prepared to accredit "tomorrow's values" as a source of constitutional judgment: his formal claim was that that had been the criterion of the Warren Court and that by its own criterion that Court had to be judged a failure. Though the point is arguable, I believe there was a good deal of prescription folded into Bickel's description. In any event others, before and after, have endorsed the method, even if Bickel did not mean to.[127]

The problems with this approach are the familiar ones, in more aggravated form. First — assuming for the moment that we really are talking about a predictive task — there is no reason to suppose that judges are well qualified to foresee the future development of popular opinion. Professor Bickel, whose historical sensitivity surely exceeded that of most lawyers and judges, fell on his face — or so at least it seems as of 1980 — explaining a decade ago how the Warren Court's great desegregation and reapportionment decisions had (already!) become irrelevant.[128] That only proves he was human — we've all mistaken ripples for waves. But that's exactly the point: prediction is a risky enterprise for anyone, and there is no warrant for an appointed judge's supposing he is so much better at it than the legislature that he is going to declare their efforts unconstitutional on the basis of his predictions.

In addition, the reference is antidemocratic on its face. Controlling today's generation by the values of its grandchildren is no more acceptable than controlling it by the values of its grandparents: a "liberal accelerator" is neither less nor more consistent with democratic theory than a "conservative brake." Superimposed on this problem is one I noted in connection with a contemporary consensus approach: the imposition of allegedly majoritarian values is a mindless way of going about protecting minorities, and stipulating that the majority is to be a future majority does not suddenly make sense of it. But even assuming that by some miracle of logic we could convince ourselves that the sensible way to protect today's minorities from today's majority is to impose on today's majority the values of tomorrow's majority, it would remain a myth that "the values of tomorrow's majority" are data that prescient courts can discover in a value-neutral way. For today's judicial decision (no matter what its source of judgment) will inevitably have an important influence on the values of tomorrow's majority.[129] The "prophecies" of people in power have an inevitably self-fulfilling character, even when what is being "prophesied" is popular opinion. This may or may not be a bad thing, but it does mean that the Court cannot be heard to plead value-neutrality on the theory that it is "taking its values from the future" rather than imposing its values *on* it: the fact that things turned out as the Supreme Court predicted may prove only that the Supreme Court is the Supreme Court. Thus by predicting the future the justices will unavoidably help shape it, and by shaping the future they will unavoidably, indeed this is the point of the methodology, shape the present. Assuming it works, that amounts to the imposition of the justices' own values. That's just what the fundamental value theorists promised they wouldn't do to us; the fact that it's done with mirrors shouldn't count as a defense.

The Odyssey of Alexander Bickel

There are a couple of reasons why Alexander Bickel has been such a central character in this chapter. He was probably the most creative constitutional theorist of the past twenty years. And he ran the gamut of fundamental-value methodologies. His career* is thus a microcosm, and it testifies to the inevitable futility of trying to answer the wrong question: "Which values, among adequately neutral and general ones, qualify as sufficiently important or fundamental or whathaveyou to be vindicated by the Court against other values affirmed by legislative acts?"[130] It wouldn't do, he acknowledged, for the justices simply to impose their own values: he recognized, as others have pretended not to, that given the enormous influence of the judiciary such a course would be fundamentally inconsistent with the first principles of our democracy. Nor did he suppose for a moment that there was some timeless set of objectively valid natural law principles out there to be discovered by judges or anyone else. And so he began his quest. He was one of the first to see that incanting "neutral principles" doesn't begin to tell you what those principles should be, and though he talked a lot about "reason" it was clear he understood that some other ingredient was needed. Tradition was too backward-looking, at least for a Robert Kennedy liberal, which is what Bickel was as late as 1968. Consensus — now that was promising, that could solve the countermajoritarian difficulty. But slowly he came to realize, though he never gave up on the idea altogether, that there probably wasn't any consensus respecting the sorts of issues that came before the Court,[131] and that even if there had been, the Court was one of the last bodies we should trust to find it.[132] Thus "the idea of progress." Bickel's posthumously published book, *The Morality of Consent*, suggests that he soon saw this too for what it was, a thinly veiled imposition of personal judicial values on the present and future.[133] What, then, to fill the breach? Unfortunately, a pastiche of themes remembered, with particular stress this time on one that hadn't much attracted the young Alex Bickel: tradition. His good friend Robert Bork explained at Bickel's Memorial Service that this Burkean ending

---

*"Tragically foreshortened" is too trite for Alex, who was never trite, in intellectual or personal style.

meant that Bickel had finally "resolved the tension" between his political liberalism and his judicial conservatism. "To read his *New Republic* piece on Edmund Burke is to see that his political philosophy had come into alignment with his legal philosophy." I remember choking as Bork said this, not because I disagreed that Bickel's politics had moved somewhat toward the end — I can't account for *The Morality of Consent* without that assumption either — but rather because of Bork's suggestion that there had been a contradiction to be resolved. For one perfectly well *can* be a genuine political liberal and at the same time believe, out of a respect for the democratic process, that the Court should keep its hands off the legislature's value judgments. I've calmed down, though, and now I can see how *someone who started with Bickel's premise*, that the proper role of the Court is the definition and imposition of values,[134] might well after a lifetime of searching conclude that since nothing else works — since there isn't any impersonal value source out there waiting to be tapped — one might just as well "do the right thing" by imposing one's own values. It's a conclusion of desperation, but in this case an inevitable desperation. No answer is what the wrong question begets.

4 Policing the Process of Representation: The Court as Referee

ALL this seems to leave us in a quandary. An interpretivist approach — at least one that approaches constitutional provisions as self-contained units — proves on analysis incapable of keeping faith with the evident spirit of certain of the provisions. When we search for an external source of values with which to fill in the Constitution's open texture, however — one that will not simply end up constituting the Court a council of legislative revision — we search in vain. Despite the usual assumption that these are the only options,[1] however, they are not, for value imposition is not the only possible response to the realization that we have a Constitution that needs filling in. A quite different approach is available, and to discern its outlines we need look no further than to the Warren Court.[2]

That Court's reputation as "activist" or interventionist is deserved. A good deal of carping to the contrary notwithstanding, however, that is where its similarity to earlier interventionist Courts, in particular the early twentieth-century Court that decided *Lochner v. New York* and its progeny, ends. For all the while the commentators of the Warren era were talking about ways of discovering fundamental values, the Court itself was marching to a different drummer. The divergence wasn't entirely self-conscious, and the Court did lapse occasionally into the language of fundamental values: it would be surprising if the thinking of earlier Courts and the writings of the day's preeminent commentators hadn't taken some toll.[3] The toll, however, was almost entirely rhetorical: the constitutional decisions of the Warren Court evidence a deep structure significantly different from the value-oriented approach favored by the academy.[4]

Many of the Warren Court's most controversial decisions concerned criminal procedure or other questions of what judicial or administrative process is due before serious consequences may be visited upon individuals — process-oriented decisions in the most ordinary sense. But a concern with process in a broader sense — with the process by which the laws that govern society are made — animated its other decisions as well. Its unprecedented activism in the fields of political expression and association obviously fits this broader pattern. Other Courts had recognized the connection between such political activity and the proper functioning of the democratic process: the Warren Court was the first seriously to act upon it. That Court was also the first to move into, and once there seriously to occupy, the voter qualification and malapportionment areas. These were certainly interventionist decisions, but the interventionism was fueled not by a desire on the part of the Court to vindicate particular substantive values it had determined were important or fundamental, but rather by a desire to ensure that the political process — which is where such values *are* properly identified, weighed, and accommodated — was open to those of all viewpoints on something approaching an equal basis.

Finally there were the important decisions insisting on equal treatment for society's habitual unequals: notably racial minorities, but also aliens, "illegitimates," and poor people. But rather than announcing that good or value X was so important or fundamental it simply had to be provided or protected, the Court's message here was that insofar as political officials had chosen to provide or protect X for some people (generally people like themselves), they had better make sure that everyone was being similarly accommodated or be prepared to explain pretty convincingly why not. Whether these two broad concerns of the Warren Court — with clearing the channels of political change on the one hand, and with correcting certain kinds of discrimination against minorities on the other — fit together to form a coherent theory of representative government, or whether, as is sometimes suggested, they are actually inconsistent impulses,[5] is a question I shall take up presently. But however that may be, it seems to be coming into focus that the pursuit of these "participational" goals of broadened access to the processes and bounty* of representative government, as opposed to the more tra-

---

*The reference here should be understood as including exemptions or immunities from hurts (punishments, taxes, regulations, and so forth) along with benefits. It is thus to patterns of distribution generally.

ditional and academically popular insistence upon the provision of a series of particular substantive goods or values deemed fundamental, was what marked the work of the Warren Court.[6] Some condemn and others praise, but at least we're beginning to understand that something different from old-fashioned value imposition was for a time the order of the day.*

The Carolene Products Footnote

The Warren Court's approach was foreshadowed in a famous footnote in *United States v. Carolene Products Co.*, decided in 1938. Justice Stone's opinion for the Court upheld a federal statute prohibiting the interstate shipment of filled milk, on the ground that all it had to be was "rational" and it assuredly was that. Footnote four suggested, however, that mere rationality might not always be enough:

> There may be narrower scope for operation of the presumption of constitutionality when legislation appears on its face to be within a specific prohibition of the Constitution, such as those of the first ten amendments, which are deemed equally specific when held to be embraced within the Fourteenth . . .
>
> It is unnecessary to consider now whether legislation which restricts those political processes which can ordinarily be ex-

*Participation itself can obviously be regarded as a value, but that doesn't collapse the two modes of review I am describing into one. As I am using the terms, value imposition refers to the designation of certain goods (rights or whatever) as so important that they must be insulated from whatever inhibition the political process might impose, whereas a participational orientation denotes a form of review that concerns itself with how decisions effecting value choices and distributing the resultant costs and benefits are made. See also p. 87n. I surely don't claim that the words have to be used thus. (There is even doubt that "participational" deserves to be recognized as a word at all.) I claim only that that is how I am using them, and that so used they are not synonyms.

If the objection is not that I have not distinguished two concepts but rather that one might well "value" certain decision procedures for their own sake, of course it is right: one might. And to one who insisted on that terminology, my point would be that the "values" the Court should pursue are "participational values" of the sort I have mentioned, since those are the "values" (1) with which our Constitution has preeminently and most successfully concerned itself, (2) whose "imposition" is not incompatible with, but on the contrary supports, the American system of representative democracy, and (3) that courts set apart from the political process are uniquely situated to "impose."

pected to bring about repeal of undesirable legislation, is to be subjected to more exacting judicial scrutiny under the general prohibitions of the Fourteenth Amendment than are most other types of legislation . . .

Nor need we enquire whether similar considerations enter into the review of statutes directed at particular religious . . . or national . . . or racial minorities . . . ; whether prejudice against discrete and insular minorities may be a special condition, which tends seriously to curtail the operation of those political processes ordinarily to be relied upon to protect minorities, and which may call for a correspondingly more searching judicial inquiry.[7]

The first paragraph is pure interpretivism: it says the Court should enforce the "specific" provisions of the Constitution.[8] We've seen, though, that interpretivism is incomplete: there are provisions in the Constitution that call for more. The second and third paragraphs give us a version of what that more might be. Paragraph two suggests that it is an appropriate function of the Court to keep the machinery of democratic government running as it should, to make sure the channels of political participation and communication are kept open. Paragraph three suggests that the Court should also concern itself with what majorities do to minorities, particularly mentioning laws "directed at" religious, national, and racial minorities and those infected by prejudice against them.

For all its notoriety and influence, the *Carolene Products* footnote has not been adequately elaborated. Paragraph one has always seemed to some commentators not quite to go with the other two.[9] Professor Lusky, who as Stone's law clerk was substantially responsible for the footnote, has recently revealed that the first paragraph was added at the request of Chief Justice Hughes.[10] Any implied substantive criticism seems misplaced: positive law has its claims, even when it doesn't fit some grander theory.[11] It's true, though, that paragraphs two and three are more interesting, and it is the relationship between those two paragraphs that has not been adequately elaborated. Popular control and egalitarianism are surely both ancient American ideals; indeed, dictionary definitions of "democracy" tend to incorporate both.[12] Frequent conjunction is not the same thing as consistency, however, and at least on the surface a principle of popular control suggests an ability on the part of a majority simply to outvote a minority and thus deprive its members of goods they desire. Borrowing Paul Freund's word,[13] I have suggested that both *Carolene Products* themes are concerned with participation: they ask us to focus not on whether this or that substantive value is unusually important or fundamental, but rather on whether the opportunity to participate either in the political processes by which values are appropriately identified and accommodated, or in the accommodation those processes have reached, has been unduly constricted. But the fact that two concepts can fit under the same verbal umbrella isn't enough to render them consistent either, and a system of equal participation in the processes of government is by no means self-evidently linked to a system of presumptively equal participation in the benefits and costs that process generates; in many ways it seems calculated to produce just the opposite effect. To understand the ways these two sorts of participation join together in a coherent political theory, it is necessary to focus more insistently than I did in Chapter 1 on the American system of representative democracy.

Representative Government

> It is a principle of general application that the exercise of a granted power to act in behalf of others involves the assumption toward them of a duty to exercise the power in their interest and behalf . . .
> We think that the Railway Labor Act imposes upon the statutory representative of a craft at least as exacting a duty to protect equally the interests of the members of the craft as the Constitution imposes upon a legislature to give equal protection to the interests of those for whom it legislates.
>
> — United States Supreme Court (1944)[14]

Representative democracy is perhaps most obviously a system of government suited to situations in which it is for one reason or another impractical for the citizenry actually to show up and personally participate in the legislative process. But the concept of representation, as understood by our forebears, was richer than this. Prerevolutionary rhetoric posited a continuing conflict between the interests of "the rulers" on the one hand, and those of "the ruled" (or "the people") on the other.[15] A solution was sought by building into the concept of representation the idea of an association of the interests of the two groups. Thus the representatives in the new government were visualized as "citizens," persons of unusual ability and character to be sure, but nonetheless "of" the people. Upon conclusion of their service, the vision continued, they would return to the body of the people and thus to the body of the ruled. In addition, even while in office, the idea was that they would live under the regime of the laws they passed and not exempt themselves from their operation: this obligation to include themselves among the ruled would ensure a community of interest and guard against oppressive legislation.[16] The framers realized that even visions need enforcement mechanisms: "some force to oppose the insidious tendency of power to separate . . . the rulers from the ruled" was required.[17] The principal force envisioned was the ballot: the people in their self-interest would choose representatives whose interests intertwined with theirs and by the critical reelection decision ensure that they stayed that way, in particular that the representatives did not shield themselves from the rigors of the laws they passed.[18]

Actually it may not matter so much whether our representatives are treating themselves the way they treat the rest of us. Indeed it may be precisely because in some ways they treat themselves better, that they seem so desperately to want to be reelected. And it may be that desire for reelection, more than any community of interest, that is our insurance policy. If most of us feel we are being subjected to unreasonable treatment by our representatives, we retain the ability — irrespective of whether they are formally or informally insulating themselves — to turn them out of office. What the system, at least as described thus far, does *not* ensure is the effective protection of minorities whose interests differ from the interests of most of the rest of us. For if it is not the "many" who are being treated unreasonably but rather only some minority, the situation will not be so comfortably amenable to political correction. Indeed there may be political pressures to *encourage* our representatives to pass laws that treat the majority coalition on whose continued support they depend in one way, and one or more minorities whose backing they don't need less favorably. Even assuming we were willing and able to give it teeth, a requirement that our representatives treat themselves as they treat most of the rest of us would be no guarantee whatever against unequal treatment for minorities.

This is not to say that the oppression of minorities was a development our forebears were prepared to accept as inevitable. The "republic" they envisioned was not some "winner-take-all" system in
which the government pursued the interests of a privileged few or
even of only those groups that could work themselves into some
majority coalition,[19] but rather—leaving slavery to one side, which
of course is precisely what they did—one in which the representatives would govern in the interest of the whole people.[20] Thus every
citizen was said to be entitled to equivalent respect, and equality was
a frequently mentioned republican concern. Its place in the Declaration of Independence, for example, could hardly be more prominent.[21] When it came to describing the actual mechanics of republican government in the Constitution, however, this concern for
equality got comparatively little explicit attention. This seems to
have been largely because of an assumption of "pure" republican
political and social theory that we have brushed but not yet stressed:
that "the people" were an essentially homogenous group whose
interests did not vary significantly.[22] Though most often articulated
as if it were an existing reality, this was at best an ideal, and the fact
that wealth redistribution of some form—ranging from fairly extreme to fairly modest proposals—figured in so much early republican theorizing,[23] while doubtless partly explainable simply in terms
of the perceived desirability of such a change, also was quite con-
sciously connected to republicanism's political theory. To the extent
that existing heterogeneity of interest was a function of wealth dis-
parity, redistribution would reduce it. To the extent that the ideal
of homogeneity could be achieved, legislation in the interest of most
would necessarily be legislation in the interest of all, and extensive
further attention to equality of treatment would be unnecessary.

The key assumption here, that everyone's interests are essentially
identical, is obviously a hard one for our generation to swallow, and
in fact we know perfectly well that many of our forebears were am-
bivalent about it too.[24] Thus the document of 1789 and 1791,
though at no point explicitly invoking the concept of equality, did
strive by at least two strategies to protect the interests of minorities
from the potentially destructive will of some majority coalition. The
more obvious one may be the "list" strategy employed by the Bill of
Rights, itemizing things that cannot be done to anyone, at least by
the federal government (though even here the safeguards turn out to

be mainly procedural). The original Constitution's more pervasive strategy, however, can be loosely styled a strategy of pluralism, one of structuring the government, and to a limited extent society generally, so that a variety of voices would be guaranteed their say and no majority coalition could dominate.[25] As Madison—pointedly eschewing the ("Chapter 3") approach of setting up an undemocratic body to keep watch over the majority's values—put it in *Federalist* 51:

> It is of great importance in a republic not only to guard the society against the oppression of its rulers, but to guard one part of the society against the injustice of the other part . . . If a majority be united by a common interest, the rights of the minority will be insecure. There are but two methods of providing against this evil: the one by creating a will in the community independent of the majority . . . the other, by comprehending in the society so many separate descriptions of citizens as will render an unjust combination of a majority of the whole very improbable, if not impracticable. The first method prevails in all governments possessing an hereditary or self-appointed authority. This, at best, is but a precarious security; because a power independent of the society may as well espouse the unjust views of the major, as the rightful interests of the minor party, and may possibly be turned against both parties. The second method will be exemplified in the federal republic of the United States.[26]

The crucial move from a confederation to a system with a stronger central government was so conceived. Madison has been conspicuously attacked for not understanding pluralist political theory,[27] but in fact there is reason to suppose he understood it rather well. His theory, derived from David Hume and spelled out at length in *The Federalist*, was that although at a local level one "faction" might well have sufficient clout to be able to tyrannize others, in the national government no faction or interest group would constitute a majority capable of exercising control.[28] The Constitution's various moves to break up and counterpoise governmental decision and enforcement authority, not only between the national government and the states but among the three departments of the national government as well, were of similar design.[29]

It is a rightly renowned system, but it didn't take long to learn that from the standpoint of protecting minorities it was not enough. Whatever genuine faith had existed at the beginning that everyone's interests either were identical or were about to be rendered so, had run its course as the republic approached its fiftieth birthday. Significant economic differences remained a reality, and the fear of legislation hostile to the interests of the propertied and creditor classes—a fear that of course had materialized earlier, during the regime of the Articles of Confederation, and thus had importantly inspired the constitutional devices to which we have alluded—surely did not abate during the Jacksonian era, as the "many" began genuinely to exercise political power.[30] The Pennsylvania Supreme Court summed it up thus in 1851:

> [W]hen, in the exercise of proper legislative powers, general laws are enacted, which bear or may bear on the whole community, if they are unjust and against the spirit of the constitution, the whole community will be interested to procure their repeal by a voice potential. And that is the great security for just and fair legislation.
>
> But when individuals are selected from the mass, and laws are enacted affecting their property, . . . who is to stand up for them, thus isolated from the mass, in injury and injustice, or where are they to seek relief from such acts of despotic power?[31]

Also relevant was the persistence of the institution of slavery. So long as blacks could conveniently be regarded as subhuman, they provided no proof that some people were tyrannizing others. Once that assumption began to blur, there came into focus another reason for doubting that the protection of the many was necessarily the protection of all.[32]

Simultaneously we came to recognize that the existing constitutional devices for protecting minorities were simply not sufficient. No finite list of entitlements can possibly cover all the ways majorities can tyrannize minorities, and the informal and more formal mechanisms of pluralism cannot always be counted on either. The fact that effective majorities can usually be described as clusters of cooperating minorities won't be much help when the cluster in question has sufficient power and perceived community of interest to advantage itself at the expense of a minority (or group of minorities) it is inclined to regard as different, and in such situations the fact that a number of agencies must concur, and others retain the right to squawk, isn't going to help much either. If, therefore, the republican ideal of government in the interest of the whole people was to be maintained, in an age when faith in the republican tenet that the people and their interests were essentially homogeneous was all but dead, a frontal assault on the problem of majority tyranny was needed. The existing theory of representation had to be extended so as to ensure not simply that the representative would not sever his interests from those of a majority of his constituency but also that he would not sever a majority coalition's interests from those of various minorities. Naturally that cannot mean that groups that constitute minorities of the population can never be treated less favorably than the rest, but it does preclude a refusal to *represent* them,[33] the denial to minorities of what Professor Dworkin has called "equal concern and respect in the design and administration of the political institutions that govern them."[34] The Fourteenth Amendment's Equal Protection Clause is obviously our Constitution's most dramatic embodiment of this ideal. Before that amendment was ratified, however, its theory was understood, and functioned as a component — even on occasion as a judicially enforceable component[35] — of the concept of representation that had been at the core of our Constitution from the beginning.

It's ironic, but the old concept of "virtual representation" is helpful here. The actual term was anathema to our forefathers, since it was invoked to answer their cries of "taxation without representation." But the concept contained an insight that has survived in American political theory and in fact has informed our constitutional thinking from the beginning. The colonists' argument that it was wrong, even "unconstitutional," to tax us when we lacked the privilege of sending representatives to Parliament was answered on the British side by the argument that although the colonies didn't actually elect anyone, they were "virtually represented" in Parliament. Manchester was taxed, it was pointed out, without the privilege of sending representatives to Parliament; yet surely, the argument concluded, no one could deny that Manchester was represented. The colonists' answer, at least their principal one, took the form of a denial not of the concept's general sense, but rather of its applicability to our case. Thus Daniel Dulany responded:

The security of the non-electors [of Manchester] against oppression is that their oppression will fall also upon the electors and the representatives . . . The electors, who are inseparably connected in their interests with the non-electors, may be justly deemed to be the representatives of the non-electors . . . and the members chosen, therefore, the representatives of both.

However,

there is not that intimate and inseparable relation between the electors of Great Britain and the inhabitants of the colonies, which must inevitably involve both in the same taxation. On the contrary, not a single actual elector in England might be immediately affected by a taxation in America . . . Even acts oppressive and injurious to an extreme degree, might become popular in England, from the promise or expectation that the very measures which depressed the colonies, would give ease to the inhabitants of Great Britain.[36]

Although the term understandably has not been revived, the protective device of guaranteeing "virtual representation" by tying the interests of those without political power to the interests of those with it, was one that importantly influenced both the drafting of our original Constitution and its subsequent interpretation. Article IV's Privileges and Immunities Clause was intended and has been interpreted to mean that state legislatures cannot by their various regulations treat out-of-staters less favorably than they treat locals. "It was designed to insure to a citizen of State A who ventures into State B the same privileges which the citizens of State B enjoy."[37] Article IV conveys no set of substantive entitlements, but "simply" the guarantee that whatever entitlements those living in a state see fit to vote themselves will generally be extended to visitors. An ethical ideal of equality is certainly working here, but the reason inequalities against nonresidents and not others were singled out for prohibition in the original document is obvious: nonresidents are a paradigmatically powerless class politically. And their protection proceeds by what amounts to a system of virtual representation: by constitutionally tying the fate of outsiders to the fate of those possessing political power, the framers insured that their interests would be well looked after. The Commerce Clause of Article I, Section 8 provides simply that Congress shall have the power to regulate commerce among the states. But early on the Supreme Court gave this provision a self-operating dimension as well, one growing out of the same need to protect the politically powerless and proceeding by the

same device of guaranteed virtual representation. Thus, for example, early in the nineteenth century the Court indicated that a state
could not subject goods produced out of state to taxes it did not impose on goods produced locally.[38] By thus constitutionally binding
the interests of out-of-state manufacturers to those of local manufacturers represented in the legislature, it provided political insurance that the taxes imposed on the former would not rise to a pro-
hibitive or even an unreasonable level.[39]

These examples involve the protection of geographical outsiders,
the literally voteless. But even the technically represented can find
themselves functionally powerless and thus in need of a sort of "virtual representation" by those more powerful than they.[40] From one
perspective the claim of such groups to protection from the ruling
majority is even more compelling than that of the out-of-stater: they
are, after all, members of the community that is doing them in.
From another, however, their claim seems weaker: they do have the
vote, and it may not in the abstract seem unreasonable to expect
them to wheel and deal as the rest of us (theoretically) do, yielding
on issues about which they are comparatively indifferent and
"scratching the other guy's back" in order to get him to scratch
theirs. "[N]o group that is prepared to enter into the process and
combine with others need remain permanently and completely out
of power."[41] Perhaps not "permanently and completely" if by that
we mean forever, but certain groups that are technically enfran-
chised *have* found themselves for long stretches in a state of persistent inability to protect themselves from pervasive forms of discriminatory treatment. Such groups might just as well be disenfranchised.

The issues adumbrated here—relating to the conditions under
which it is appropriate constitutionally to bind the interests of the
majority to those of some minority with which no felt community of
interests has naturally developed—obviously need a good deal more
attention, and they shall receive it in Chapter 6. The point that is
relevant here is that even before the enactment of the Equal Protection Clause, the Supreme Court was prepared at least under certain
conditions to protect the interests of minorities that were not literally voteless by constitutionally tying their interests to those of
groups that did possess political power—and, what is the same
thing, by intervening to protect such interests when it appeared that
such a guarantee of "virtual representation" was not being pro-

vided. In the landmark case of *McCulloch v. Maryland*, decided in 1819, the Court invalidated a state tax on the operations of all banks (preeminently including the Bank of the United States) not chartered by the state legislature. Toward the end of Chief Justice Marshall's Court opinion, there appears a potentially baffling qualification: "This opinion . . . does not extend to a tax paid by the real property of the bank, in common with the other real property within the state, nor to a tax imposed on the interest which the citizens of Maryland may hold in this institution, in common with other property of the same description throughout the state."[42] What ever did he have in mind? It can't have been that he knew the sorts of property taxes mentioned were in fact less burdensome, for nothing in his opinion had indicated that the tax the Court was invalidating was in fact disabling or even burdensome. Indeed it was at the heart of his argument that no such showing was necessary: "the power to tax involves the power to destroy" and a little tax on bank operations was declared as impermissible as a big one. A tax on the land on which the local branch of the Bank of the United States sits also has the potential to destroy, however. *Either* tax, if it got out of hand—and there was no indication that either had—could destroy the Bank.

By now we should be in a position to spot the trick right away: it lies in Marshall's indication that the real estate tax would have to be "in common with the other real property within the state," the tax on any interest held by citizens "in common with other property of the same description throughout the state." The unity of interest with all Maryland property owners assured by this insistence on equal treatment would protect the Bank from serious disablement by taxes of this sort. The power to tax real or personal property *is* potentially the power to destroy. But people aren't lemmings, and while they may agree to disadvantage themselves somewhat in the service of some overriding social good, they aren't in the habit of destroying themselves en masse.[43]

The tax in issue, on the operations of banks not chartered by the state, presented a different configuration of interests. Naturally the Bank of the United States didn't have a vote in the Maryland legislature, but no corporation did. The interests of organizations generally have to be protected by persons whose interests are tied up with theirs—officers, employees, stockholders—and in these respects there is no reason to suppose the Bank of the United States was more impoverished than any other organization. Thus the Bank was not voteless, at least not voteless in any sense that other corporations were not. Yet the tax on bank operations was invalidated, and the reason it was is quite obvious: this was a tax exclusively on banks, indeed exclusively on banks not chartered by the state. The Bank of the United States may have had a "vote" as effective as that of any other single corporation, but it was clear nonetheless that with regard to a tax on the operations of non-state-chartered banks it would find itself in a perpetually losing situation politically, since at best—though it appears even this was lacking—its only allies on this issue would be a couple of wildcat banks. Here too there is reason to suppose that constitutional salvation would have been found only in a genuine guarantee of virtual representation—if, for example, the Bank's operations had been taxed only as part of a tax equally affecting all business operations in Maryland.[44]

I certainly do not mean to suggest that *McCulloch* was a direct precursor of the *Carolene Products* footnote, generally heralding the special judicial protection of discrete and insular minorities: it is most unlikely that the Bank would have received this special solicitude had it not been a federal instrumentality. The Court's discussion is instructive nonetheless. It suggests by its reference to the property taxes the clear assumption of even that early day that representatives were expected to represent the entirety of their constituencies without arbitrarily severing disfavored minorities for comparatively unfavorable treatment. And it suggests by its invalidation of the bank operations tax its further assumption that at least in some situations judicial intervention becomes appropriate when the existing processes of representation seem inadequately fitted to the representation of minority interests, even minority interests that are not voteless. I do not suggest that these themes were very often made explicit before the Civil War, but the frequency of their invocation is not to the present point. Whatever may have been the case before, the Fourteenth Amendment quite plainly imposes a judicially enforceable duty of virtual representation of the sort I have been describing. My main point in using the examples has been to suggest a way in which what are sometimes characterized as two conflicting American ideals—the protection of popular government on the one hand, and the protection of minorities from denials of equal concern and respect on the other — in fact can be understood as arising from a common duty of representation. Once again, Madison said it early and well:

> I will add, as a fifth circumstance in the situation of the House of Representatives, restraining them from oppressive measures, that they can make no law which will not have its full operation on themselves and their friends, as well as on the great mass of society . . . If it be asked, what is to restrain the House of Representatives from making legal discriminations in favor of themselves and a particular class of the society? I answer: the genius of the whole system; the nature of just and constitutional laws; and above all, the vigilant and manly spirit which actuates the people of America . . . [45]

The remainder of this chapter will comprise three arguments in favor of a participation-oriented, representation-reinforcing approach to judicial review. The first will take longer than the others, since it will necessitate a tour, albeit brisk, of the Constitution itself. What this tour will reveal, contrary to the standard characterization of the Constitution as "an enduring but evolving statement of general values,"[46] is that in fact the selection and accommodation of substantive values is left almost entirely to the political process and instead the document is overwhelmingly concerned, on the one hand, with procedural fairness in the resolution of individual disputes (process writ small), and on the other, with what might capaciously be designated process writ large* — with ensuring broad participation in the processes and distributions of government.[47] An argument by way of *ejusdem generis* seems particularly justified in this case, since the constitutional provisions for which we are attempting to identify modes of supplying content, such as the Ninth Amendment and the Privileges or Immunities Clause, seem to have been included in a "we must have missed something here, so let's trust our successors to add what we missed" spirit.[48] On my more expansive days, therefore, I am tempted to claim that the mode of re-

---

*I don't mean to be hanging any of the argument on this characterization. See p. 75n. It is true, however, that the approach I shall recommend is more thoroughgoingly process-oriented in elaboration than might be supposed even from the discussion thus far. See generally Chapter 6.

view developed here represents the ultimate interpretivism.* Our review will tell us something else that may be even more relevant to the issue before us — that the few attempts the various framers *have* made to freeze substantive values by designating them for special protection in the document have been ill-fated, normally resulting in repeal, either officially or by interpretative pretense. This suggests a conclusion with important implications for the task of giving content to the document's more open-ended provisions, that preserving fundamental values is not an appropriate constitutional task.

The other two arguments are susceptible to briefer statement but are not less important. The first is that a representation-reinforcing approach to judicial review, unlike its rival value-protecting approach, is not inconsistent with, but on the contrary (and quite by design) entirely supportive of, the underlying premises of the American system of representative democracy. The second is that such an approach, again in contradistinction to its rival, involves tasks that courts, as experts on process and (more important) as political outsiders, can sensibly claim to be better qualified and situated to perform than political officials.

The Nature of the United States Constitution

> *In the United States the basic charter of the law-making process is found in a written constitution . . . [W]e should resist the temptation to clutter up that document with amendments relating to substantive matters . . . [Such attempts] involve the obvious unwisdom of trying to solve tomorrow's problems today. But their more insidious danger lies in the weakening effect they would have on the moral force of the Constitution itself.*
>
> *—Lon Fuller* [49]

Many of our colonial forebears' complaints against British rule were phrased in "constitutional" terms. Seldom, however, was the claim

---

*As I've indicated, I don't think this terminological question is either entirely coherent or especially important. Obviously the approach recommended is neither "interpretivist" in the usual sense (of treating constitutional clauses as self-contained units) nor "noninterpretivist" in the usual sense (of seeking the principal stuff of constitutional judgment in one's rendition of society's fundamental values rather than in the document's broader themes). What counts is not whether it is "really" a broad interpretivism or rather a position that does not fall entirely in

one of deprivation of some treasured good or substantive right: the American colonists, at least the white males, were among the freest and best-off people in the history of the world, and by and large they knew it.[50] "Constitutional" claims thus were often jurisdictional —that Parliament lacked authority, say, to regulate the colonies' "internal commerce"—the foundation for the claim being generally that we were not represented in Parliament.[51] (Obviously the colonists weren't any crazier about being taxed than anyone else is, but what they damned as tyrannical was taxation *without representation.*) Or they were arguments of inequality: claims of entitlement to "the rights of Englishmen" had an occasional natural law flavor, but the more common meaning was that suggested by the words, a claim for equality of treatment with those living in England.[52] Thus the colonists' "constitutional" arguments drew on the two participational themes we have been considering: that (1) their input into the process by which they were governed was insufficient, and that (partly as a consequence) (2) they were being denied what others were receiving. The American version of revolution, wrote Hannah Arendt, "actually proclaims no more than the necessity of civilized government for all mankind; the French version . . . proclaims the existence of rights independent of and outside the body public . . ."[53]

The theme that justice and happiness are best assured not by trying to define them for all time, but rather by attending to the governmental processes by which their dimensions would be specified over time, carried over into our critical constitutional documents. Even our foremost "natural law" statement, the Declaration of Independence, after adverting to some admirable but assuredly open-ended goals—made more so by using "the pursuit of happiness" in place of the already broad Lockean reference to "property"[54]— signals its appreciation of the critical role of (democratic) process:

---

either camp, but whether it is capable of keeping faith with the document's promise in a way I have argued that a clause-bound interpretivism is not, and capable at the same time of avoiding the objections to a value-laden form of noninterpretivism, objections rooted most importantly in democratic theory. In that regard the two arguments that close this chapter, those addressed explicitly to consistency with democratic theory and the relative institutional capacities of legislatures and courts, seem at least as important as the argument from the nature of the Constitution (which given the complexity of the document must be a qualified one in any event).

> We hold these truths to be self-evident, that all men are created
> equal, that they are endowed by their creator with certain un-
> alienable rights; that among these are life, liberty, and the pur-
> suit of happiness; that *to secure these rights governments are
> instituted among men, deriving their just powers from the
> consent of the governed* . . .[55]

The Constitution, less surprisingly, begins on the same note, not one
of trying to set forth some governing ideology—the values mentioned in the Preamble could hardly be more pliable—but rather
one of ensuring a durable structure for the ongoing resolution of
policy disputes:

> We the People of the United States, in Order to form a more
> perfect Union, establish Justice, insure domestic Tranquility,
> provide for the common defence, promote the general Wel-
> fare, and secure the Blessings of Liberty to ourselves and our
> Posterity, do ordain and establish this Constitution for the
> United States of America.

I don't suppose it will surprise anyone to learn that the body of the
original Constitution is devoted almost entirely to structure, explaining who among the various actors—federal government, state
government; Congress, executive, judiciary—has authority to do
what, and going on to fill in a good bit of detail about how these
persons are to be selected and to conduct their business. Even provisions that at first glance might seem primarily designed to assure or
preclude certain substantive results seem on reflection to be principally concerned with process. Thus, for example, the provision that
treason "shall consist only in levying War against [the United
States], or in adhering to their Enemies, giving them Aid and Com-
fort," appears at least in substantial measure to have been a precursor of the First Amendment, reacting to the recognition that persons
in power can disable their detractors by charging disagreement as
treason.[56] The prohibitions against granting titles of nobility seem
rather plainly to have been designed to buttress the democratic ideal
that all are equals in government.[57] The Ex Post Facto and Bill of
Attainder Clauses prove on analysis to be separation of powers provisions, enjoining the legislature to act prospectively and by general
rule (just as the judiciary is implicitly enjoined by Article III to act
retrospectively and by specific decree).[58] And we have seen that the
Privileges and Immunities Clause of Article IV, and at least in one

aspect — the other being a grant of congressional power — the Commerce Clause as well, function as equality provisions, guaranteeing virtual representation to the politically powerless.

During most of this century the Obligation of Contracts Clause has not played a significant role.[59] Powerful arguments have been made that the clause was intended importantly to limit the extent to which state governments could control the subjects and terms of private contracts.[60] Early in the nineteenth century the Supreme Court rejected this broad interpretation, however, holding that the clause affected only the extent to which the legislature could alter or overrule the terms of contracts in existence at the time the statute was passed, and thus did not affect what legislation could say about future contracts.[61] What's more, though there have been signs of stiffening in the past two years,[62] the Court in general has not been very energetic about protecting existing contracts either, holding in essence that legislatures can alter them so long as they do so reasonably (which virtually denudes the clause of any independent function).[63] It is tempting to conclude that the Court's long-standing interpretation of the clause as protecting only existing contracts reduces it to just another hedge against retroactive legislation and thus, like the Ex Post Facto Clause, essentially a separation of powers provision. That conclusion, however, is a little quick. Legislation effectively overruling the terms of an existing contract is not really "retroactive" in the ex post facto sense of attaching untoward consequences to an act performed before it was enacted; rather it refuses to recognize a prior act (the making of the contract) as a defense to or exemption from a legal regime the legislature now wishes to impose.[64] Thus both interpretations of the clause recognize the existence of a contract as a special shield against legislative regulation of future behavior, though on the long-accepted narrow interpretation only contracts already in existence can serve thus.

At this point another temptation arises, to characterize the Contracts Clause as serving an institutional or "separation of powers" function of cordoning off an extragovernmental enclave, in this case an enclave of decision via contract, to serve as a counterpoise to governmental authority.[65] The problem with this account is not that it does not fit, but rather that it will *always* fit: it is difficult to imagine any purported constitutional right that cannot be described as creating a private space where actions antithetical to the wishes of our elected representatives can be taken. For this reason the account seems incapable of serving as a meaningful explanation (or as a basis from which broader constitutional themes can responsibly be extrapolated).[66] Thus whichever interpretation of the clause was in fact intended, it is difficult to avoid the conclusion that in the Contracts Clause the framers and ratifiers meant to single out for special protection from the political processes—though note that in this case it is only the *state* political processes—a substantive value that is not wholly susceptible to convincing rationalization in terms of either the processes of government or procedure more narrowly conceived. On the broad and rejected interpretation, that value is contract, the ability to arrive at binding agreements. On the narrower and received interpretation, applying the clause only to contracts in existence at the time of the legislation—which I should reiterate is an interpretation the Court has not, at least until very recently, pursued very enthusiastically either—what is protected is a somewhat narrower reliance interest, an assurance that by entering into a contract one can render oneself immune from future shifts in the identity or thinking of one's elected representatives.

This needn't throw us into a tailspin: my claim is only that the original Constitution was principally, indeed I would say overwhelmingly, dedicated to concerns of process and structure and not to the identification and preservation of specific substantive values. Any claim that it was exclusively so conceived would be ridiculous (as would any comparable claim about any comparably complicated human undertaking). And indeed there are other provisions in the original document that seem almost entirely value-oriented, though my point, of course, is that they are few and far between.* Thus "corruption of blood" is forbidden as a punishment for treason. Punishing people for their parents' transgressions is outlawed as a substantively unfair outcome: it just can't be done, irrespective of procedures and also irrespective of whether it is done to the children of all offenders. The federal government, along with the states, is

---

*I realize that by stressing the few occasions on which values *were* singled out for protection, I run the risk of conveying the impression that that is the character of much of the Constitution. My point of course is quite the opposite, but I'm not sufficiently sadistic to list all the provisions that are obviously concerned only with process. If you find yourself thinking I'm not making my case here, please read a few pages of the Constitution to assure yourself that I could.

precluded from taxing articles exported from any state. Here too an outcome is simply precluded; what might be styled a value, the economic value of free trade among the states, is protected.[67] This short list, however, covers just about all the values protected in the original Constitution—save one. And a big one it was. Although an understandable squeamishness kept the word out of the document, *slavery* must be counted a substantive value to which the original Constitution meant to extend unusual protection from the ordinary legislative process, at least temporarily. Prior to 1808, Congress was forbidden to prohibit the slave trade into any state that wanted it,[68] and the states were obliged to return escaping slaves to their "homes."[69]

The idea of a bill of rights was not even brought up until close to the end of the Constitutional Convention, at which time it was rejected. The reason is not that the framers were unconcerned with liberty, but rather that by their lights a bill of rights did not belong in a constitution, at least not in the one they had drafted. As Hamilton explained in *Federalist* 84, "a minute detail of particular rights is certainly far less applicable to a Constitution like that under consideration, which is merely intended to regulate the general political interests of the nation . . . "[70] Moreover, the very point of all that had been wrought had been, in large measure, to preserve the liberties of individuals. "The truth is, after all the declamations we have heard, that the Constitution is itself, in every rational sense, and to every useful purpose, *a Bill of Rights.*"[71] "The additional securities to republican government, to liberty, and to property, to be derived from the adoption of the plan under consideration, consist chiefly in the restraints which the preservation of the Union will impose on local factions . . . in the prevention of extensive military establishments . . . in the express guarantee of a republican form of government to each [state]; in the absolute and universal exclusion of titles of nobility . . ."[72]

Of course a number of the state ratifying conventions remained apprehensive, and a bill of rights did emerge. Here too, however, the data are unruly. The expression-related provisions of the First Amendment—"Congress shall make no law . . . abridging the freedom of speech, or of the press; or the right of the people peaceably to assemble, and to petition the Government for a redress of grievances"—were centrally intended to help make our governmental processes work, to ensure the open and informed discussion of political issues, and to check our government when it gets out of bounds.[73] We can attribute other functions to freedom of expression, and some of them must have played a role,[74] but the exercise has the smell of the lamp about it: the view that free expression per se, without regard to what it means to the process of government, is our preeminent right has a highly elitist cast. Positive law has its claims, and I am not suggesting that such other purposes as are plausibly attributable to the language should not be attributed: the amendment's language is not limited to political speech and it should not be so limited by construction (even assuming someone could come up with a determinate definition of "political"). But we are at present engaged in an exploration of what sort of document our forebears thought they were putting together, and in that regard the linking of the politically oriented protections of speech, press, assembly, and petition is highly informative.

The First Amendment's religious clauses — "Congress shall make no law respecting an establishment of religion, or prohibiting the free exercise thereof" — are a different matter. Obviously part of the point of combining these cross-cutting commands was to make sure the church and the government gave each other breathing space: the provision thus performs a structural or separation of powers function.[75] But we must not infer that because one account fits the data it must be the only appropriate account, and here the obvious cannot be blinked: part of the explanation of the Free Exercise Clause has to be that for the framers religion was an important substantive value they wanted to put significantly beyond the reach of at least the federal legislature.

The Second Amendment, protecting "the right of the people to keep and bear Arms," seems (at least if that's all you read) calculated simply to set beyond congressional control another "important" value, the right to carry a gun. It hasn't been construed that way, however, and instead has been interpreted as protecting only the right of state governments to keep militias (National Guards) and to arm them. The rationalization for this narrow construction has ordinarily been historical, that the purpose the framers talked most about was maintaining state militias. However, a provision cannot responsibly be restricted to less than its language indicates simply because a particular purpose received more attention than

others (and in fact that favored purpose of today's firearms enthusi-
asts, the right of *individual* self-protection, was mentioned more
than a couple of times). Arguments can be right for the wrong reasons, however, and though the point is debatable,[76] the conclusion
here is probably correct. The Second Amendment has its own little
preamble: "A well regulated Militia, being necessary to the security
of a free State, the right of the people to keep and bear Arms, shall
not be infringed." Thus here, as almost nowhere else,[77] the framers
and ratifiers apparently opted against leaving to the future the attribution of purposes, choosing instead explicitly to legislate the
goal in terms of which the provision was to be interpreted.

The Third Amendment, undoubtedly another of your favorites,
forbids the nonconsensual peacetime quartering of troops. Like the
Establishment of Religion Clause, it grew largely out of fear of an
undue influence, this time by the military: in that aspect it can be
counted a "separation of powers" provision. Again, however, one
cannot responsibly stop there. Other provisions provide for civilian
control of the military, and although that is surely one of the purposes here, there is obviously something else at stake, a desire to protect the privacy of the home from prying government eyes, to say
nothing of the annoyance of uninvited guests. Both process and
value seem to be involved here.

Amendments five through eight tend to become relevant only
during lawsuits, and we tend therefore to think of them as procedural—instrumental provisions calculated to enhance the fairness
and efficiency of the litigation process. That's exactly what most of
them are: the importance of the guarantees of grand juries, criminal and civil petit juries, information of the charge, the right of con-
frontation, compulsory process, and even the assistance of counsel
inheres mainly in their tendency to ensure a reliable determination.[78] Unconcerned with the substance of government regulation,
they refer instead to the ways in which regulations can be enforced
against those they cover. Once again, however, that is not the whole
story. The Fifth Amendment's privilege against self-incrimination
surely has a lot to do with wanting to find the truth: coerced confes-
sions are less likely to be reliable. But at least as interpreted,[79] the
privilege needs further rationalization than that: the argument runs
that there is simply something immoral—though it has proved
tricky pinning down exactly what it is—about the state's asking

somebody whether he committed a crime and expecting him to answer. The same amendment's guarantee against double jeopardy gets complicated. Insofar as it forbids retrial after acquittal, it seems a largely procedural protection, designed to guard against the conviction of innocent persons. But insofar as it forbids additional prosecution after conviction or added punishment after sentence, it performs the quite different (and substantive) function, which obviously is present in the acquittal situation too, of guaranteeing a sense of repose, an assurance that at some definable point the defendant can assume the ordeal is over, its consequences known.[80]

The Fourth Amendment provides: "The right of the people to be secure in their persons, houses, papers, and effects, against unreasonable searches and seizures, shall not be violated, and no Warrants shall issue, but upon probable cause, supported by Oath or affirmation, and particularly describing the place to be searched, and the persons or things to be seized." This provision most often becomes relevant when a criminal defendant tries to suppress evidence seized as the fruit of an illegal search or arrest, but it would be a mistake to infer from that that it is a purely procedural provision. In fact (as thus enforced by the exclusionary rule) it *thwarts* the procedural goal of accurately determining the facts, in order to serve one or more other goals felt to be more important.[81] The standard line is that that other, more important goal is privacy, and surely privacy is sometimes implicated.[82] But the language of the amendment reaches further — so for that matter did the customs abuses we know had a lot to do with its inclusion — and when it is read in its entirety the notion of "privacy" proves inadequate as an explanation. The amendment covers seizures of goods and arrests ("seizures of the person") along with searches, and it does not distinguish public episodes from private: a completely open arrest or seizure of goods is as illegal as a search of a private area if it is effected without probable cause. It thus "protects individual privacy against certain kinds of governmental intrusion, but its protections go further, and often have nothing to do with privacy at all."[83]

A major point of the amendment, obviously, was to keep the government from disrupting our lives without at least moderately convincing justification. That rationale intertwines with another — and the historic customs abuses are relevant here too — namely, a fear of official discretion. In deciding whose lives to disrupt in the ways the amendment indicates — that is, whom to search or arrest or whose goods to seize — law enforcement officials will necessarily have a good deal of low visibility discretion. In addition they are likely in such situations to be sensitive to social station and other factors that should not bear on the decision. The amendment thus requires not simply a certain quantum of probability but also when possible, via the warrant requirement, the judgment of a "neutral and detached magistrate." From this perspective, which obviously is only one of several, the Fourth Amendment can be seen as another harbinger of the Equal Protection Clause, concerned with avoiding indefensible inequities in treatment. The Eighth Amendment's ban on "cruel and unusual punishments" is even more obviously amenable to this account. Apparently part of the point was to outlaw certain understood and abhorred forms of torture, but the decision to use open-ended language can hardly have been inadvertent.[84] It is possible that part of the point also was to ban punishments that were unusually severe in relation to the crimes for which they were being imposed. But much of it surely had to do with a realization that in the context of imposing penalties too there is tremendous potential for the arbitrary or invidious infliction of "unusually" severe punishments on persons of various classes other than "our own."[85]

On first reading, the Fifth Amendment's requirement that private property not be taken for public use without just compensation may appear simply to mark the substantive value of private property for special protection from the political process (though, on the face of the document, from only the state political process). Again, though, we must ask why. Because property was regarded as unusually important? That may be part of the explanation, but note that property is not shielded from condemnation by this provision. On the contrary, the amendment assumes that property will sometimes be taken and provides instead for compensation. Read through it thus emerges — and this account fits the historical situation like a glove[86] — as yet another protection of the few against the many, "a limit on government's power to isolate particular individuals for sacrifice to the general good."[87] Its point is to "spread the cost of operating the governmental apparatus throughout the society rather than imposing it upon some small segment of it."[88] If we want a highway or a park we can have it, but we're all going to have to share the cost rather than imposing it on some isolated individual or group.*

With one important exception, the Reconstruction Amendments do not designate substantive values for protection from the political process.[89] The Fourteenth Amendment's Due Process Clause, we have seen, is concerned with process writ small, the processes by which regulations are enforced against individuals. Its Privileges or Immunities Clause is quite inscrutable, indicating only that there should exist some set of constitutional entitlements not explicitly enumerated in the document: it is one of the provisions for which we are seeking guides to construction. The Equal Protection Clause is also unforthcoming with details, though it at least gives us a clue: by its explicit concern with equality among the persons within a state's jurisdiction it constitutes the document's clearest, though not sole, recognition that technical access to the process may not always be sufficient to guarantee good-faith representation of all those putatively represented.[90] The Fifteenth Amendment, forbidding abridgment of the right to vote on account of race, opens the process to persons who had previously been excluded and thus by another strategy seeks to enforce the representative's duty of equal concern and respect. The exception, of course, involves a value I have mentioned before, slavery. The Thirteenth Amendment can be forced into a "process" mold—slaves don't participate effectively in the political process—and it surely significantly reflects a concern with equality as well. Just as surely, however, it embodies a substantive judgment that human slavery is simply not morally tolerable. Thus at no point has the Constitution been neutral on this subject. Slavery was one of the few values the original document singled out for protection from the political branches; *non*slavery is one of the few values it singles out for protection now.

What has happened to the Constitution in the second century of

---

*This view of the clause is also of some assistance in deciding whether a given government action should be counted a taking in the first place as opposed to, say, a regulation or a tax. In recent discussions of this issue the Court has begun to ask whether the measure under review singles out a minority for unusually harsh treatment or rather affects a class sufficiently generalized to have a fair shot at protecting itself politically. E.g., Penn Central Transp. Co. v. New York City, 438 U.S. 104, 132 (1978).

our nationhood, though ground less frequently plowed, is most instructive on the subject of what jobs we have learned our basic document is suited to. There were no amendments between 1870 and
1913, but there have been eleven since. Five of them have extended
the franchise: the Seventeenth extends to all of us the right to vote
for our Senators directly, the Twenty-Fourth abolishes the poll tax
as a condition of voting in federal elections, the Nineteenth extends
the vote to women, the Twenty-Third to residents of the District of
Columbia, and the Twenty-Sixth to eighteen-year-olds. Extension
of the franchise to groups previously excluded has therefore been
the dominant theme of our constitutional development since the
Fourteenth Amendment, and it pursues both of the broad constitutional themes we have observed from the beginning: the achievement of a political process open to all on an equal basis and a consequent enforcement of the representative's duty of equal concern and
respect to minorities and majorities alike. Three other amendments
— the Twentieth, Twenty-Second, and Twenty-Fifth — involve Presidential eligibility and succession. The Sixteenth, permitting a federal income tax, adds another power to the list of those that had
previously been assigned to the central government.* That's it, save
two, and indeed one of those two did place a substantive value beyond the reach of the political process. The amendment was the
Eighteenth, and the value shielded was temperance. It was, of
course, repealed fourteen years later by the Twenty-First Amendment, precisely, I suggest, because such attempts to freeze substantive values do not belong in a constitution. In 1919 temperance obviously seemed like a fundamental value; in 1933 it obviously did
not.

What has happened to the Constitution's other value-enshrining
provisions is similar, and similarly instructive. Some surely have survived, but typically because they are so obscure that they don't
become issues (corruption of blood, quartering of troops) or so in-
terlaced with procedural concerns they seem appropriate in a constitution (self-incrimination, double jeopardy). Those sufficiently

*Moreover, the amendment most likely (though perhaps not likely enough) to
become the Twenty-Seventh, the Equal Rights Amendment, is a guarantor of fair
distribution akin to the Equal Protection Clause: it does not designate any substantive values as worthy of constitutional protection.

conspicuous and precise to be controvertible have not survived.[91] The most dramatic examples, of course, were slavery and prohibition. Both were removed by repeal, in one case a repeal requiring unprecedented carnage. Two other substantive values that at least arguably were placed beyond the reach of the political process by the Constitution have been "repealed" by judicial construction—the right of individuals to bear arms, and freedom to set contract terms without significant state regulation.[92] Maybe in fact our forebears did not intend very seriously to protect those values, but the fact that the Court, in the face of what must be counted at least plausible contrary arguments, so readily read these values out of the Constitution is itself instructive of American expectations of a constitution. Finally, there is the value of religion, still protected by the Free Exercise Clause. Something different has happened here. In recent years that clause has functioned primarily to protect what must be counted as discrete and insular minorities, such as the Amish, Seventh Day Adventists, and Jehovah's Witnesses. Whatever the original conception of the Free Exercise Clause, its function during essentially all of its effective life has been one akin to the Equal Protection Clause and thus entirely appropriate to a constitution.

Don't get me wrong: our Constitution has always been substantially concerned with preserving liberty. If it weren't, it would hardly be worth fighting for. The question that is relevant to our inquiry here, however, is how that concern has been pursued. The principal answers to that, we have seen, are by a quite extensive set of procedural protections, and by a still more elaborate scheme designed to ensure that in the making of substantive choices the decision process will be open to all on something approaching an equal basis, with the decision-makers held to a duty to take into account the interests of all those their decisions affect. (Most often the document has proceeded on the assumption that assuring access is the best way of assuring that someone's interests will be considered, and so in fact it usually is. Other provisions, however—centrally but not exclusively the Equal Protection Clause—reflect a realization that access will not always be sufficient.) The general strategy has therefore not been to root in the document a set of substantive rights entitled to permanent protection. The Constitution has instead proceeded from the quite sensible assumption that an effective majority will not inordinately threaten its own rights, and has sought to assure that such a majority not systematically treat others less well than it treats itself—by structuring decision processes at all levels to try to ensure, first, that everyone's interests will be actually or virtually represented (usually both) at the point of substantive decision, and second, that the processes of individual application will not be manipulated so as to reintroduce in practice the sort of discrimination that is impermissible in theory. We have noted a few provisions that do not comfortably conform to this pattern. But they're an odd assortment, the understandable products of particular historical circumstances—guns, religion, contract, and so on—and in any event they are few and far between. To represent them as a dominant theme of our constitutional document one would have to concentrate quite single-mindedly on hopping from stone to stone and averting one's eyes from the mainstream.

The American Constitution has thus by and large remained a constitution properly so called, concerned with constitutive questions. What has distinguished it, and indeed the United States itself, has been a process of government,[93] not a governing ideology.[94] Justice Linde has written: "As a charter of government a constitution must prescribe legitimate processes, not legitimate outcomes, if like ours (and unlike more ideological documents elsewhere) it is to serve many generations through changing times."[95]

Democracy and Distrust

As I have tried to be scrupulous about indicating, the argument from the general contours of the Constitution is necessarily a qualified one. In fact the documentary dictation of particular substantive outcomes has been rare (and generally unsuccessful), but our Constitution is too complex a document to lie still for *any* pat characterization. Beyond that, the premise of the argument, that aids to construing the more open-ended provisions are appropriately found in the nature of the surrounding document, though it is a premise that seems to find acceptance on all sides, is not one with which it is impossible to disagree. Thus the two arguments that follow, each overtly normative, are if anything more important than the one I have just reviewed. The first is entirely obvious by now, that unlike an approach geared to the judicial imposition of "fundamental values," the representation-reinforcing orientation whose contours I have sketched and will develop further is not inconsistent with, but on the contrary is entirely supportive of, the American system of representative democracy. It recognizes the unacceptability of the claim that appointed and life-tenured judges are better reflectors of conventional values than elected representatives, devoting itself instead to policing the mechanisms by which the system seeks to ensure that our elected representatives will actually represent. There may be an illusion of circularity here: my approach is more consistent with representative democracy because that's the way it was planned. But of course it isn't any more circular than setting out to build an airplane and ending up with something that flies.

The final point worth serious mention is that (again unlike a fundamental-values approach) a representation-reinforcing approach assigns judges a role they are conspicuously well situated to fill.* My reference here is not principally to expertise. Lawyers *are* experts on process writ small, the processes by which facts are found and contending parties are allowed to present their claims. And to a degree they are experts on process writ larger, the processes by which issues of public policy are fairly determined: lawyers do seem genuinely to have a feel, indeed it is hard to see what other special value they have, for ways of insuring that everyone gets his or her fair say. But too much shouldn't be made of this. Others, particularly the full-time participants, can also claim expertise on how the political process allocates voice and power. And of course many legislators are lawyers themselves. So the point isn't so much one of expertise as it is one of perspective.

The approach to constitutional adjudication recommended here is akin to what might be called an "antitrust" as opposed to a "regulatory" orientation to economic affairs[96] — rather than dictate sub-

---

*For reasons that are currently obscure, I went through a period of worrying that the orientation here recommended might mean less protection for civil liberties. (Of course it would deny the opportunity to create rights out of whole cloth: that is much of its point and strength. What I had in mind was the possibility that the *same* freedoms might systematically come out thinner if derived from a participational orientation than they would if protected on the ground that they are "good.") Reflection has convinced me that just the opposite is true, that freedoms are more secure to the extent that they find foundation in the theory that supports our entire government, rather than gaining protection because the judge deciding the case thinks they're important. Cf. C. Black, *Structure and Relationship in Constitutional Law* 29-30 (1969). Indeed, the only remotely systematic "Carolene Products" Court we have had was also clearly the most protective of civil liberties.

stantive results it intervenes only when the "market," in our case the political market, is systemically malfunctioning. (A referee analogy is also not far off: the referee is to intervene only when one team is gaining unfair advantage, not because the "wrong" team has scored.) Our government cannot fairly be said to be "malfunctioning" simply because it sometimes generates outcomes with which we disagree, however strongly (and claims that it is reaching results with which "the people" really disagree—or would "if they understood"—are likely to be little more than self-deluding projections). In a representative democracy value determinations are to be made by our elected representatives, and if in fact most of us disapprove we can vote them out of office. Malfunction occurs when the *process* is undeserving of trust, when (1) the ins are choking off the channels of political change to ensure that they will stay in and the outs will stay out, or (2) though no one is actually denied a voice or a vote, representatives beholden to an effective majority are systematically disadvantaging some minority out of simple hostility or a prejudiced refusal to recognize commonalities of interest, and thereby denying that minority the protection afforded other groups by a representative system.[97]

Obviously our elected representatives are the last persons we should trust with identification of either of these situations. Appointed judges, however, are comparative outsiders in our governmental system, and need worry about continuance in office only very obliquely. This does not give them some special pipeline to the genuine values of the American people: in fact it goes far to ensure that they won't have one. It does, however, put them in a position objectively to assess claims—though no one could suppose the evaluation won't be full of judgment calls—that either by clogging the channels of change or by acting as accessories to majority tyranny, our elected representatives in fact are not representing the interests of those whom the system presupposes they are.

Before embarking on his career-long quest for a satisfactory approach to constitutional adjudication, Alexander Bickel described the challenge thus:

> The search must be for a function . . . which is peculiarly suited to the capabilities of the courts; which will not likely be performed elsewhere if the courts do not assume it; which can be so exercised as to be acceptable in a society that generally

shares Judge Hand's satisfaction in a "sense of common venture"; which will be effective when needed; and whose discharge by the courts will not lower the quality of the other departments' performance by denuding them of the dignity and burden of their own responsibility.[98]

As quoted, it's a remarkably appropriate set of specifications, one that fits the orientation suggested here precisely. Unfortunately, by adding one more specification (where I have put the elipsis) and thereby committing himself to a value orientation—"which might (indeed must) involve the making of policy, yet which differs from the legislative and executive functions"—he built in an inescapable contradiction and thereby ensured the failure of his enterprise.

5 Clearing the Channels
of Political Change

VIRTUALLY everyone agrees that the courts should be heavily involved in reviewing impediments to free speech, publication, and political association. Those who think of themselves as interpretivists naturally make much of the language of the First Amendment: "Congress shall make no law . . . abridging the freedom of speech, or of the press, or the right of the people peaceably to assemble, and to petition the Government for a redress of grievances." Justice Black used to italicize "*no* law," and he had a point: language that strong demands to be taken seriously. The other words are less comforting, though, and more than the specific language and legislative history of the amendment is needed to get us very far at all. "Congress" does not on its face refer to the President, the courts, or the legions that manage the Executive Branch, and "law" only arguably includes administrative orders or congressional investigations. Freedom of political association, which (without serious controversy) has been held to be fully protected, is not even mentioned in the document; and of course the states are not directly covered by the First Amendment. It requires a theory to get us where the Court has gone. That theory has been the right one, that rights like these, whether or not they are explicitly mentioned, must nonetheless be protected, strenuously so, because they are critical to the functioning of an open and effective democratic process.

Judicial review in this area must involve, at a minimum, the elimination of any inhibition of expression that is unnecessary to the promotion of a government interest. This sort of review has several names—"overbreadth,"[1] "less restrictive alternative," "tight fit," even the doctrine that "administrative convenience" cannot count as a governmental justification here[2]—but it all comes to much the same thing: that false-positives are not to be tolerated, that no one's

First Amendment freedoms are to be inhibited unless the inhibition of his or her freedom in particular is necessary to serve the interest the state is invoking. Temptingly manageable as this sort of "means scrutiny" may sound, however, it cannot be enough. In *United States v. Robel*, decided at the height of the Court's infatuation with "overbreadth" analysis, Chief Justice Warren suggested for the majority that such analysis really does not concern itself with the *strength* of the government's interest at all, but involves instead an almost mechanical pruning of superfluous restraints: "It has been suggested that this case should be decided by 'balancing' the governmental interest, expressed in [the statute] against the First Amendment rights asserted by the appellee. This we decline to do . . . We have ruled only that the Constitution requires that the conflict between congressional power and individual rights be accommodated by legislation drawn more narrowly to avoid the conflict."[3] That may be good propaganda, but it does not accurately reflect what was going on in *Robel* and similar cases. Legislatures do not engage in the wholly gratuitous inhibition of expression (or for that matter of anything), and to trim what is literally surplussage would be to trim nothing. The real point of an overbreadth holding, therefore, has to be that at the outer reaches of the prohibition in issue, a significant inhibition has been imposed, not for no reason, but for a relatively insignificant reason. The evaluation takes place "at the margin," comparing the incremental promotion of the government's interest effected by covering the fringe cases with the incremental threat to free expression posed by such coverage. It is thus likely to involve more commensurable factors than an up-or-down balance on the entirety of the statute.[4] But it remains evaluation nonetheless.[5]

I can certainly understand the instincts that might incline one to minimize the number of occasions on which the judiciary becomes involved in assessing the importance of the interest the state adduces to support its regulation. But some attention to that question is unavoidable — precisely because legislatures don't engage in wholly gratuitous suppression — if there is to be review at all. Moreover, the theory that demands review in the first place demands that it attend to ends. Courts must police inhibitions on expression and other political activity because we cannot trust elected officials to do so: ins have a way of wanting to make sure the outs stay out. Of course that means the ins should not be permitted to inhibit expression for no reason at all. But to mean anything it must also mean that they should not be permitted to inhibit it for some flimsy reason that in fact is being used as a pretext. But even this cannot be enough. Perspective is critical, and one whose continued authority depends on the silencing of other voices may well *in all good faith* be able to convince himself that a reason a more objective observer would label inadequate is in fact compelling.

So long as the constitutional test is geared to the threat posed by the specific communication in issue, however, courts will tend to be swept along by the same sorts of fears that moved the legislators and the prosecutorial authorities, and the First Amendment is likely to end up a very theoretical barrier. The Supreme Court's first significant encounter with this amendment came in a series of cases involving prosecutions under the Espionage Act of 1917. Speaking for a unanimous Court, Justice Holmes made clear that his approach was one geared to the specific threat the communication in issue posed. "We admit that in many places and in ordinary times the defendants in saying all that was said in the circular would have been within their constitutional rights. But the character of every act depends upon the circumstances in which it is done." This general approach was specified in the famous clear and present danger test: "The question in every case is whether the words used are used in such circumstances and are of such a nature as to create a clear and present danger that they will bring about the substantive evils that Congress has a right to prevent."[6] The clear and present danger test has been the object of considerable liberal nostalgia, and on its surface seems at least moderately demanding.[7] The problem is that the defendants in the three cases in which it was introduced all ended up going to prison for quite tame and ineffectual expression.* In fact they went to prison *for ten years*. It was all quite understand-

---

*Thus the defendant in the landmark, Schenck v. United States, 249 U.S. 47 (1919), went to prison for printing and circulating a pamphlet addressed to conscripts that "said 'Do not submit to intimidation,' but in form at least confined itself to peaceful measures such as a petition for the repeal of the act." Id. at 51. A week later the Court affirmed the conviction of Eugene V. Debs for giving a speech in which he was imprudent enough to say "that he had to be prudent and might not be able to say all that he thought, thus intimating to his hearers that they might infer that he meant more," and continued with "personal experiences and illustrations of the growth of socialism, a glorification of minorities, and a prophecy of the success of the international socialist crusade, with the interjection that 'you need to know that you are fit for something better than slavery and cannon fodder.' " Debs v. United States, 249 U.S. 211, 213-14 (1919).

able, though: the nation was at war, the sentiments expressed by the defendants were unpopular ones, and it can't be too surprising that the justices were prepared to entertain every presumption in favor of their dangerousness.

Between the two World Wars the Court performed better (which also is quite understandable). Justice Holmes, joined now by Justice Brandeis, began in a series of dissents to put some teeth into his clear and present danger test, and by the late 1920s and the 1930s a majority of the Court began reversing some convictions. The Communist scare that followed the Second World War and continued into the 1950s, however, snapped the country generally, and the Court along with it, back into earlier form. Of course to convict the Communists the clear and present danger test had to be modified somewhat (to eliminate the requirement that the threat be immediate), and in 1951, in *Dennis v. United States*, it was. The test now, we were told, was whether "the gravity of the 'evil,' discounted by its improbability, justifies such invasion of free speech as is necessary to avoid the danger."[8] Of course that was quite understandable: if an immediate but fairly minor threat—such as inducing a few people not to submit to conscription—can justify an "invasion of free speech," why shouldn't a less immediate but more serious evil—such as an attempted overthrow of the government—count as well? Concurring separately in *Dennis*, Justice Frankfurter went further. Why, he asked, wasn't the proper test simply a straightforward balance between the costs and benefits of suppressing the communication, without the pretense of a mathematical formula? Well, that too makes a lot of sense: in fact the Court's rendition, with its critical references to "discount" and "justification," amounts to nothing different. But Frankfurter wasn't through: if the test is really just a balance of the pros and cons of suppressing the expression in issue, what warrant had the Court to substitute its judgment for that of the political branches? After all, the Congress was, if anything, in a better position to amass and assess all the facts bearing on the gravity of the Communist threat. In fact the Frankfurter approach—ad hoc balancing tempered with substantial deference to the legislative judgment—was the one the Court ended up buying for a time, and it wasn't until we were well into the 1960s (and out of the spell of McCarthyism) that our national self-confidence returned to the point where the Court could be counted on to invalidate legislation making criminals of Communists.

This is all familiar history. It is all quite understandable. And it all mocks our commitment to an open political process. The First Amendment simply cannot stand on the shifting foundation of ad hoc evaluations of specific threat. The trick, of course, is to find something better. Justices Black and Douglas used to claim, though Black more insistently than Douglas, that they were "absolutists," by which they said they meant that speech could *never* be officially punished or otherwise deterred. That does indeed sound better than what the Court has given us over the years: there are precious few, if indeed there are any, First Amendment claims that have reached the Court whose vindication would have seriously imperiled the republic or anything else. That's not the right comparison, though: if all the claims raised had been successful, others more problematic would have been made, and I at least begin to get nervous about, say, false advertising for quack cancer cures or the printing of a (previously undisclosed) formula for the hydrogen bomb. A case can be made—in fact one has, eloquently, by Charles Black—that even though a justice must know deep down that no one can *really* mean there can be no restrictions on free speech, there is value in his putting it that way nonetheless.[9] Most of us aren't justices, however, so we should face the validity of such an "absolutist" approach head-on and recognize that one simply cannot be granted a constitutional right to stand on the steps of an inadequately guarded jail and urge a mob to lynch the prisoner within.[10] To judge from performances elsewhere, Justice Douglas would say that that was "speech brigaded with action" and therefore not protected,[11] while Justice Black would call it "speech plus" or perhaps simply "not speech" and similarly deny it protection.[12] The justices do themselves no credit here, for "answers" like this are simply not responsible. They refuse to display whatever reasoning in fact underlies the denial of protection, and by their transparent lack of principle substantially attenuate whatever hortatory value there was in the pronouncement that speech is always protected. We can all agree that it would be better to put extra guards on the jail and let the hothead have his say. But that's not always possible, and when it is not he simply cannot be granted a constitutional right to make his speech. For that assuredly is what it is: its likely effectiveness, and that is what we fear, does not make it any less a speech.

That doesn't exhaust the alternatives, however. Another, more viable, form of "absolutism" is possible, one that does not purport to hold all expression or speech constitutionally immune to government regulation, but rather immunizes all expression *save that which falls within a few clearly and narrowly defined categories.* No responsible approach to the problem can be oblivious to the dangers certain types of expression pose: our lynch mob example teaches us that. What distinguishes this "unprotected messages" approach from the various "specific threat" approaches that have so ill served the cause of freedom, however, is that here the consideration of likely harm takes place at wholesale, in advance, outside the context of specific cases. The question will run whether, for example, "advocacy of illegal activity" should be cordoned off as an unprotected category (in order to handle cases like the lynch mob)? That one is obviously much too broad:[13] as we shall see, the Court has narrowed it substantially, to "incitement of immediate lawless action." The categories of unprotected messages once fixed, however, likely effect drops out of the calculation, and expression that does not fall within one of the categories is simply protected, irrespective of the identity of the speaker and the audience.

This won't always work either, though. Let's take a message that could not conceivably fall within anyone's notion of an appropriately unprotected category: I can think of no better example than "Ely for Congress." That one's simply protected, regardless of context, right? Well, not quite. Suppose I hire a sound-truck and blast it forth. Perhaps I have that constitutional right. Suppose, however, I buy a bullhorn and aim it at your bedroom window at three in the morning (or smarter still my opponent does): "Ely for Congress—I know you're in there—Ely for Congress!" That can't be a constitutional right, protected as the message obviously has to be. Neither have I a constitutional right to shout "Ely for Congress" at a cardiac patient, to hold an "Ely for Congress" rally in Times Square at noon, let alone to firebomb the Post Office to dramatize the postal service plank of my platform. The "absolutely protected" character of the message cannot insulate these forms of expression from regulation: context—the threat the particular expressive event poses—obviously is relevant and sometimes will be dispositive.[14]

The debate on the First Amendment has proceeded on the assumption that the two general approaches I have noted—what I have been calling the "specific threat" approach (which includes clear and present danger as well as ad hoc balancing) and the "unprotected messages" approach (which I have suggested is the only intelligible form of "absolutism")—are mutually exclusive general approaches to the entire range of problems that arise under the amendment. Each side, by concentrating on certain cases, has been able to make the other look quite bad—an "unprotected messages" approach virtually unintelligible, a "specific threat" approach virtually useless. I would like to suggest, however, that the First Amendment will best be served if the two approaches are treated as complementary rather than contending, each with its own legitimate and indispensable role in protecting expression.[15]

Where the evil the state is seeking to avert is one that is independent of the message being regulated, where it arises from something other than a fear of how people will react to what the speaker is saying—as is true of the examples cited in the paragraph before last—a "specific threat" approach is the only one that can be coherent.[16] The regulation at issue will necessarily be one that applies across the board, not just to a particular view or family of views thought to be unusually dangerous. (If it's of the latter sort, it should be treated by the other test.) That obviously diminishes the dangers we saw in applying "specific threat" tests to communications regarded as threatening because of their content, dangers of conscious or unconscious exaggeration on the part of political officials and understandable acquiescence on the part of the judiciary. It isn't quite that neat, of course: the regulation of certain forms of communication for reasons other than their content may discriminate de facto (or even intentionally, though in a way that may not be provable) against certain clusters of messages. Sound-trucks, for example, are more frequently resorted to by those whose access to more expensive and less annoying media is limited. That surely is something that belongs in the calculation: a more serious threat should be required when there is doubt that the speaker has other effective means of reaching the same audience.[17] However, there simply is no intelligible way of dealing with cases where the harm arises other than from the message that does not attend to context and involve an assessment of the particular threat posed by the communication in issue.

Where the evil the state is seeking to avert is one that is thought to arise from the particular dangers of the message being conveyed, however, the hazards of political distortion and judicial acquiescence are at their peak. The message being regulated will obviously be one with which those imposing the regulation are markedly unsympathetic. Justice Frankfurter's final point was somewhat exaggerated, of course: unelected judges are likely to be somewhat more objective than elected officials about the dangers posed by an alien view, and thus even if it were true that a balancing test was the only one intelligible in these circumstances there would remain *some* point in granting the judiciary a genuine power of review. However, judges by and large are drawn from the same political and social ranks as elected officials, and are subject to many of the same anxieties. If the history we briefly reviewed teaches us anything, it is that attempts to evaluate the threat posed by the communication of an alien view inevitably become involved with the ideological predispositions of those doing the evaluating, and certainly with the relative confidence or paranoia of the age. If the First Amendment is even to begin to serve its central function of assuring an open political dialogue and process, we must seek to minimize assessment of the dangerousness of the various messages people want to communicate. That means, where state officials seek to silence a message because they think it's dangerous, that we insist that the message fall within some clearly and narrowly bounded category of expression we have designated in advance as unentitled to protection. One doesn't have to be much of a lawyer to recognize that even the clearest verbal formula can be manipulated. But it's a very bad lawyer who supposes that manipulability and infinite manipulability are the same thing. An "unprotected messages" approach cannot guarantee liberty—nothing can—but it's the surest hedge against judicial capitulation that humans have available. As Judge Learned Hand put it (early in his career[18]) in a letter to Zechariah Chafee, Jr.:

I am not wholly in love with Holmesy's test and the reason is this. Once you admit that the matter is one of degree, while you may put it where it genuinely belongs, you so obviously make it a matter of administration, i.e. you give to Tomdickandharry, D.J., so much latitude [here Hand wrote and struck out "as his own fears may require"] that the jig is at once up. Besides even their Ineffabilities, the Nine Elder Statesmen, have not shown themselves wholly immune from the "herd instinct" and what seems "immediate and direct" to-day may seem very remote next year even though the circumstances surrounding the utter-

ance be unchanged. I own I should prefer a qualitative formula, hard, conventional, difficult to evade. If it could become
sacred by the incrustations of time and precedent it might be
made to serve just a little to withhold the torrents of passion to
which . . . democracies [are] subject . . .[19]

The Supreme Court has long understood the first half of this
analysis. In *Prince v. Massachusetts*,[20] decided in 1944, it upheld
the application of the state's child labor law to a child distributing
Jehovah's Witness literature. Obviously the state was thereby inhib-
iting the communication of a message that must count as protected
by anyone's definition. But the evil the state was trying to avert was
one that would have been equally implicated had the child been
engaged in work with no communicative component whatever, and
thus the consideration of context was entirely appropriate. Similarly, by employing what amounts to a balancing test to permit at
least limited municipal regulation of sound-trucks,[21] the Court has
permitted some restriction of expression. But again, the values the
state seeks to protect by such regulation, values of quiet and repose,
would be threatened as much by meaningless moans and static
(which is usually how it comes out anyway) as by a political message.* This approach to First Amendment problems not involving
the regulation of particular messages on the ground that they are
dangerous was reaffirmed by the Warren Court.[22]

That's the easy half, however: in fact we've seen that into the
1960s the Court followed this approach of considering context and

---

*The dichotomy suggested has the additional virtue of dissolving the supposed
"speech-conduct" problem. A political assassination, or the breaking of the induction center's windows in protest against the draft, obviously has important elements
of expression, but just as obviously cannot be granted First Amendment protection.
The usual temptation has been to set such cases aside on the ground that they involve "conduct" rather than "speech," or perhaps "action" rather than "expression." It's true that the expression is accomplished by action, indeed that both the
activities mentioned are entirely nonverbal. But so are many other acts the Court
would properly recognize as protected expression: a salute, the raising of a clenched
fist, the wearing of an armband. What relevantly distinguishes the assassination
and the window breaking from the others is not that they are not expressive, but
rather that the harm they cause does not flow from the message the act conveys. An
assassination or a window breaking is harmful even if no ones sees an expressive element in it; an armband can lead to trouble only if people know what it means. See
generally Ely, "Flag Desecration: A Case Study in the Roles of Categorization and
Balancing in First Amendment Analysis," 88 *Harv. L. Rev.* 1482 (1975).

essentially balancing in *all* First Amendment cases. What is heartening is that toward the end of the Warren era the Court, led in this by Justice Harlan, gave evidence of beginning to understand that where expression is inhibited because of the perceived dangerousness of the message a quite different approach, one geared to unprotected categories of expression, is needed to secure our First Amendment freedoms. In *Cohen v. California* the Court reversed the conviction of a young man who felt he could adequately convey his feelings only by parading about in a jacket bearing the legend "Fuck the Draft." Unlike the cases we have just considered, the harms on the basis of which the state was proceeding in *Cohen*, harms of shock and offense, flowed entirely from the communicative content of Cohen's message. (Had his "audience" been unable to read English, there obviously would have been no occasion for state intervention.) Appropriately, the Court indicated that an "unprotected messages" approach was in order and concluded that Cohen's message fit within no such category.[23] To reach this result it had to reject one category the state proffered and narrow two others the Court has long recognized. The state argued that Cohen's words — at least where they were thrust upon a nonvolunteering audience — were "offensive" and I have no doubt they must have seemed so to Justice Harlan, who wrote for the majority. His opinion was wise enough to recognize, however, that what seems offensive to me may not seem offensive to you, and indeed that much valuable free speech, speech that has awakened the public to outrages it had previously been taking for granted, very likely was of a sort that many would have found offensive. The dangers of censorship of both cognitive and emotive content thus led the Court to refuse to cordon off "offensive language" as a category of unprotected speech. "Fighting words" have long been recognized as an unprotected category, but Harlan's opinion made clear that that phrase was no longer to be understood as a euphemism for controversial or dirty talk but was to require instead a quite unambiguous invitation to a brawl. "Obscenity" or highly erotic material is also unprotected — for reasons it is difficult to make convincing — but as Justice Harlan suggested, anyone who gets aroused by the legend on Cohen's jacket is in serious trouble. His communication thus fitting within no appropriate category of unprotected messages, Cohen's conviction was reversed.

  Brandenburg v. Ohio, decided two years earlier, followed a similar "unprotected messages" approach.[24] It seems a more important case, however, since the category on which it concentrated (and which it substantially constricted) may be the most sensitive of all. Invalidating Ohio's Criminal Syndicalism Act, a unanimous Court declared that "the constitutional guarantees of free speech and free press do not permit a State to forbid or proscribe advocacy of the use of force or of law violation except where such advocacy is directed to inciting or producing imminent lawless action . . . "[25] Now this is very potent stuff, which would have demanded the contrary result in the early Espionage Act cases and the later Communist cases as well.[26] We can't know that the Court will have the fortitude to hold fast through the next period of panic, but it has raised the odds considerably by deciding the case on this basis rather than simply observing that in context Brandenburg's speech posed no great danger.

It is important that the distinction I have suggested not be misunderstood as, or telescoped into, one simply between "permissive review" and "strict review." Of course the review recommended is stricter for situations where expression is being inhibited on the theory that the message is dangerous, but to say that is to say too little, to run the risk of converting that stricter brand of review— and unfortunately a few recent decisions seem to do just this[27]— into simply a more demanding sort of balancing or specific harm test. That's importantly different from what is recommended here, however, since it has been my point that where allegedly dangerous views are concerned, a specific harm test *of any sort* is likely to erode in times of perceived crisis. To construe the form of review that is appropriate when messages are proscribed on the theory that they are dangerous as anything short of an "absolute" protection of all speech that does not fall within some unprotected category is to miss the central point of the discussion.

The point can be defeated just as easily, of course, by defining the categories of unprotected speech either too vaguely, thereby inviting a different sort of erosion, or too broadly, thereby diminishing the set of protected messages.[28] Neither should we forget the other side of the dichotomy and allow the review of measures that are geared to something other than the perceived dangerousness of the message to degenerate into what is essentially a "reasonableness" test. Measures concerned "merely" with noise control, traffic control, and the like may not be intelligibly reviewable by any approach that excludes the consideration of context, but they nonetheless have the potential of seriously disabling free expression. Courts therefore have no choice but to analyze them in terms of specific harm, but they should employ the strictest available sort of specific harm test, one that seriously insists on a clear and present danger of a serious evil. The reasons that clear and present danger tests tend almost inevitably to degenerate into flabby balancing tests in situations involving allegedly subversive, seditious, or inflammatory expression *are* substantially attenuated where the evil feared is unrelated to the content of the expression. But courts must nonetheless guard against slippage in all contexts.

Thus while an "unprotected messages" approach may not be appropriate in cases that do not involve the suppression of expression because of its content, "strict review" is always appropriate where free expression is in issue. As Josiah Quincy observed at the outset, and is if anything truer today, "[i]t is much easier to restrain liberty from running into licentiousness than power from swelling into tyranny and oppression."[29] While I don't begin to buy the radical cant that this is an oppressive society compared to others, we're certainly in no danger of too much political freedom. Allowing people to assault our eardrums with outrageous and overdrawn denunciations of institutions we treasure will inconvenience, annoy, and infuriate us on occasion, even set us to wondering about the stability of our society: that's exactly what such messages are meant to do, and exactly the price we shouldn't think twice about paying. By silencing such people we may be protecting something, but we certainly won't be protecting "the American way." In 1980 most people who have thought about the issue appreciate this. The hard part will be to sustain that appreciation through our future periods of actual or perceived crisis. Maybe we won't be able to, but we increase the chances by using today to build protective barriers around free expression as secure as words can make them.

The Right to Vote

Although the right to vote[30] seems equally central to a right of participation in the democratic process, there is less consensus among commentators on the propriety of judicial activism in the voting area. It is tempting to suppose that this is because the right to vote is not mentioned explicitly in the Constitution—at least the right to vote in state elections isn't[31]—but we know that won't wash. Freedom of association is not mentioned in the First Amendment or anywhere else, and neither speech nor association is mentioned in the Fourteenth, yet those have quite properly been protected. Also, those who object to active review in voting cases tend as often as not to be people who are untroubled by "substantive due process" elsewhere: something like "contraception, yes—voting, no" is not that uncommon a constellation.[32] It should be clear from what has gone before that I think that's exactly upside down: unblocking stoppages in the democratic process is what judicial review ought preeminently to be about, and denial of the vote seems the quintessential stoppage.*

Sometimes the voting cases, the malapportionment cases in particular, are praised on the ground that they took care of a problem the legislatures had refused to do anything about. That is true, but it is a dangerously incomplete account. There are many things legislatures "haven't done anything about" that should be left in precisely that condition. A more complete account of the voting cases is that they involve rights (1) that are essential to the democratic process and (2) whose dimensions cannot safely be left to our elected representatives, who have an obvious vested interest in the status quo.[33] Chief Justice Warren wrote for the Court in *Kramer v. Union Free School District No. 15:*

> [W]hen we are reviewing statutes which deny some residents the right to vote, the general presumption of constitutionality afforded state statutes and the traditional approval given state classifications if the Court can conceive of a "rational basis" for the distinctions made are not applicable . . . The presumption of constitutionality and the approval given "rational" classifications in other types of enactments are based on an assumption that the institutions of state government are structured so as to represent fairly all the people. However, when the challenge to the statute is in effect a challenge of this basic assumption, the assumption can no longer serve as the basis for presuming constitutionality.[34]

---

*Other practices that go to the core of the right of the people to choose their representatives and express their preferences are the denial of places on the ballot to minor parties and the refusal to seat representatives the people have selected. The Warren Court moved quite actively into both these areas too.

Why, then, the resistance in so many quarters to active judicial review in the voting area? In fact most of the fire has been directed at the malapportionment cases, which we shall get to presently. Justice Harlan had a more fundamental objection, however — one that goes to voter qualification cases equally — and that was that the Equal Protection Clause, which is the provision under which the Court has decided both kinds of cases, simply had not been intended by its framers to apply to voting.[35] In fact the legislative history is not as clear as Harlan claimed it was,[36] but it does seem probable that most of the framers (and ratifiers) of the Fourteenth Amendment did not specifically anticipate that its first section would be applied to voting rights.[37] The problem comes in what Harlan thought that observation proved.* Why on this of all issues should

---

*An alternative answer to Justice Harlan's objection is that reliance on the Equal Protection Clause, in either the voter qualification or the malapportionment cases, may have been unnecessary. The right to vote in various federal elections is adverted to in several constitutional provisions, and whatever additional content Article IV's Republican Form of Government Clause may have, at a bare minimum it means that states must hold popular elections. See, e.g., In re Duncan, 139 U.S. 449, 461 (1891). One of the things we mean by labeling something a right is that it shall not be denied, or granted in only watered-down form, to some subset of persons unless there is a good reason for doing so.

As regards state elections (though not federal) there is an apparent problem with this alternate line of defense, namely that the Supreme Court has historically characterized claims arising under the Republican Form Clause as presenting "political questions" unfit for judicial resolution. In fact, as Professor Wiecek's book on the clause has demonstrated, that generalization is rooted in a category mistake. The early case of Luther v. Borden, 7 How. 1 (1849), involving an attempt to get the Court to decide under the Republican Form Clause which of two contending governments was the "real" government of Rhode Island, did involve a situation whose political tangle the Court probably was wise to leave to Congress. It was, however, a gross mistake of logic to infer, as subsequent cases did, that all cases brought under the Republican Form Clause must therefore also present political questions. See generally W. Wiecek, *The Guarantee Clause of the U.S. Constitution* (1972). In fact it seems likely that this unfortunate doctrine — that all Republican Form cases are necessarily cases involving political questions — will wholly pass from the scene one of these days. Friend and foe alike have come to recognize the obvious, that although the various state voting rights cases decided by the Warren and Burger Courts have been styled as equal protection decisions, they cannot comfortably be understood without a strong injection of the view that the right to vote in state elections is a rather special constitutional prerogative, a view that cannot be teased out of the language of equal protection alone and in textual terms is most naturally assignable to the Republican Form Clause.

In arguing that the Equal Protection Clause was not intended to apply to voting, Justice Harlan placed heavy reliance on a statement of Congressman Bingham: "*The second section excludes the conclusion that by the first section suffrage is subjected to congressional law*; save, indeed, with this exception, that as the right of

we get hung up — why, in particular, should Justice Harlan get hung up[38] — on the specific intentions of the framers?[39] As we have seen, the overriding intention of those who wrote and ratified the Equal Protection Clause was apparently to state a general ideal whose specific applications would be supplied by posterity. They surely entertained no specific intention that the Equal Protection Clause would cover antimiscegenation laws, or for that matter segregated schooling either. But as Chief Justice Warren so correctly put it in *Brown v. Board of Education*, the legislative history relating specifically to schooling, and he might have added the legislative history bearing on all specific applications, was "inconclusive."[40] Unjustified discriminations in the distribution of the franchise fit comfortably within the language of — and just as obviously violate the ideal expressed by — the Equal Protection Clause (and for that matter the Republican Form of Government Clause as well). That is what should count as important.*

---

the people in each State to a republican government and to choose their Representatives in Congress is [one] of the guarantees of the Constitution, by this amendment a remedy might be given directly for a case supposed by Madison, where treason might change a State government from a republican to a despotic government, and thereby deny suffrage to the people." Reynolds v. Sims, 377 U.S. 533, 598-99 (1964) (Harlan, J., dissenting). The italics are Harlan's, and they should not distract the eye from what follows. Of course it is most unlikely that Bingham had in mind any of the situations involved in the modern cases in adverting to the possibility that a denial of the franchise could violate either the Republican Form Clause or the provisions providing for the election of members of Congress: to reach such cases those provisions must be given a line of growth. But Harlan's claim was that §1 of the Fourteenth Amendment just doesn't apply to voting, and to that the nonitalicized portion of Bingham's statement (whose italicized portion Harlan's argument needs) is fatal. In fact several members of the Thirty-Ninth Congress expressed their understanding that the Republican Form Clause gave Congress power to void certain voter qualifications. See Van Alstyne, "The Fourteenth Amendment, the Right to Vote, and the Understanding of the Thirty-Ninth Congress," 1965 *Sup. Ct. Rev.* 33, 50-51, 63-65. That alone is damaging, but Bingham's statement twists the knife by adding that §1 of the Fourteenth Amendment provides additional remedies for such claims.

*The lack of any specific expectation that the Fourteenth Amendment would be applied to voting seems unusually irrelevant in light of the ratification of the Fifteenth Amendment two years later. If any potential extension of the franchise was giving the backers of the Fourteenth Amendment cause for reservation about the possibility that it might be applied to voting, it was a potential extension of the franchise to blacks. See Oregon v. Mitchell, 400 U.S. 112, 174 (1970) (Harlan, J., concurring in part and dissenting in part); cf. R. Berger, *Government by Judiciary* (1977). That, however, was the very extension effected by the Fifteenth Amend-

The sort of review that is appropriate in cases involving voter qualifications is related to that which is appropriate in First Amendment contexts. We cannot trust the ins to decide who stays out, and it is therefore incumbent on the courts to ensure not only that no one is denied the vote for no reason, but also that where there is a reason (as there will be) it had better be a very convincing one. Thus in *Carrington v. Rash*,[41] decided in 1965, the Court invalidated a Texas law denying the franchise to those who had moved into the state on military service, and in *Harper v. Virginia Board of Elections*,[42] decided a year later, it struck down Virginia's poll tax. Each of these voter qualifications, the Court said, was irrational. But neither really was that. Military personnel do tend to be more transient than others and in addition might well, as the state argued, end up dominating the politics of a town in or near which a military base is located. It may also be true, or at least it is not irrational to think so, that persons of some wealth tend to be more "responsible" citizens or, more plausibly still, that the willingness to pay a fee for voting is some reflection of serious interest in the election. So the language of irrationality was hyperbole, and the real point in each case was that a group of persons—the military in one case, those so poor that a fee might be a deterrent in the other—was being frozen out of the decision process for an insufficiently compelling reason.[43]

"Malapportionment," where one person's vote counts only a fraction (and sometimes it was a very small fraction) of another's, involves the same principle. Half a vote is only half a vote, a sixth of a vote is scarcely better than no vote at all, and here again those in power have a vested interest in keeping things the way they are.[44] Yet it is the malapportionment decisions that have borne the brunt of the commentators' criticism.[45] Justice Frankfurter used to say that reapportionment was a "political thicket" that the courts should avoid.[46] The critics love to quote him, but in truth the meaning of the point is blurred. Sometimes it has meant that there can be no administrable standard for determining the legality of apportionments.[47] At least in the present context of this dispute, however,

---

ment, which recent studies have shown was supported by essentially the same people as the Fourteenth. See note 70 to Chapter 2. In any event the reservation was not expressed in the Fourteenth Amendment and is unusually inconsistent with the ideal it expresses.

that is nothing short of silly. For the very standard the Court chose in the landmark *Reynolds v. Sims*[48] (the very standard that was anathema to Frankfurter and his successor in criticism here, Justice Harlan) — the "one person, one vote" standard — is certainly administrable. In fact administrability is its long suit, and the more troublesome question is what else it has to recommend it. On other occasions the "thicket" criticism has signaled a "realist's" point, that a reapportionment order is one unusually calculated to get the Court in trouble, dangerously to decrease its prestige.[49] I have suggested that this is a questionable basis on which to make or criticize constitutional law. Anyhow, the critics were wrong on this one: the equal weighting of everyone's vote turned out to be a notion with which most people could sympathize,[50] and in any event a legislature, once reapportioned, will lack incentive to "re-malapportion" itself and indeed will probably have little but praise for the Court's initiative in this area. (What the critics missed is that the incentive of elected representatives is not necessarily toward malapportionment but rather toward maintaining whatever apportionment, good or bad, it is that got and keeps them where they are.) So that version of the "thicket" criticism, whether or not it ever had colorable validity, is yesterday's news. In 1967 Louis Jaffe, characteristically candid in his refusal to "revise and extend" his earlier remarks, confessed: "At least some of us who shook our heads over *Baker v. Carr* are prepared to admit . . . that it has not impaired, indeed that it has enhanced the prestige of the Court."[51]

However, the usual demand of the Equal Protection Clause is simply that the discrimination in question be rationally explainable. Chief Justice Warren's opinion for the Court in *Reynolds* tried to suggest that any deviation from a one person, one vote standard was irrational, but that is nonsense. Various states, and the federal government as well, often and permissibly give special breaks to certain groups in our society. Farmers, for example, frequently receive special governmental favors — subsidies, tax breaks, even exemptions from antitrust and other criminal statutes[52] — as a way of fostering a strong agricultural economy. Another entirely rational way of pursuing the same goal is to give rural areas more legislative representatives per unit of population.

There is indeed a problem with this sort of defense, but it's not that it isn't rational, or even that it is incapable of meeting the rightfully stronger demand the Court has imposed in the voting area. The problem instead, if you will, is that such defenses work too well, that they can readily be pushed to the point of justifying governmental systems that we all would recognize as inconsistent with the plan of our Constitution. If protecting the agricultural economy is truly important to a state, and it obviously is to some, it would not be illogical to give farmers 90 percent of the effective voting power even though they make up only 10 percent of the population. That is too much for everyone, however. It was obviously to cope with such extended inferences that Justice Stewart, dissenting in *Reynolds* and its companion cases, added to the baseline equal protection requirement, that distinctions in voting strength be rationally defensible, the additional demand that the plan at issue "must be such as not to permit the systematic frustration of the will of a majority of the electorate of the State."[53]

Now obviously that qualification did not arise from anything in or about the Fourteenth Amendment or existing equal protection lore: defensible distinctions typically survive, without the interposition of any such backstop. It came instead from certain assumptions about the sort of representative government the Constitution contemplates, assumptions it is most comfortable to assign to the Republican Form of Government Clause. Thus, to be intelligible, *Reynolds v. Sims*, its majority and dissenting opinions alike, must be approached as the joint product of the Equal Protection and Republican Form Clauses. Maybe, therefore, we can make some headway toward justifying, at least toward understanding, the one person, one vote principle if we direct some attention to the Republican Form Clause. Relevant building blocks are certainly available. Discussions of the meaning of "democracy," no matter how scrupulous they are about noting the existence of some variations in understanding, seem invariably to include political equality, or the principle that everyone's vote is to count for the same, in their core definition.[54] Nor is this an understanding recently arrived at: many among the framers stressed the importance to the system they were forging of the equal representation of equal population groups.[55]

However, it is the United States Constitution we are expounding, and it doesn't say this, but indicates instead that states are to maintain a "Republican Form of Government." And while it is true that many among the framers indicated their understanding that that term connoted what we would now call a representative democracy, for others it appears to have required only that the government not be a monarchy.[56] Of course the latter view only sets a floor, and a system of representative democracy complete with political equality would obviously be consistent with both. Neither is there anything special about the Republican Form Clause that suggests that a line of growth or development (like that the Court has given virtually every other constitutional phrase) would be inappropriate.[57] It is a clear if common error to suppose, however, that the fact that it would not do violence to a provision to move to a meaning we favor can alone constitute a sufficient justification for the move. "One person, one vote" is certainly a principle the Republican Form Clause is capable of containing, but so is Stewart's weaker "simply don't systematically frustrate the majority will" approach. What are lacking still are the reasons that justify choosing the former over the latter.

In judging the propriety of such a line of growth it is surely appropriate, indeed I should think it imperative, to look to the ways our constitutional document has developed over the two centuries since the Republican Form Clause was drafted. Not only has the Fourteenth Amendment underscored our commitment to equality in the distribution of various goods — particularly, one has to suppose, those that are crucial to one's ability to protect oneself respecting the distribution of all others — but several other amendments, in fact most of the recent ones, have extended the franchise to persons who previously had been denied it, thereby reflecting a strengthening constitutional commitment to the proposition that all qualified citizens are to play a role in the making of public decisions. Valuing a vote thus granted at a fraction of the votes of others obviously undercuts the commitment this constitutional development reflects. Now we're getting somewhere, though Justice Stewart still has an answer left: of course, I should think his response would run, the general ideal these constitutional provisions combine to generate is one of at least rough equality in terms of one's influence on governmental choices, but influence can be exerted in many ways. Some groups have unusual access to, say, the state executive, or the city governments, or the media, and it is therefore not unreasonable — indeed it may ultimately serve the cause of real equality — to compensate for such comparative advantages by granting others advantages when it comes to the weighting of votes for, say, legislative officials. Urban working people, the idea might run in a given state, do not need the same clout in the legislature the farmers have, since they historically have had an effective pipeline to the governor.[58]

The issue thus focused, we are in a better position to understand the Court's conclusion that one person, one vote was the only acceptable standard for courts to apply. The Court itself does not appear to have been entirely self-conscious about its reasoning, or at least it did not share it, but the explanation must be that given by Professor Deutsch, that Justice Stewart's "in-between" standard would have involved the Court in difficult and unseemly inquiries into the power alignments prevalent in the various states whose plans came before it.

> [T]he formula espoused by Stewart . . . would . . . require the Court to canvass the actual workings of the floor leadership in the legislative branches, the mechanisms of party control not only over voters and the city government but also over elected representatives—in short, the details of the petty corruption and networks of personal influence that all too often constitute critical sources of power in municipal politics. Given the Court's institutional arrangements, however, it could investigate these matters only by requiring lower courts to build records on these issues . . . Even assuming that the evidence was available and would be forthcoming, is it likely that our society could accept, as a steady diet, the spectacle of the judiciary solemnly ruling on the accuracy of a political boss's testimony concerning the sources of his power over voters and the degree of control that he exercised over elected officials?[59]

It thus turns out that there were two ways to avoid the unadministrability thicket. One was to stay out of the area altogether. That would have meant, however, that the ins would simply have gone on maintaining their positions by valuing one person's vote at a sixth of another's.[60] Everyone without a strong personal stake in the status quo granted that that was no more compatible with the underlying theory of our Constitution than taking away some people's votes altogether. So the Court entered, and *precisely because of considerations of administrability*, soon found itself with no perceived alternative but to move to a one person, one vote standard.[61] Actually this move was characteristic of the Warren Court, which on several occasions adopted what seemed on the surface the more intrusive rule on the theory that it would be less intrusive in practice. Part of the theory behind *Gideon v. Wainwright*,[62] requiring appointed counsel in all felony cases, was that the previously prevailing "special circumstances rule," though requiring counsel on fewer occasions, in fact had repeatedly resulted in messy and friction-generating factual inquiries into every case.[63] *Miranda v. Arizona*,[64] requiring a set list of warnings to precede every police interrogation, was similarly motivated. Sometimes more is less.[65]

Toward a Visible Legislative Process

So far in this chapter I have been concerned, as the Supreme Court has been primarily concerned, with assuring the free and effective popular choice of our representatives. But popular choice will mean relatively little if we don't know what our representatives are up to. Recently the Court has begun to react to this realization, or at least it has been tinkering with the Equal Protection Clause in ways that are difficult to explain in any other terms. Traditionally the Court has stood ready to invoke in a classification's defense any nonforbidden goal that might conceivably have generated it, whether or not it was mentioned at the time the law was passed or even cited by the state's lawyer.[66] In the past few years, however—following a suggestion of Gerald Gunther[67]—the Court has taken to indicating that at least in certain contexts classifications will be upheld only by virtue of their relation to "articulated" purposes, those that have been "identified by the State."[68] The Court has been somewhat uneven on the subject of just who has to have articulated the purpose—the legislature, the state courts, or the attorney arguing the case for the state[69]—and in fact it seems to ignore the entire doctrine more often than it invokes it.[70] By canvassing the various forms the doctrine might take, we shall be able to understand the hesitancy.

The goal of the exercise, one of flushing out legislative purposes so that the voters can better react to them, seems entirely laudable and in addition is an appropriately constitutional concern. The problem is that the more one tries to specify a way in which the Court might participate in forcing articulation, the clearer it seems to become that none exists whose costs will not exceed its benefits. In terms of promoting political accountability it is difficult to imagine any difference whatever between the Court's traditional practice of upholding a classification by reference to a purpose it itself hypothesizes, and its upholding it by reference to a purpose the state's lawyer puts in his or her brief or argument. To a purpose supplied either way the legislator standing for reelection will be able to respond if so inclined, "That's what *they* said; the reasons for my vote were different." If the idea is that the state's lawyer will hesitate to rely on a purpose he or she isn't sure the legislature had in mind, it seems to ignore the dynamics of the litigation process. The lawyer wants to win, and in order to do so is likely to be willing to rely on any purpose that will help — that is, any that is not flat-out unconstitutional.[71] After all, the lawyer is not *endorsing* the purpose, but only speculating on what another group of persons might have had in mind.[72] As far as the state judges are concerned (assuming the case in fact came up through the state court system), it enhances neither their state's image nor, usually, their personal careers to strike down local laws (or to set them up for invalidation by the Supreme Court).

But even if this kind of incentive to protect the products of the local legislature were lacking, we would still generally expect state courts (and surely state attorneys general) to attribute the purpose or purposes necessary to save the classification in issue. For the purpose that will most comfortably establish the rationality of a classification — that is, the purpose that fits its terms most closely — is most likely to be the purpose that actually generated it.* Thus, far from

---

*It is for this reason that analyses that purport to test a classification against the purposes that "actually" inspired it will necessarily be charades, invalidations on such grounds inevitably unconvincing. See, e.g., Eisenstadt v. Baird, 405 U.S. 438 (1972), rejecting the state supreme court's conclusion that the deterrence of premarital sex was one purpose of a state law forbidding unmarried persons to obtain contraceptives for the prevention of pregnancy, and consequently voiding the law as irrational. This is certainly not to say that the purpose that actually generated the classification is constitutionally irrelevant. If that purpose was unconstitutional, the classification should fall. See generally Chapter 6. If it wasn't, though, it can serve no further candid constitutional function: in particular it cannot meaningfully serve as the measure of the classification, since the fit between the classification and the purpose(s) that actually generated it will invariably be close. See generally Note, "Legislative Purpose, Rationality, and Equal Protection," 82 *Yale L. J.* 123 (1972). See also Trimble v. Gordon, 430 U.S. 762, 783 (1977) (Rehnquist, J., dissenting): complainant invoking such a test must schizophrenically "first convince this Court that the legislature had a particular purpose in mind in enacting the law, and then convince it that the law was not at all suited to the accomplish-

its taking a court determined to uphold the statute at all costs to conclude that the purpose that is most helpful constitutionally is probably the one that inspired it, it would usually take a court hell-bent on invalidation to reach any other conclusion.[73] (And if the relevant purpose is somewhat embarrassing politically, well, again, the court isn't endorsing it, but simply speculating that it may have played a role.) The only cases in which an articulation requirement would make a difference here, therefore—cases where the state court or the government's lawyer refuses to credit as possible the only purpose that can save the statute—would be cases in which we would have to question their motives for doing so.

We are thus driven to the conclusion a naive observer would have arrived at forthwith: that if what we're trying to achieve by imposing an articulation requirement is more candor on the part of our elected representatives, the only sensible requirement is some sort of articulation *by those representatives*. The most obvious specification of that requirement would be that to be invocable the purpose must appear somewhere in the legislative history. We may not, of course, be dealing with a state legislature whose debates are recorded but rather with, say, a town council or administrative board, and neither, to my knowledge, are the deliberations of the executive before a bill is signed often preserved. But arguably those are details: if the general idea makes sense it could simply become the responsibility of those who make the law to get their purposes recorded in some form that can be presented to the federal courts. Somewhat more serious is the fact, known to everyone who has participated in a group deliberation of any kind, that people often vote for measures for reasons sufficient to themselves even though no one else has put those reasons on the record. Again, I suppose, the answer is that there will simply have to be a change, though there surely are costs

---

ment of that purpose." The proposal we are now examining is different, seeking to enhance accountability by refusing to sustain a classification in terms of a purpose that has not been articulated. My suggestion, however, is that insofar as articulation by the state court system or the state's counsel is allowed to count, this approach too, responsibly applied, will collapse into a system of measuring classifications against their actual motivations—which is to say that in the absence of provable unconstitutional motivation nothing will be invalidated—since responsible courts and counsel will attribute to a classification that permissible purpose that best explains it.

—a good deal of cumbersome and costly litigation until people get the idea, and a good deal of cumbersome and costly recordation of everyone's purposes once they do.

And what positive difference would this make? The system once understood, the more politically embarrassing (though most to the point, and thus in court potentially most helpful) statements of purpose — "This is to ensure a vital embalming industry" — could be articulated by lame ducks or those from safe districts, leaving everyone else free to explain his vote in his own terms. Maybe then we will have to require something more authoritative — a committee report perhaps (placing on those not on the committee the burden of getting to its staff and convincing them to include those purposes they wish to have included). That would likely result in a laundry list of purposes, however, or more likely a few so all-encompassing in their generality that they could plausibly be used in every report the committee issues.[74] It is difficult to imagine that accountability would be significantly enhanced by such a system: an individual legislator would remain free to disavow some of the purposes listed and to attribute others that seem useful to his or her understanding of the boilerplate.*

*It may appear at this point that I am assuming bad faith, and that certainly is a part of my concern. I'm sure, however, that there are numerous legislators who would not want to mislead concerning their purposes. (Of course there has never been anything to prevent such people from detailing their purposes, yet one will search the legislative records in vain for many startling displays of candor. Presumably those most scrupulous about "laying it all out" for the voters are also those whose purposes are least likely to be crass.) I'm not at all convinced, however, that the concerns expressed are applicable only to situations of bad faith, principally because choices among various purposes for the same piece of legislation — unlike, say, choices between two inconsistent pieces of legislation or two conflicting interpretations of a single law — are not either-or choices. Whenever there are two or more compatible explanations for a course of action it will be difficult for anyone, including the actor, to be clear about what "really" generated it, and it is simple human nature to want to believe that the more laudable purpose played a (the) significant role. Beyond that, it is a rare motivation that is so crassly political that it cannot *itself* be characterized, both externally and internally, as laudable. Thus one might vote for a law permitting only optometrists to replace lenses in part to please the optometrists' lobby, but quite honestly rationalize the vote not simply on the ground that optometrists are more likely to have the training to make sure it is done right, but also on the ground that the maintenance of a "healthy" optometric profession is important. Since the latter can also be viewed as a public health purpose, one can in all good faith represent one's *entire* concern as having been with public health.

Requiring that the purpose be stated in a preamble or elsewhere in the statute itself might at first blush appear calculated to reduce the individual legislator's ability thus to escape personal accountability: after all, he *voted* for the thing, didn't he? In fact this approach would seem to carry serious additional costs. Much valuable legislative time would be consumed debating the question, not simply of what sort of regulation should be imposed, but in addition of what purposes should be noted in the bill. Beyond that, much legislation that must be counted desirable in the sense that a majority of legislators favor it might well never get passed at all, due to a lack of enactable agreement on purposes. To avoid that, legislatures would have to fall into, and courts would have to validate, the sort of pattern I sketched as likely respecting committee reports, one of appending boilerplate so flabby—of course this is what preambles already tend to be—that accountability will not be significantly promoted.[75]

Thus, while I share the instinct that animated Professor Gunther's suggestion and that seems intermittently to be moving the Court, I'm skeptical that a method of forcing articulation of purposes can be developed that will be both workable and helpful. The next question is how greatly that conclusion ought to upset us, and my answer, for several reasons, is that it may matter very little. I say this not because I believe the voters don't care where their representatives stand on the issues. Of course many other factors have much to do with political success, but it also seems pretty clear that our representatives act on the assumption that the stands they take will importantly affect their future success,[76] and I'm aware of no reason to doubt on this score their judgment of their constituents. Neither is my point that most people don't very effectively keep abreast of how their representatives are voting on various bills, let alone what they're saying about them. In fact a good number do keep up—with intermittent help from the media—on those issues about which they care most intensely. But for the others, one important function of campaigns is to give an opponent a strong incentive to check up on his or her rival's record and bring it to the public's attention. Neither, finally, is the point that I am skeptical about the possibility of determining people's intentions, even the intentions of people functioning in groups as large as legislative assemblies. Quite the contrary, such inquiries permeate my approaches to constitutional interpretation and enforcement. But as I stressed in Chapter 2 (in discussing whether the language of the Fourteenth Amendment should be either expanded or contracted to fit certain alleged but unenacted conceptions of its framers) and as will also become clear in Chapter 6 (when I turn to the possibility of invalidating statutes for unconstitutional motivation), the inquiry's most important ingredient by far must be the actual terms of the law or provision in issue, read in light of its foreseeable effects and a healthy dose of common sense, and not, though it can help occasionally, its legislative history.

That realization seems critical to the present question as well. We have seen that court-induced articulation of purposes is likely to be so vague or all-inclusive as to be peculiarly unhelpful. But even if a way could be found to make it more informative, it would help the voters at the point where they least need help. If, say, the law in question provides that only licensed taxidermists will be allowed to stuff birds, opponents will characterize it — irrespective of what appears in the preamble or the legislative history — as a sellout to a powerful special interest group, and defenders will argue that there are plausible health and safety reasons for not letting every Tom, Dick, and Harriet go around stuffing birds, and perhaps that the nation needs a stable taxidermy industry. It is likely that the average voter could use some help evaluating the strength of these arguments, since on their strength will likely depend one's assessment of the contenders' wisdom and good faith. An articulation of purposes requirement won't help with that, however: it will simply bring the range of possible justifications to the surface. That, however, the voter — certainly with the help of the incumbent and his opponent — seems fully capable of doing simply by looking at the face of the law.*

In fact, I would argue, the common case of nonaccountability involves not a situation where the legislature has drawn a distinction whose range of informing purposes won't be readily apparent, but rather a situation where the legislature (in large measure precisely in order to escape accountability) has refused to draw the legally oper-

*To the extent that the drive for an articulation requirement is based on the assumption that the average voter is too naive to detect handouts or cross-subsidies to powerful interest groups, it is the assumption that seems naive. What is hard to sell in America today is the claim that legislators ever vote in the public interest.

ative distinctions, leaving that chore to others who are not politically accountable. Perhaps, therefore, the most effective way to get our representatives to be clearer about what they are up to in their legislation is to get them to legislate.

Toward a Legislative Lawmaking Process

In theory it is the legislature that makes the laws and the administrators who apply them.[77] Anyone who has seen Congress in action, however — I am not much acquainted with state legislatures but assume a number of them are similar in this regard[78] — will know that the actual situation is very nearly upside down. Much of the typical representative's time is consumed, not with considering legislation, but rather with running errands (big and small) for his or her constituents — "making calls to public agencies on behalf of businessmen and interested parties back home, introducing private bills to permit alien relatives of constituents to enter or remain in the country and answering the huge quantity of mail that comes in."[79] This is not to say that our representatives are unconcerned with substantive questions. But often that concern is expressed not in the form of legislation but rather by second-guessing the decisions of executive and administrative officials — questioning them at hearings and in various less formal ways. Much of the law is thus effectively left to be made by the legions of unelected administrators whose duty it becomes to give operative meaning to the broad delegations the statutes contain. The point is not that such "faceless bureaucrats" necessarily do a bad job as our effective legislators. It is rather that they are neither elected nor reelected, and are controlled only spasmodically by officials who are. (In the federal executive, of course, the only elected officials are the President and the Vice President.)

The reasons things got switched around are not hard to discern. One is that it is simply easier, and it pays more visible political dividends, to play errand-boy-cum-ombudsman than to play one's part in a genuinely legislative process. How much more comfortable it must be simply to vote in favor of a bill calling for safe cars, clean air, or nondiscrimination, and to leave to others the chore of fleshing out what such a mandate might mean. How much safer, too — and here we get to the nub. For the fact seems to be that on most hard issues our representatives quite shrewdly prefer not to have to stand up and be counted but rather to let some executive-branch bureaucrat, or perhaps some independent regulatory commission, "take the inevitable political heat."[80] As Congressman Levitas put it, "When hard decisions have to be made, we pass the buck to the agencies with vaguely worded statutes."[81] And as Congressman Flowers added, what comes later is a virtually no-loss situation: "[T]hen we stand back and say when our constituents are aggrieved or oppressed by various rules and regulations, 'Hey, it's not me. We didn't mean that. We passed this well-meaning legislation, and we intended for those people out there . . . to do exactly what we meant, and they did not do it.' "[82]

Now this is wrong, not because it isn't "the way it was meant to be"—in some circumstances there may be little objection to institutions' trading jobs—but rather because it is undemocratic, in the quite obvious sense that by refusing to legislate, our legislators are escaping the sort of accountability that is crucial to the intelligible functioning of a democratic republic. There was a very brief period when the Supreme Court took all this rather seriously. In *Panama Refining Co. v. Ryan*[83] and *A.L.A. Schechter Poultry Corp. v. United States*,[84] both decided in 1935, it struck down laws for "invalid delegation," that is, for passing the decision authority on to other persons without a "standard'" or "intelligible principle" to guide their policy choices. Coming along when it did, the nondelegation doctrine became identified with others that were used in the early thirties to invalidate reform legislation, such as substantive due process and a restrictive interpretation of the commerce power—in fact *Schechter* itself featured the latter as an alternative holding—and when those doctrines died the nondelegation doctrine died along with them. (It was, of course, part of the New Deal religion that policy should be made by "experts.") Since that time Congress has quite commonly by statute said to administrative officials, in essence, "Find the problems in this area and solve them," and the Court, when the question has even been raised, has upheld the delegation. Writing in 1974, Justice Marshall accurately summarized the doctrine's contemporary standing: "The notion that the Constitution narrowly confines the power of Congress to delegate authority to administrative agencies, which was briefly in vogue in the 1930's, has been virtually abandoned by the Court for all practical purposes

. . . This doctrine is surely as moribund as the substantive due process approach of the same era — for which the Court is fond of writing an obituary . . . if not more so."[85] "If not more so" is right, given the prior year's abortion decision.

It's a case of death by association, though. There can be little point in worrying about the distribution of the franchise and other personal political rights unless the important policy choices are being made by elected officials. Courts thus should ensure not only that administrators follow those legislative policy directions that do exist — on that proposition there is little disagreement — but also that such directions are given.[86] The reason this isn't a popular idea[87] probably has mainly to do with its history, but sometimes reasons are given. One is that the world is a complicated and volatile place and therefore detailed legislative instructions would simply prove unworkable.[88] To this two different answers seem appropriate. The first is that most legislatures, certainly the Congress, can call on staffs as expert as those the administrators have available,[89] and that at least in the federal government they are also entitled to the assistance of the executive departments' technical staffs. The second and more fundamental answer is that the nondelegation doctrine, even at its high point, never insisted either on more detail than was feasible or that matters be settled with more permanence than the subject matter would allow. Policy direction is all that was ever required, and policy direction is what is lacking in much contemporary legislation.

It is thus a second objection to the nondelegation doctrine that is more often billed as dispositive, namely that it often will not be politically convenient for legislators to resolve issues of policy. The point is one that has been reiterated, but never more succinctly than it was recently by Richard Stewart: "Individual politicians often find far more to be lost than gained in taking a readily identifiable stand on a controversial issue of social or economic policy."[90] It's an argument, all right, but for which side? That legislators often find it convenient to escape accountability is precisely the reason *for* a nondelegation doctrine. Were it to turn out that legislators forced to govern wouldn't have the courage to do so energetically, that would often be too bad — though administrators with formless delegations often and understandably don't turn out to be so active themselves[91] — but at least it would be our system. Much as liberals may not like it, one reason we have broadly based representative assemblies is to await something approaching a consensus before government intervenes.[92] As Judge Wright put it in 1972: "An argument for letting the experts decide when the people's representatives are uncertain or cannot agree is an argument for paternalism and against democracy."[93]

The recent attention given the problem of ventilating legislative purposes is healthy; in fact it is critical to representative government. However, the track down which the Court and the commentators are proceeding is one that may not lead anywhere, since there is serious doubt that there is any effective way of getting our representatives to set down their purposes in a form that will tell us anything we cannot learn from the face of legislation. The problem seems more basic, and may lie not in a propensity to make politically controversial decisions without telling us why, but rather in a propensity not to make politically controversial decisions — to leave them instead to others, most often others who are not elected or effectively controlled by those who are. If we can just get our legislators to legislate we'll be able to understand their goals well enough. I'm not saying we may not still end up with a fair number of clowns as representatives, but at least then it will be because clowns are what we deserve.

6 Facilitating
the Representation
of Minorities

Some commentators have suggested that the Court's role in protecting minorities should consist only in removing barriers to their participation in the political process.[1] We have seen, however — and the realization is one that threads our constitutional document — that the duty of representation that lies at the core of our system requires more than a voice and a vote. No matter how open the process, those with most of the votes are in a position to vote themselves advantages at the expense of the others, or otherwise to refuse to take their interests into account. " 'One person, one vote,' under these circumstances, makes a travesty of the equality principle."[2] Not long ago the assurances of pluralist political theory, that any group whose members were not denied the franchise could protect itself by entering into the give and take of the political marketplace, dominated academic political science.[3] Recently, however, pluralism has come under powerful attack, as more stress has been placed on the undeniable concentrations of power, and inequalities among the various competing groups, in American politics.[4] Of course the pluralist model does work sometimes, and minorities *can* protect themselves by striking deals and stressing the ties that bind the interests of other groups to their own. But sometimes it doesn't, as the single example of how our society has treated its black minority (even after that minority had gained every official attribute of access to the process) is more than sufficient to prove.

One thing we know the Constitution, the Equal Protection Clause in particular, cannot mean is that everyone is entitled to equal treatment by every law. In fact much of the point of most laws is to sort people out for differential treatment, often quite seriously differential treatment. Neither can the Constitution coherently be interpreted as outlining some "appropriate" distributional pattern against which actual allocations of hurts and benefits can be traced to see if they are constitutional.[5] The constitutionality of most distributions thus cannot be determined simply by looking to see who ended up with what, but rather can be approached intelligibly only by attending to the process that brought about the distribution in question—by what Robert Nozick has called a "historical" (as opposed to an "end result") approach.[6] This is not the way one should approach a law withholding something to which the Constitution gives us a presumptive constitutional entitlement, such as the right to vote. That right simply cannot be denied (unless the state's lawyer can come up with a compelling justification for doing so). The Court's job in such cases is to look at the world as it exists and ask whether such a right is in fact being abridged, and if it is, to consider what reasons might be adduced in support of the deprivation, without regard to what actually occasioned it.* To the extent that there is a stoppage, the system is malfunctioning, and the Court should unblock it without caring how it got that way. Benefits— goods, rights, exemptions, or whatever—that are not essential to political participation or explicitly guaranteed by the language of the Constitution, however, we can call constitutionally gratuitous— though obviously they may be terribly important—and malfunction in their distribution can intelligibly inhere only in the process that effected it. (The distributional pattern can provide powerful evidence of what that process is likely to have been, of course.) I am aware that at this point this general conclusion is unlikely to seem any more than plausible, if indeed it seems that, but I believe it will become more convincing as I develop the ways in which such a process-oriented system of review would operate.

Legislative (and Administrative) Motivation

For years the Supreme Court has gone back and forth on the question of whether an official act should be invalidated because it was undertaken for an unconstitutional reason,[7] and it has continued to vacillate lately. As recently as 1971 it indicated that "no case in this Court"—surely that historical claim was wrong—"has held that a

---

*Of course, a distrust of the self-serving motives of those in power significantly animates the entire enterprise.

legislative act may violate equal protection solely because of the motivations of the men who voted for it"[8] and went on to deny the relevance of a strong showing of racial motivation in the closing of Jackson, Mississippi's municipal swimming pools (which had recently been ordered integrated). In two cases decided in 1976 and 1977, however, the Court has gone just the other way, indicating that "[p]roof of racially discriminatory intent or purpose is required to show a violation of the Equal Protection Clause."[9] Plainly the question is one that gives the Court (and others) trouble. On reflection, though, it's not clear why it should.

Suppose a sergeant in the National Guard has to pick three members of his six-man squad for an especially hazardous assignment quelling a civil disturbance, and ends up picking Winken, Blinken, and Nod. The Constitution obviously would not be offended if those three were picked because they had scored highest on their riflery tests. It would even, presumably, be constitutional to pick them at random. Suppose, however, they were selected because they were Poles, or Methodists, or Republicans—or indeed simply because the sergeant liked the other three members of his squad better. Under these circumstances, our intuition tells us that Winken, Blinken, and Nod have been treated unconstitutionally. Of course the problems of proof in such a case could be monumental (especially if the three chosen were in fact the three best shots), but notice what the example suggests—that the very same governmental action can be constitutional or unconstitutional depending on why it was undertaken. This makes theoretical sense too. It is inconsistent with constitutional norms to select people for unusual deprivation on the basis of race, religion, or politics, or even simply because the official doing the choosing doesn't like them.[10] When such a principle of selection has been employed, the system has malfunctioned: indeed we can accurately label such a selection a denial of due process. Perhaps a properly functioning system would have generated the same result, perhaps it wouldn't. But that typically is true when due process has been denied, and the remedy, save only in cases of clearly nonprejudicial error, is to reject the product of the malfunctioning process and start over.[11]

The reasons usually given for refusing to look at motivation were summarized in Justice Black's opinion for the Court in the Jackson pool case:

First, it is extremely difficult for a court to ascertain the motivation, or collection of different motivations, that lie behind a
legislative enactment . . . It is difficult or impossible for any
court to determine the "sole" or "dominant" motivation behind
the choices of a group of legislators. Furthermore, there is an
element of futility in a judicial attempt to invalidate a law because of the bad motives of its supporters. If the law is struck
down for this reason, rather than because of its facial content
or effect, it would presumably be valid as soon as the legislature
or relevant governing body repassed it for different reasons.[12]

There's something of a cheat on the first point here. The considerations that make motivation relevant argue not for the discovery of
the "sole" motivation (is there ever just one?) or even the "dominant"
motivation (whatever that might mean),[13] but rather for asking
whether an unconstitutional motivation appears materially to have
influenced the choice: if one did, the procedure was illegitimate —
"due process of lawmaking" was denied[14] — and its product should
be invalidated. But Black's more general point is right: determining
whether an illegitimate motivation influenced a decision can be very
difficult. Indeed it will be next to impossible for a court responsibly
to conclude that a decision was affected by an unconstitutional
motivation whenever it is possible to articulate a plausible legitimate
explanation for the action taken.[15] But what does that prove? Only
that it often will not be possible responsibly to conclude that the
challenged action was the product of an unconstitutional motivation,
not that the inquiry should not be undertaken. Moreover, we shall
see from a review of some of the decided cases that there *will* be situations, more than a few, where in fact there won't exist an alternative legitimate explanation of the action in question, and where
therefore a responsible inference that the action was unconstitutionally motivated will be possible. Black's "futility" point obviously is
closely related, and the appropriate answer is much the same. The
idea is that sometimes an action invalidated because it was undertaken for unconstitutional reasons will be able to be retaken, this
time putatively on legitimate grounds the courts will have to credit.
This won't happen very often, however, for two reasons. First, the
reasons that led the court to conclude in the first case that the action
was inspired by an illicit motivation will rightly make it somewhat
skeptical of claims of a subsequent change of heart. Second, a claim

of change of heart will be plausible only where there exists a plausible legitimate explanation of the action in question, and as I have noted the existence of that explanation will in all likelihood have precluded a finding of unconstitutional motivation in the first place. But suppose from time to time an action previously invalidated for unconstitutional motivation is retaken and upheld: so what? We don't regard the system as having failed when a person whose conviction was reversed because the jury was biased is reconvicted by an unbiased jury on remand: indeed we regard it as vindicated.[16]

The point is one that has proved elusive, though, so it is well to review some of the decided cases here.[17] Two conclusions should emerge, and they are the two that probably need to emerge if the skeptical are to be convinced: first, that there are real-world cases where an unconstitutional motivation, even on the part of a legislature, can quite confidently be inferred,[18] and second, that there will be cases your intuition tells you involve unconstitutional action that cannot be responsibly rationalized on anything *but* a motivation theory. Let's start with a recurrent situation, the selection of jury panels. It has been settled for a century that, to make out a claim of racial or other unconstitutional discrimination in the selection of a jury panel, a complainant must prove intentional discrimination, and will succeed if he does. As Justice Douglas put it in 1970: "We have often said that no jury need represent proportionally a cross-section of the community . . . Jury selection is largely by chance; and no matter what the race of the defendant, he bears the risk that no racial component, presumably favorable to him, will appear on the jury that tries him. The law only requires that the panel not be purposely unrepresentative."[19] Naturally the inference of unconstitutional motivation is most likely to arise, as it will in most of our cases, from the pattern of impact. Nor is a convincing rebuttal of a striking statistical case of jury discrimination likely to be forthcoming. But impact alone is not the constitutional point, and in the rare case where imbalanced statistics *can* be explained — as where the state can convincingly prove that an inordinately high percentage of "white names" just happened to be picked at random from the city directory — the claim will be rejected.

Unconstitutionally motivated *legislative* actions are similarly unconstitutional.[20] In 1957 the Alabama Legislature redrew, by statute, the boundary lines of the City of Tuskegee so as to change

its shape from a square to an "uncouth twenty-eight-sided figure"
and, in the process, to exclude all but a handful of the city's four
hundred previously resident black voters. In 1960, in *Gomillion v.
Lightfoot*, the Supreme Court unanimously invalidated Alabama's
action, stating that "[a]cts generally lawful may become unlawful
when done to accomplish an unlawful end."[21] The demonstration
that the act was the product of an unconstitutional motivation was
obviously overwhelming: in fact the state did not offer a rebuttal,
but argued instead that the Court shouldn't reach the question.
Eight years later in *United States v. O'Brien*, the Court, in one of its
periodic denials that official motivation is relevant, asserted that
Gomillion stood "not for the proposition that legislative motive is a
proper basis for declaring a statute unconstitutional, but that the
inevitable effect of a statute on its face may render it unconstitutional."[22] That's gibberish, though, as the Court has since recognized. There are many cities and voting districts throughout the
United States whose residents are predominantly or even exclusively
white (not to mention those whose residents are largely Protestant,
Catholic, Jewish, conservative, liberal, Republican, or Democratic),
and a number of them are abutted by communities that are entirely
different. To require, in the absence of proof of intentional discrimination, that they somehow be more nearly "equalized" would be
to take a step the Court has consistently refused — one of forcing
government officials to determine and take into account the races
(and so forth) of everyone who will be affected by a proposed action
and juggle it so that the numbers come out (about?) even.[23] Thus in
Wright v. Rockefeller,[24] decided in 1964, the Court rejected a claim
of racial discrimination respecting the abutting Seventeenth and
Eighteenth Congressional Districts in New York, one of which was
94.9 percent white and the other of which was 86.3 percent black
and Puerto Rican, on the ground that intentional discrimination
had not been proved. In my opinion the two dissenters, Douglas and
Goldberg, got the better of the factual dispute, but what is important here is that their argument too was one sounding in intentional
racial selection, not a contention that disproportionate impact
alone, without an inference of racial motivation, could add up to a
constitutional violation.

There is nothing in the reasoning that establishes the relevance of
unconstitutional motivation that limits it to cases involving racial

discrimination. In *Epperson v. Arkansas*, decided in 1968, the Court invalidated as an establishment of religion a statute prohibiting the teaching in Arkansas's public schools of the theory that humankind evolved from other species of life, explicitly resting its holding on the conclusion that the law had been passed in order to promote fundamentalist Christianity.[25] Neither was this reliance on motivation unnecessary, for the result cannot be justified in terms of the law's impact alone. Biology generally, or the study of all theories of human origins, could under most circumstances constitutionally be eliminated entirely, even though that would mean the students would never be exposed to Darwin's theory.[26] There are, moreover, numerous philosophical and scientific theories that undoubtedly would undercut a fundamentalist's faith as much as or more than the theory of evolution, but *Epperson* obviously cannot mean that a school is obligated to teach them all. However, a moment's reflection on the significance of evolution to twentieth-century assumptions about our origins is enough to establish the soundness of the Court's inference of religious motivation. The exclusion of evolution and only evolution plainly resulted from more than an arbitrary reaction to the realization that the curriculum had to be closed somewhere, and no other explanation was suggested.

The motivation of government officials will also be relevant in some cases involving freedom of speech, press, and association, though not in all. Where the government is simply obliged to respect a certain right it must do so, and the reasons why it didn't are not constitutionally relevant. Where the good or right whose distribution is in issue is not one whose provision or accommodation is affirmatively required, however, it nonetheless remains true that the government, in distributing that good, must be neutral as among political faiths, just as it must be neutral as among races and religions. In such cases official motivation becomes critical. There is not, for example, any constitutional requirement that a municipal stadium be provided every time a political group wants to hold a rally—there may not even *be* a stadium—and if there are more applications than can be accommodated it would be perfectly constitutional to draw straws to decide which ones to grant, even though that might well mean that certain "viewpoints" were selected more often than others. (Think of the nightmare that would be involved, a nightmare quite flagrantly jeopardizing First Amendment values, were state officials instead to attempt to categorize the views of the applicants and allocate permission so as to make it all come out "even.") If, however, it can be proven that the officials are granting applications so as systematically to favor or disfavor a certain viewpoint or family of viewpoints or indeed that they have instituted a given method of selection with the expectation that it will have that effect, a constitutional violation will have been made out.

Oestereich v. Selective Service Board, decided in 1968, is essentially our National Guard case. It involved a young man who returned his draft registration certificate to the government as an expression of his opposition to the war in Vietnam, whereupon the draft board declared him a delinquent and changed his classification from IV-D to I-A. The ground on which the case was decided involved no consideration of the motivation of the board; there simply was no statutory authority, the Court held, for declaring Oestereich a delinquent and reclassifying him. However, the Court went on:

> We deal with conduct of a local Board that is basically lawless. It is no different in constitutional implications from a case where induction of an ordained minister or other clearly exempt person is ordered (a) to retaliate against the person because of his political views or (b) to bear down on him for his religious views or his racial attitudes or (c) to get him out of town so that the amorous interests of a Board member might be better served.[27]

The reference to persons "clearly exempt" makes this technically a trivial statement; if one is statutorily exempt he cannot be inducted regardless of motivation. But the Court's reference to "constitutional implications" obviously suggests more than this, that a draft board is constitutionally precluded from selecting from among the pool of those statutorily eligible on the basis of belief or expression (or, the Court correctly adds, to serve the personal interests of Board members). This conclusion is plainly correct, but again it is one that cannot be sustained without reference to motivation.[28] Even if it could be demonstrated that those inducted were largely or even exclusively persons who had expressed opposition to the war, the selection would not offend the Constitution if the board could prove that it had in fact been random, or made in accord with some legitimate criterion of selection such as health or age. When, however, an in-

ductee can prove that he was selected on the basis of a constitutionally impermissible criterion, he is entitled to relief.

In *Grosjean v. American Press Company*, decided in 1936, the
Supreme Court invalidated a Louisiana license tax of 2 percent of
the advance receipts of all periodicals whose circulation exceeded
20,000 per week, of which there were 13 (out of 163) in the state.
The *O'Brien* Court, struggling to establish the irrelevance of motivation, characterized *Grosjean* thus: "[T]he Court, having concluded that the right of publications to be free from certain kinds of
taxes was a freedom of the press protected by the First Amendment,
struck down a statute which on its face did nothing other than impose just such a tax."[29] The *Grosjean* opinion is a masterpiece of
ambiguity, and it does contain language arguing that taxes on newspapers had historically been viewed as suspect. It is clear, however,
that the Court did not intend to void all taxes on the gross income of
periodicals.[30] We shall see that the tax in fact bore most heavily on
papers which had taken an anti-administration line. But this effect
cannot be sufficient per se to invalidate it, any more than the gradu-
ated income tax is unconstitutional because its impact is to tax Republicans more heavily.[31] The right theory thus seems to be the one
the Court actually invoked, that if it can be demonstrated that the
class of those taxed was closed where it was in order to discourage or
punish certain ideas, the classification could not stand.

> The tax here involved is bad not because it takes money from
> the pockets of the appellees. If that were all, a wholly different
> question would be presented. It is bad because, in the light of
> its history and of its present setting, it is seen to be a deliberate
> and calculated device in the guise of a tax to limit the circula-
> tion of information to which the public is entitled in virtue of
> the constitutional guaranties.[32]

The Court supported this allegation of illicit motivation with only
the following: "The form in which the tax is imposed is in itself suspicious. It is not measured or limited by the volume of advertisements. It is measured alone by the extent of the circulation of the
publication in which the advertisements are carried, with the plain
purpose of penalizing the publishers and curtailing the circulation
of a selected group of newspapers."[33] However, the fact that the cut-
off was geared to circulation rather than advertising volume does
not demonstrate on its face an intent to disfavor those espousing cer-

tain ideas: in some contexts it might cut quite the other way. The fact that only 13 of 163 periodicals were affected may be somewhat suspicious. Much more important, the record (though not the opinion) reveals that 12 of the 13 periodicals whose circulation exceeded that figure had been taking positions antagonistic to the Long machine. However, 20,000 circulation (unlike 28 sides to a voting district) is not an inherently suspicious figure, and absent some further evidence, coincidence would have been an arguable explanation.

To understand fully the confidence with which the Court arrived at its conclusion of illicit motivation, it is necessary to delve still further into the record. A circular signed by Senator Long and Governor Allen, and distributed to the legislature at the time the bill was under consideration, explained the bill's aim: "It is a system that these big Louisiana newspapers tell a lie every time they make a dollar. This tax should be called a tax on lying, two cents per lie." Of the one cooperative newspaper whose circulation exceeded 20,000 Long had this to say: "Well, we tried to find a way to exempt the 'Lake Charles American-Press' from the advertising tax, but did not think we could do it, but we would have done it if we could."[34] Of course one always has to be careful of legislative history: what motivates one legislator to make a speech about a statute is not necessarily what motivates his or her colleagues to enact it. *Grosjean*, however, is an unusual case, one in which reference to the remarks of two (critical) persons seems sufficient to seal an already plausible inference of unconstitutional legislative motivation. The issue facing the Court was not which of two criteria of selection, one legitimate and one impermissible, was employed, but rather whether the choice of the 20,000 cutoff resulted from an impermissible criterion of choice on the one hand or essentially random selection on the other. Long's publicized statements, coupled with the crucial fact that the statute's effects were consistent with the aim he stated, constitute compelling evidence that 20,000 was not chosen without reference to the ideas espoused by the papers in question. More underlay the choice than a feeling that a line had to be drawn somewhere.

A point already alluded to should be underscored, since a failure to heed it—and who knows where the Court will run in its new-found enthusiasm for motivation analysis—could prove disastrous to our constitutional liberties. In this chapter I am concerned not with benefits to which we have a substantive constitutional entitlement, but rather with those to which we do not. (The benefit may be strictly comparative, as in *Grosjean* an exemption from a governmentally imposed deprivation.) Analysis of official motivation is appropriate only here, only where the claim is that a benefit that is "constitutionally gratuitous" in this sense has been improperly withheld,[35] and my point has been that the fact that something is not a constitutional right does not mean it can be distributed (explicitly or not) on an unconstitutional basis. However, where what is denied is something to which the claimant has a constitutional right — because it is granted explicitly by the terms of the Constitution or is essential to the effective functioning of a democratic government (or both) — the reasons it was denied are irrelevant.[36] What justifications counsel for the state can articulate in support of its denial or nonprovision may become important in court, but the reasons that actually inspired the denial never can: to have a constitutional right to something is to have a claim on it irrespective of why it is denied. It would be a tragedy of the first order were the Court to expand its burgeoning awareness of the relevance of motivation into the thoroughly mistaken notion that a denial of a constitutional right doesn't count as such unless it was intentional.

Suspicious Classification

Justice Black's point persists, though: it *will* be difficult to prove unconstitutional official motivation. That doesn't prove what he thought it did, that the Court shouldn't look, but it does indicate that more is needed if the rights of minorities are to be adequately protected. Given that unconstitutionality in the distribution of benefits that are not themselves constitutionally required can intelligibly inhere only in the way the distribution was arrived at, does this mean the ball game is over? It doesn't, for the more familiar doctrine of "suspect classifications," though not generally so understood, turns out on analysis to function as a handmaiden of motivation analysis.

The doctrines support each other in this way. The goal the classification in issue is likely to fit most closely, obviously, is the goal the legislators actually had in mind.[37] If it can be directly identified and is one that is unconstitutional, all well and good: the classification is unconstitutional. But even if such a confident demonstration of motivation proves impossible, a classification that in fact was unconstitutionally motivated will nonetheless — thanks to the indirect pressure exerted by the suspect-classification doctrine — find itself in serious constitutional difficulty. For an unconstitutional goal obviously cannot be invoked in a statute's defense. That means, where the real goal was unconstitutional, that the goal that fits the classification best will not be invocable in its defense, and the classification will have to be defended in terms of others to which it relates more tenuously. Where the requirement is simply the Court's standard call for a "rational" relation between classification and goal, that will seldom matter: even if the goal the classification fits best is disabled from invocation, there will likely be other permissible goals whose relation to the classification is sufficiently close to be called rational.[38] The "special scrutiny" that is afforded suspect classifications, however, insists that the classification in issue fit the goal invoked in its defense more closely than any alternative classification would. There is only one goal the classification is likely to fit *that* closely, however, and that is the goal the legislators actually had in mind. If that goal cannot be invoked because it is unconstitutional, the classification will fall. Thus, functionally, special scrutiny, in particular its demand for an essentially perfect fit, turns out to be a way of "flushing out" unconstitutional motivation,[39] one that lacks the proof problems of a more direct inquiry and into the bargain permits courts (and complainants) to be more politic, to invalidate (or attack) something for illicit motivation without having to come right out and say that's what they're doing.[40]

Considered in isolation, the combination of demands that prevailing doctrine imposes on suspect classifications — that the state (1) come up with a goal of substantial weight and (2) show that the classification fits that goal with virtual perfection — is easy to regard as a patchwork without pattern. Once the suspect classification doctrine is put in proper context as a roundabout variant of motivation analysis, however, this combination of demands can be understood to make good functional sense. The crucial step is to think ourselves out of the two-stage metaphysic that has dominated the cases and the literature here, wherein one first decides whether the classification in issue is suspect, and if it is, next insists — in an analytically separate operation—that it meet the extraordinary demands of fit and weight. Sense can be made of the package only if we recognize that it *is* a package, and understand the unusual fit and weight requirements not as new demands piled on as a sort of penalty for being suspect, but rather as ways of extending the initial inquiry, of determining whether the initial suspicions aroused by the classification are well founded or rather on fuller exploration can be allayed.

To take the clearest case of a classification that should count as suspect, assume you have before you a law that classifies in racial terms to the disadvantage of a minority. Naturally you suspect (*le mot juste*) that the law's motivation was that most naturally suggested by its terms, a simple desire to disadvantage the minority in question. But the state wishes to dispute that point, and so you listen. What would it take to allay your suspicion? To start with, a goal the classification fits as well as it fits the goal of comparatively disadvantaging the minority affected. For if it turns out that the classification fits the invidious goal more closely than it fits the goal the state now comes up with, you will ask why they didn't classify in terms more germane to the goal they are now arguing, and your suspicion that the goal suggested by the face of the statute was the real one will hardly be allayed. If, however, the goal the state is arguing fits the classification as well as the invidious one you started out suspecting was really operative—note that, at least in the case of a de jure racial classification, this necessarily means that there was no more direct way of reaching the goal the state is arguing—you should begin to pause. I say "begin" because another element should be required before your suspicion is allayed, and it turns out to be the other element the Court has in fact required, that the goal the state is arguing possess some degree of substantiality.

This latter requirement has been subjected to two sorts of criticism, each quite understandable in light of the Court's failure to connect the notions of suspect classification and unconstitutional motivation: that it doesn't provide a standard (how important is important enough?),[41] and that it bears no functional relation to the evil perceived here, which has to do, after all, with the terms of the classification and not with the importance of the good or burden whose distribution is being limited.[42] But once the connection is made, this requirement too makes sense, and in terms that suggest a standard. For even a perfect fit between the classification in issue and the goal the state is arguing shouldn't be enough to allay your initial suspicion if that goal is so unimportant that you have to suspect it's a pretext that didn't actually generate the choice. Professor Brest poses the case of a school principal who seats the blacks on one side of the stage at the graduation ceremony and the whites on the other, and defends it in aesthetic terms.[43] There may be nothing wrong with the *fit*, but the goal is so trivial in context that you have to believe it's a rationalization for a racially motivated choice. Contrast the case where the prison warden temporarily separates the black and white prisoners in order to quell a race riot.[44] There too the fit is essentially perfect (given the need for an instantaneous response[45]) and beyond that the goal, of preserving the lives and limbs of prisoners of both races, is one we can count as compelling—which we are now in a position to define functionally, in terms of whether the claim that it was the actual motivation is credible.[46] Thus despite the Court's failure to defend them and despite their apparent unrelatedness, the two requirements of special scrutiny, requirements of tight fit and substantial weight, turn out to be the sensible ones—once the critical connection is made between the doctrine of suspect classification and that of unconstitutional motivation.

During the Warren era, the Supreme Court was quite adventurous in expanding the set of suspect classifications beyond the core case of race. Laws classifying to the comparative disadvantage of aliens, persons of "illegitimate" birth, even poor people, were all at one time or another approached as suspect. The Burger Court has also paid lip service to the general idea. In fact Justice Blackmun was the first ever—apart, of course, from Justice Stone's original *Carolene Products* footnote—to indicate in an Opinion of the Court that "discrete and insular" minorities are entitled to special constitutional protection from the political process.[47] However, the Burger Court's performance on this score has not matched its rhetoric. Since he came on the Court, Justice Rehnquist has been campaigning to reduce the set of suspect classifications to race and "its first cousin," national origin,[48] and his campaign seems to be succeeding. Though here as elsewhere there are exceptions, the retreat from the once glittering crusade to extend special constitutional protection to the poor has turned into a rout.[49] There were, however, unusual conceptual problems with that campaign that were never satisfactorily worked out, and in fact that retreat was well begun at the end of the Warren era.[50] On other fronts, however, the retreats have been the Burger Court's own. The recent record has been inconsistent respecting laws classifying to the comparative disadvantage of "illegitimates," and in general tends in the direction of less protection.[51] Laws disadvantaging aliens seemed for a time even more securely in the "suspect" column: in fact it was in this context that Justice Blackmun put the modern Court's imprimatur upon the "discrete and insular minorities" formula. In 1978, however, they too seem to have been removed (or at least the situation was substantially confused).[52]

The reason Justice Rehnquist gives for wanting to cut the list back to race and national origin is one allegedly grounded in original intent, that those are the classifications the framers of the Fourteenth Amendment would have wanted to subject to unusual scrutiny. Although race was the subject that most occupied the framers (and undoubtedly the ratifiers as well), the decision not to limit the amendment to race, and thus to leave open at least the possibility of a line of growth, seems rather clearly to have been conscious. Of course Justice Rehnquist has a point, and it has been also the point of much of this book, that that doesn't mean that all bets are off, that we can therefore do with the amendment whatever we please: only those classifications that are "like race" in some relevant sense can responsibly be accorded similar treatment. But even Justice Rehnquist understands that it would be untrue to the amendment's spirit to limit its reach to just those classifications the framers talked about: if that were an appropriate methodology we would have to consider seriously the possibility that only blacks (and not other racial minorities) should receive protection, and surely we would be unjustified in expanding the list to cover national origin. The justice thinks he sees a family resemblance between national origin and race, but classifications aren't really the same thing as people and it takes a theory to make one classification the "first cousin" of another. It's true, only "racelike" classifications should be regarded as suspect, but we have to figure out what "racelike" should mean in this context.

It's probably because Court and commentator alike have failed here, at the level of theory, that Justice Rehnquist is steadily gaining his way. Factors are frequently mentioned in the literature that in an intuitive way do seem to have something to do with the point — and on further analysis we'll see that in oblique ways some of them do — but somehow none is quite capable of convincing us that it *is* the point. Thus, for example, it is often said that the immutability of the classifying trait ought to make a classification suspect.[53] That doesn't generate a list as long as its proponents seem to think it does. Alienage (usually)[54] and poverty (at least theoretically) are escapable conditions; so also, at least under the laws in issue in most of the landmark cases, were the legal deprivations that derived from being "illegitimate";[55] and I suppose even gender is becoming an alterable condition. That pares us down pretty close to Rehnquist's short list, which really shouldn't count as an objection, though I can assure you it would for most of those who propose immutability as the criterion. There is a real objection, though, and that is that no one has bothered to build the logical bridge, to tell us exactly *why* we should be suspicious of legislatures that classify on the basis of immutable characteristics. Surely one has to feel sorry for a person disabled by something that he or she can't do anything about, but I'm not aware of any reason to suppose that elected officials are unusually unlikely to share that feeling. Moreover, classifications based on physical disability and intelligence are typically accepted as legitimate, even by judges and commentators who assert that immutability is relevant. The explanation, when one is given, is that *those* characteristics (unlike the one the commentator is trying to render suspect) are often relevant to legitimate purposes.[56] At that point there's not much left of the immutability theory, is there?

A number of commentaries, purporting to find support in *Brown v. Board of Education*, argue that classifications disfavoring racial minorities are suspect because they "will usually be perceived as a stigma of inferiority and a badge of opprobrium."[57] This confuses two issues and thus misreads *Brown*.[58] Feelings of opprobrium *are* relevant to determining whether a classification the state claims is "harmless," such as "separate but equal" schooling, in fact inflicts harm on one or the other class. But *Brown* was unusual in that respect: the existence of comparative harm to one of the classes distinguished by a governmental classification is rarely an issue. Neither can the idea be that the presence of stigma is necessary in order to establish some requisite *amount* of harm. That account would make sense if the Court followed the practice of reviewing more strenuously those distinctions that hurt more, which it doesn't.

A taxation distinction worth $1,000,000 receives about the same review as one worth $100 — that is, virtually none.

An account that seems more to the point, one to which I've alluded several times, is that attributed to Justice Stone's *Carolene Products* footnote and recently paraphrased for the Court (before its about-face on alienage) by Justice Blackmun: "Aliens as a class are a prime example of a 'discrete and insular' minority . . . for whom . . . heightened judicial solicitude is appropriate . . . "[59] Justice Rehnquist (and others) have objected on grounds of indeterminacy, suggesting that it "would hardly take extraordinary ingenuity for a lawyer to find 'insular and discrete' minorities at every turn in the road."[60] This is certainly true if one makes the reference narrow enough. In a sense the complainant in every case speaks for such a group: he wouldn't be in court if the class in which the legislature had placed him had not been, on at least one occasion, a political minority (they lost), both discrete (they're the ones on the disfavored side of the statutory line) and insular (they couldn't gather enough allies to defeat the legislation). But obviously that isn't what Justice Stone meant. His reference was rather to the sort of "pluralist" wheeling and dealing by which the various minorities that make up our society typically interact to protect their interests, and constituted an attempt to denote those minorities for which such a system of "mutual defense pacts" will prove recurrently unavailing.

But even understood thus, a "discrete and insular minorities" approach, at least one that refuses to attend to *why* the minority in question is discrete and insular, also turns out to be less than entirely tenable. Perhaps the most obvious objection is one it is always easy to make, that courts aren't qualified to engage in this kind of practical political analysis. Alienage may seem an easy case — since aliens typically can't vote — but beyond that the going gets tough. Should the inquiry turn out to be constitutionally appropriate, however, we would want to ask — even admitting courts will have trouble (which may just mean that they should intervene only in reasonably clear cases) — whether any other institution is better situated to make it, and the answer to that question seems clearly to be no. The whole point of the approach is to identify those groups in society to whose needs and wishes elected officials have no apparent interest in attending. If the approach makes sense, it would not make sense to assign its enforcement to anyone but the courts.

There are more serious objections, however. The first is that the formula at least arguably fails to cover the one group everyone seems to agree should be extended special protection under the Fourteenth Amendment, namely blacks. "[I]f indeed there are groups that have no voice or visibility and that, in an almost literal sense, cannot make themselves heard, it is by no means clear that the urban black is among them. Numerically, blacks approach a majority in many large cities and are an increasingly formidable voting bloc in most. Numbers aside, they speak with a voice ever more audible . . . "[61] And that was written in 1972, four years before the election of Jimmy Carter. Whatever that election may or may not eventually turn out to have delivered, it did seem to demonstrate the ability of blacks to pool their political interests with those of other groups. Let us pray the day will come when we can agree that the need to pursue the amendment's historic core purpose of protecting blacks is so obsolete it can be disregarded. It would take an extraordinary insensitivity, however, to suppose that today is that day. A theory that excludes blacks from its protection, as one geared exclusively to political insularity seems to, is at least in need of some reexamination.[62]

No matter how clear the examples, however, arguments geared to what will and won't be covered must always fail wholly to satisfy: if a theory is sound, we should live with the results. But though the general idea here may be clear enough—courts should protect those who can't protect themselves politically—the justification for it isn't. In a way it is of the essence of democracy to allow the various persons and groups that make up our society to decide which others they wish to combine with in shaping legislation. We are not all the same in all respects, and on certain subjects our interests in fact do differ substantially. There is thus no way to exclude a priori—as the theory as elaborated so far does—the possibility that there may exist groups or interests with which others will refuse to combine politically for perfectly respectable reasons.

An added element is therefore needed, that the minority in question be one that is barred from the pluralist's bazaar, and thus keeps finding itself on the wrong end of the legislature's classifications, for reasons that in some sense are discreditable. Standard renditions of what we think of as the *Carolene Products* approach, such as the one by Justice Blackmun quoted above, do not include this element: "discrete and insular minorities" are simply entitled to "heightened judicial solicitude." Justice Stone's original, however, was richer than this, indicating that *"prejudice against discrete and insular minorities* may be a special condition, which tends to curtail the operation of those political processes ordinarily to be relied upon to protect minorities . . . " Now "prejudice" is a mushword in its own right, one we shall have to clarify, but it does supply the element that is missing in the usual rendition. For whatever else it may or may not be, prejudice is a lens that distorts reality. We are a nation of minorities and our system thus depends on the ability and willingness of various groups to apprehend those overlapping interests that can bind them into a majority on a given issue; prejudice blinds us to overlapping interests that in fact exist. As Frank Goodman put it so well eight years ago: "Race prejudice divides groups that have much in common (blacks and poor whites) and unites groups (white, rich and poor) that have little else in common than their antagonism for the racial minority. Race prejudice, in short, provides the 'majority of the whole' with that 'common motive to invade the rights of other citizens' that Madison believed improbable in a pluralistic society."[63]

Switching the principal perspective thus, from the purely political to one that focuses more on the psychology of decision, possesses the additional virtue of relating rather directly to what we found to be the functional significance of a theory of suspect classifications, one of flushing out unconstitutional motivations. "Prejudice" has a lot to do with that; discreteness and insularity don't seem to (except derivatively, to the extent that they are likely to reflect and engender prejudiced behavior). That connection also puts us in a position to begin to specify the meanings of prejudice relevant in this context. If the doctrine of suspect classifications is a roundabout way of uncovering official attempts to inflict inequality for its own sake — to treat a group worse not in the service of some overriding social goal but largely for the sake of simply disadvantaging its members — it would seem to follow that one set of classifications we should treat as suspicious are those that disadvantage groups we know to be the object of widespread vilification, groups we know others (specifically those who control the legislative process) might wish to injure.[64]

Note that the inquiry suggested is not whether there exists *unjustified* widespread hostility toward the group disadvantaged by the official act in issue — that would constitute a straightforward invitation to second-guess the legislative judgment — but simply whether there exists widespread hostility. There is a good deal of discretion in that inquiry too, of course, and courts must be scrupulous not simply to legislate there either. Later on I shall suggest a refinement that should help bridle the inquiry. For the moment, though, it may help to recall that all that labeling a classification "suspect" means functionally is that a prima facie case has been made out and that the inquiry into its suspiciousness should continue. If it turns out directly to pursue a substantial goal (other than the impermissible one of simply disadvantaging those it disadvantages), it will survive. Thus, for example, burglars are certainly a group toward which there is widespread societal hostility, and laws making burglary a crime certainly do comparatively disadvantage burglars. Such laws plainly should survive, however. There is so patently a substantial goal here, that of protecting our homes by penalizing those who break and enter them, and the fit between that goal and the classification is so close, that whatever suspicion such a classification might under other circumstances engender[65] is allayed so immediately it doesn't even have time to register.

Although there is more to be said about what factors properly give rise to suspicion, we have reached a point where the appeal (and limitations) of a reference to the immutability of the classifying characteristic can begin to be put in perspective. A law making burglary a crime is not suspicious — or, if you prefer, the suspicion is immediately allayed — because the goal of making life unpleasant for burglars is immediately translatable into the goal of discouraging people from breaking into our homes. It would not make sense, however, to defend a law disadvantaging blacks on the ground that we are trying to discourage people from being black. The ability to frame the point of a classification harming (or subsidizing) a certain group in terms of a desire to discourage people from joining (or encourage people to join) that group obviously depends on the mutability of the characteristic that forms the basis of classification. We shouldn't go overboard and conclude that classification on the basis of an immutable characteristic is always suspicious: that would follow only if increasing or decreasing the incidence of the classifying characteristic were the only legitimate governmental end. Forbidding blind people to pilot airplanes will do little to encourage eyesight, but such a prohibition will obviously stand nonetheless, since the classification fits perfectly a different goal, one I need hardly argue is important. Immutability thus cannot be the talisman that some have tried to make it, but it isn't entirely irrelevant either, since classifications geared to characteristics it is not within the power of the individual to change will not be amenable to immediate and innocent explanation in terms of altering the classifying characteristic's incidence.

An account mentioned with increasing frequency, and indeed it does seem more to the point, is that classifications rooted in "stereotypes" should be regarded as suspicious.[66] Stated this way, without elaboration, it cannot do. The dictionary tells us that a stereotype is "a fixed or conventional notion or conception, as of a person, group, idea, etc., held by a number of people, and allowing for no individuality . . . "[67] Legislation on the basis of "stereotype" is thus legislation by generalization, the use of a classification believed in statistical terms to be generally valid without leaving room for proof of individual deviation. That, however, is the way legislation ordinarily proceeds, as in most cases it must. Consider a familiar example, a statute that permits optometrists, but not opticians, to duplicate lenses.[68] Now suppose an optician wishes to demonstrate that although it may be true that *most* optometrists are better qualified to duplicate lenses than *most* opticians, *he* in fact is as well or better qualified to duplicate lenses than a number of optometrists he could name. The proffered proof would be rejected, on the theory that legislative classification on the basis of admittedly imperfect comparative generalizations (stereotypes) must be tolerated: unbearable cost would result were the government obligated to create procedures for deciding every case on its individual merits.* Pushed to this concession, our optician might next argue that although classifications rooted in comparative generalization are generally permis-

---

*Proceeding on the basis of general rule rather than ad hoc determination also reduces the discretion of the decision-maker and thus helps protect individuals and minority groups from invidious discrimination. See also pp. 172-177; Cleveland Bd. of Education v. LaFleur, 414 U.S. 632, 658 (1974) (Rehnquist, J., dissenting): "Most students of government consider the shift from this sort of determination, made on an *ad hoc* basis by the King's representative, to a relatively uniform body of rules enacted by a body exercising legislative authority, to have been a significant step forward in the achievement of a civilized political society."

sible, the unfairness that results to a number of individuals, himself included, from *this* classification is so great that it cannot be justified by the savings it effects. If the fit between classification and goal could be made tighter at no cost, the court might label the classification "irrational" and demand that it be made more discerning.[69] But where, as in virtually every case involving real legislation, a more perfect fit would involve some added cost — either the cost of permitting some unqualified people to practice or the cost of creating a case-by-case test of qualification — the Court ordinarily, and rightly, refuses to second-guess the legislative cost-benefit balance.

So stereotypes, at least in the ordinary sense of that term, are the inevitable stuff of legislation. If the concept is to provide us with anything beyond a basis for begging questions, it has to be refined, so as to separate, if you will, the acceptable stereotypes from the unacceptable. The approach that may initially seem most attractive would be to treat as suspicious those stereotypical generalizations to which there exist unusually high numbers or percentages of counterexamples.[70] (Coming up with a formula will obviously be difficult, but we need worry about that only if the general idea makes sense.) This has a nice objective ring to it: of course, the idea would run, the Court shouldn't simply invalidate those generalizations it doesn't like, but there can be little objection to its moving against those that are unusually inaccurate. It won't work, though; generalizations cannot be intelligibly evaluated simply in terms of the number or percentage of false-positives they entail. Sometimes, as in the case of capital punishment, any nontrivial incidence of counterexample would be intolerable. Other times, as where we are trying to keep those susceptible to heart attacks from piloting commercial airliners, a quite high percentage, surely sometimes more than half, is entirely appropriate. A determination of the acceptable incidence of counterexample must therefore involve, at a minimum, a comparison of the costs to those "wrongfully" excluded or included with the costs to the rest of us, sometimes in time and money but often also in increased risk, of trying to tune the system more finely.[71] A mode of review geared to whether the incidence of counterexample is "too high" is thus indistinguishable from the unacceptable theory that courts should intervene in the name of the Constitution whenever they disagree with the cost-benefit balance the legislature has struck.

We therefore had it wrong, but, it turns out, not by very much.

The cases where we ought to be suspicious are not those involving a generalization whose incidence of counterexample is "too high," but rather those involving a generalization whose incidence of counterexample is significantly higher than the legislative authority appears to have thought it was. No matter how many considerations may have entered into the cost-benefit balance, a misapprehension regarding the incidence of counterexample (or for that matter the cost of individualized determination) will have distorted the entire decision. Just as we would want reconsidered any important decision that was made under the influence of an erroneous assumption about the relevant facts, so should we here.[72] Of course this variety of prejudice is not the same as the sort of "first degree" prejudice discussed earlier,[73] but it implicates equal protection concerns in a related way. To disadvantage a group essentially out of dislike is surely to deny its members equal concern and respect, specifically by valuing their welfare negatively. However, to disadvantage—in the perceived service of some overriding social goal—a thousand persons that a more individualized (but more costly) test or procedure would exclude, under the impression that only five hundred fit that description, is to deny the five hundred to whose existence you are oblivious *their* right to equal concern and respect, by valuing their welfare at zero.

The rub comes in how the Court should go about identifying such situations. Just leaving it to their gestalt judgment seems obviously unacceptable, too close to simply handing over an unbridled power of substantive review. (I am not suggesting bad faith here, but a justice whose instinct is to disagree with the legislative cost-benefit balance is likely in all good faith to suppose the legislature "must have" overestimated the statistical validity of the generalization on the basis of which it appears to have acted.) The Court should therefore look not simply to the legislative product here, but to the process that generated it, to see whether it can identify some factor or factors that suggest the likelihood of such legislative misapprehension. In a recent dissent Justice Stevens made just such an attempt, suggesting that we should be especially wary of legislation rooted in generalizations that have become traditional. "For a traditional classification is more likely to be used without pausing to consider its justification than is a newly created classification. Habit, rather than analysis, makes it seem acceptable and natural . . ."[74] This surely has the ultimate point right, that what we are after are legis-

lative generalizations there is reason to suppose were seriously mis-
conceived, and Stevens must also be congratulated for attempting to
put that inquiry on an objective basis that transcends mere substantive disagreement. Unfortunately the specifics of his point seem
questionable. The fact that a generalization has long and often been
invoked by a variety of people may indeed not be the strongest argument in its favor, but in the abstract it doesn't seem like an argument against it either. Some time-honored generalizations *are* unusually inaccurate, but others are not.

In deciding how much presumptive credit to extend a given generalization in our everyday lives, we would want to know where it
came from — who came up with it and whether it is one that serves
their interests. This commonsense insight, again tempered with
others, seems relevant to the constitutional inquiry as well. The
choice between classifying on the basis of a comparative generalization and attempting to come up with a more discriminating formula
always involves balancing the increase in fairness that greater indi-
vidualization will produce against the added costs it will entail.
Where the generalization involved is one that serves the interests of
the decision-makers, however, certain dangers that are inherent in
any balancing process are significantly intensified. Where it tangi-
bly enhances their fortunes, the dangers may be most obvious — on
the one hand that the costs of treating others as they are treating
themselves are likely to be overestimated, and on the other that the
validity of the generalization being proffered as the basis of classification is likely to be overestimated, thus resulting in an under-
valuation of the interest in individual fairness. But even where no
tangible gain can be identified, there are psychic rewards in self-
flattering generalizations.[75] For years social psychologists have
understood[76] — and it would be pretty obvious even if they hadn't
pointed it out — that "[t]he easiest idea to sell anyone is that he is
better than someone else,"[77] and it's a rare person who isn't delighted to hear and prone to accept comparative characterizations
of ethnic or other groups that suggest the relative superiority of
those groups to which he belongs.[78] The phenomenon is one that is
observable among children,[79] and it persists into adulthood, largely,
it seems, as a means of ego preservation. "Ever since Aristotle divided
the human race into natural masters and natural slaves, dominant
classes have fed their self-esteem by claiming they were on top and

others on the bottom because such was the natural or God-given order of things."[80]

Thus generalizations to the effect, say, that whites in general are smarter or more industrious than blacks, men more stable emotionally than women, or native-born Americans more patriotic than Americans born elsewhere, are likely to go down pretty easily—and in fact we know they have—with groups whose demography is that of the typical American legislature. Few will suppose there aren't counterexamples, but the overall validity of such a generalization is likely to be quite readily accepted. By seizing upon the positive myths about the groups to which they belong and the negative myths about those to which they don't, or for that matter the realities respecting some or most members of the two classes, legislators, like the rest of us, are likely to assume too readily that not many of "them" will be unfairly deprived, nor many of "us" unfairly benefited, by a classification of this type. Generalizations of the opposite sort, which attribute superiority to a group to which most legislators do not belong—say, that blacks are better basketball players or that Jews are better students—are a different matter. A generalization of this sort may occasionally find grudging acceptance, but here we can be sure that the imperfect, statistical nature of the claim will be well appreciated, and in addition that there will be explanations—in both these examples, that it has to do with "the way they are brought up"—that will prevail in the legislature to assure an individualized test or at least that the statutory presumption will be rebuttable.[81] A statutory distinction built on a comparison of the qualifications of optometrists and opticians occupies an in-between position, since neither of the groups being compared is one to which most of the legislators belong.* Such a law—and most legislative

---

*Actually such a law is unlikely to provide that optometrists can duplicate lenses and opticians cannot, but rather that no one but an optometrist can do so. The generalization on which it is built is therefore literally one that attributes a comparative inferiority to everyone (including most members of the legislature) who is not an optometrist, and not just to opticians. Since, however, the typical legislator's self-image is unlikely to include the fact he is a nonoptometrist in the same way it does, say, the fact he is white, cf. R. Lane and D. Sears, *Public Opinion* 40 (1964), the comparison will probably be *perceived* as one between optometrists and others who are arguably qualified (such as opticians) and not one between optometrists and people "like us." It obviously is the legislator's likely perception of the situation

classifications are of this "they-they" contour — may lack the special safeguard that a self-deprecating generalization seems to provide, but it also lacks the unusual dangers of self-serving generalization and is consequently correctly classified as constitutionally unsuspicious.

We have seen already how the mutability of the classifying characteristic will often render a classification immediately defensible in terms of a legitimate social goal and thus allay any incipient suspicion. We are now in a position to understand how mutability (or something like it) may be relevant in another way as well, one that bears on the likelihood that the decision-maker's ability to generalize will be distorted by his or her perspective.* For example it is at least arguable that the facts that all of us once were young, and most expect one day to be fairly old, should neutralize whatever suspicion we might otherwise entertain respecting the multitude of laws (enacted by predominantly middle-aged legislatures) that comparatively advantage those between, say, 21 and 65 vis-à-vis those who are younger or older.[82] It is not quite the same thing as immutability, of course: alienage generally is an escapable condition, so in theory are poverty and perhaps even gender. But nonetheless, and it is this that seems more relevant, most legislators have never been alien, poor, or female. They all were young, though, a fact that may enhance their objectivity about just what the difference entails.[83]

One can empathize without having been there, though, and at this point a reference to discreteness and insularity reasserts its rele-

---

that is critical here. If in fact he were to regard the classification as self-deprecating, that perception would enhance its nonsuspiciousness. But that seems a strained characterization.

*So long as the notion of "stigma" is invoked to signal a special kind of *harm* resulting from the law in issue, it seems irrelevant to the question of suspiciousness. Insofar as it signals the attitudes that "normals" are likely to entertain respecting the stigmatized individual, however, its relation to a theory of suspiciousness oriented to the perspective of the decision-maker and the consequent likelihood of overgeneralization becomes obvious. "The attitudes we normals have toward a person with a stigma, and the actions we take in regard to him, are well known . . . [W]e believe the person with a stigma is not quite human . . . We construct a stigma-theory, an ideology to explain his inferiority and account for the danger he represents . . . We tend to impute a wide range of imperfections on the basis of the original one . . ." E. Goffman, *Stigma* 5 (1963). See also Karst, "Foreword: Equal Citizenship under the Fourteenth Amendment," 91 *Harv. L. Rev.* 1, 7 (1977).

vance.[84] Though theoretically indefensible in its usual free-standing form, it can quite sensibly augment and qualify an approach geared to the distorting effect of perspective. To render the concept useful, though, we have to recognize and break apart its two components, the political and the social. Political access is surely important, but (so long as it falls short of majority control) it cannot alone protect a group against the first type of prejudice we examined, out-and-out hostility, nor will it even serve effectively to correct the subtler self-aggrandizing biases of the majority. If voices and votes are all we're talking about, prejudices can easily survive (and even on occasion be exacerbated):[85] other groups may just continue to refuse to deal, and the minority in question may just continue to be outvoted.* Discreteness and insularity have a social component as well, however — of course the two will often go hand in hand — and it is that component that seems more relevant to the amelioration of cooperation-blocking prejudice. Increased social intercourse is likely not only to diminish the hostility that often accompanies unfamiliarity, but also to rein somewhat our tendency to stereotype in ways that exaggerate the superiority of those groups to which we belong. The more we get to know people who are different in some ways, the more we will begin to appreciate the ways in which they are not,[86] which is the beginning of political cooperation.

On this analysis discrimination against aliens seems a relatively easy case (and the Court's apparent turnabout on the issue in 1978 thus mistaken). Aliens cannot vote in any state, which means that any representation they receive will be exclusively "virtual." That fact should at the very least require an unusually strong showing of a favorable environment for empathy, something that is lacking here. Hostility toward "foreigners" is a time-honored American tradition.[87] Moreover, our legislatures are composed almost entirely of citizens who have always been such. Neither, finally, is the exaggerated stereotyping to which that situation lends itself ameliorated

---

*This is why legislation discriminating against racial minorities correctly continues to merit special scrutiny despite the fact that some of them, blacks notably, have become far-from-inaudible political forces. It is also why any claim that serious enforcement of the sorts of rights discussed in Chapter 5 would dispense with the need for the sort of analysis pursued in this chapter would be unduly optimistic, however tempting aesthetically.

by any substantial degree of social intercourse between recent immigrants and those who make the laws.

Except for the official lack of the vote, a similar analysis seems to apply to the poor. This observation isn't likely to possess a great deal of relevance to the present point, however, since laws that actually classify on the basis of wealth, drawing on some comparative generalization about the relative characteristics of the poor on the one hand and those who more nearly resemble the legislators on the other, are extremely rare. (Actually, there was such a case of de jure discrimination within recent memory, and the Court upheld the legislation![88]) What typically disadvantage the poor are various failures on the part of the government (or anybody else) to alleviate their poverty by providing one or another good or service. Now it is true that in order to merit suspicion a law need not necessarily discriminate explicitly against a disfavored group: that was the point of the earlier discussion of motivation.[89] However, failures to provide the poor with one or another good or service, insensitive as they may often seem to some of us, do not generally result from a sadistic desire to keep the miserable in their state of misery, or a stereotypical generalization about their characteristics, but rather from a reluctance to raise the taxes needed to support such expenditures — and at all events they will be susceptible to immediate translation into such constitutionally innocent terms.* A theory of suspicious classification will thus be of only occasional assistance to the poor, since their problems are not often problems of classification to begin with.

Homosexuals for years have been the victims of both "first-degree prejudice" and subtler forms of exaggerated we-they stereotyping. It appears, however, that quite a substantial percentage of the population is "gay," and most of us must therefore interact with homosexuals quite frequently. According to our analysis shouldn't that serve substantially to neutralize our prejudices? In this case it doesn't, since a person's homosexuality is not normally a characteristic of which others who are not gay themselves become aware sim-

---

*Whipsaws between what is and is not provided may, however, be sufficiently flagrant to demonstrate an intention to discriminate, not against the poor, but rather against the exercise of a certain constitutional right. See, e.g., Maher v. Roe, 432 U.S. 464 (1973) (upholding state funding of childbirth but not abortion), discussed further in note 38 to this chapter.

ply, say, by working with him or her. Our stereotypes — whether to the effect that male homosexuals are effeminate, females "butch"; that they are untrustworthy, unusually menacing to children, or whatever — are likely to remain fixed, given our obliviousness to the fact that the people around us may well be counterexamples.

Of course there are many characteristics that are not apparent on the surface. An example, unfortunately autobiographical, is high blood pressure. You might have known me for years without knowing I had high blood pressure, with the result that I (and others like me) could not have served as counterexamples to your stereotype that people with that particular affliction are invariably obese, red-faced, hyperactive, prone to panic (or if not those, then black). Yet it would be nonsense to treat a disqualification based on high blood pressure as constitutionally suspicious. It is true that a majority of people do not have it and probably are unaware of the extent to which they are surrounded by people who do. It is also true, however, that there are a good number of us — about 35 million in the United States — interacting with you daily, perhaps even marrying your children, and should one of you even announce your over-drawn stereotype, let alone try to legislate on the basis of it, you would rightly expect us to say "Hold it, Lester, there are lots of us with high blood pressure who don't fit your generalization," or to bear the consequences of keeping silent.

So how about homosexuals? There are plenty of them too, inter-acting with us daily, and if they choose not to correct our stereotype, that's fine, but why should we let them seek salvation in the courts when we act on the basis of it? The mistake here is a variation on the mistake of *Plessy v. Ferguson*,[90] wherein the Court assured the na-tion that if blacks were insulted by segregation, that was their choice, not a legally cognizable injury. The reason homosexuals don't say "Hold it, Lester, *I'm* gay, and my wrist's not the least bit limp," is that because of the prejudices of many of the rest of us there would be serious social costs involved in such an admission.[91] It is therefore a combination of the factors of prejudice and hidea-bility that renders classifications that disadvantage homosexuals suspicious.[92] Prejudices can sometimes be defeated by sufficient social contact, and the invisibility of the classifying characteristic is not ordinarily a factor there is any reason to count as constitution-ally consequential. But when these factors combine, the very prejudice that appropriately gives rise to suspicion in the first place also serves to diminish the likelihood of its neutralization by social non-insularity.[93]

The case of women is timely and complicated.* Instances of first-degree prejudice are obviously rare,[94] but just as obviously exaggerated stereotyping — typically to the effect that women are unsuited to the work of the world and therefore belong at home — has long been rampant throughout the male population and consequently in our almost exclusively male legislatures in particular. It may all be in apparent good humor, even perceived as protective, but it has cost women dearly. Absent a strong demonstration of mitigating factors, therefore, we would have to treat gender-based classifications that act to the disadvantage of women as suspicious. If the stereotyping has been clear, however, so has the noninsularity of the group affected. The degree of contact between men and women could hardly be greater, and neither, of course, are women "in the closet" as homosexuals historically have been. Finally, lest you think I missed it, women have about half the votes, apparently more. As if it weren't enough that they're not discrete and insular, they're not even a minority!

Despite that seeming avalanche of rebuttal, there remains something that seems right in the claim that women have been operating at an unfair disadvantage in the political process, though it's tricky pinning down just what gives rise to that intuition. It is tempting to observe that although women may be a majority, they haven't in any real sense *consented* to the various instances of gender-based legislation. Voters, female and male alike, are typically confronted not with single-issue referenda but rather with packages of attitudes, packages we call candidates. Most women are not injured in any direct way by laws that classify on the basis of sex — depriving women, say, of the opportunity to tend bar, guard railroad crossings, or administer estates — and the fact that they help elect representatives who are unprepared to repeal such laws may mean only that there are other issues about which they feel more strongly. This

---

*Ratification of the Equal Rights Amendment would moot the issue. At the moment that seems unlikely. It is true, however, that much of the state legislation that would otherwise be in issue (notably that mandating employment discriminations) has been preempted by federal legislation (notably Title VII of the Civil Rights Act of 1964).

may indeed be so, but the argument changes the rules.* Once we start to shift from a focus on whether something is blocking the opportunity to correct the stereotype reflected in the legislation, to one that attempts to explain why those who have that opportunity have chosen to pursue other goals instead, we begin to lose our way, to permit our disagreement with the substantive merits of the legislation to take the place of what is *constitutionally* relevant, an inability to do anything about it. That answer triggers a more promising inquiry, though — whether it is fair to say that women have "chosen" not to avail themselves of their opportunities, either by voting or by personally influencing those men with whom they come in contact, to correct the exaggerated stereotype that many men hold and on the basis of which they have often legislated. A major reason for lack of action on either of these fronts, or so at least it can plausibly be argued, has been that many women have *accepted* the overdrawn stereotype and thus have seen nothing to "correct" by vote or personal persuasion, and by their example may even have acted so as to reinforce it. That could, of course, imply that it wasn't so exaggerated a stereotype after all, but it could mean something else too, that our society, including the women in it, has been so pervasively dominated by men that women quite understandably have accepted men's stereotypes, of women as well as on other subjects.[95]

The general idea is one that in some contexts has merit. A sufficiently pervasive prejudice can block its own correction not simply by keeping its victims "in the closet" but also by convincing even them of its correctness. In *Castaneda v. Partida*, decided in 1977, the Court held that a prima facie case of intentional discrimination against Mexican-Americans in the selection of grand jurors was not constitutionally affected by the fact that Mexican-Americans enjoyed "governing majority" status in the county involved. Concurring, Justice Marshall gave the reason why: "Social scientists agree that members of minority groups frequently respond to discrimination and prejudice by attempting to disassociate themselves from the

---

*It is also undercut, in a way the one that follows it is not, by polls indicating that a higher percentage of men than women support the Equal Rights Amendment (a fairly good referendum on the sorts of laws we are talking about). See, e.g., *Washington Post*, August 16, 1978, at A5, col. 6 (NBC News poll); *People*, March 5, 1979, at 33.

group, even to the point of adopting the majority's negative attitudes towards the minority."[96] Nor does this insight seem relevant
only to numerical minorities: slaves outnumbered masters in the
antebellum South, and outnumbered whites generally in some
states, but that apparently didn't keep many of them from assimi-
lating much of the mythology used to legitimate their enslave-
ment.[97]

To apply all this to the situation of women in America in 1980,
however, is to strain a metaphor past the breaking point. It is true
that women do not generally operate as a very cohesive political
force, banding together to elect candidates pledged to the "woman's
point of view." Constitutional suspiciousness should turn on evidence of blocked access, however, not on the fact that elections are
coming out "wrong." There is an infinity of groups that do not act
as such in the political marketplace, but we don't automatically
infer that they have a "slave mentality." The cause, more often, is
that (sensibly or not) the people involved are not in agreement over
the significance of their shared characteristic. Thus in assessing suspiciousness it cannot be enough simply to note that a group does not
function as a political bloc. A further reference to the surrounding
conditions must be had, to see if there are systemic bars (and I'm
obviously not suggesting they need be official ones) to access. On
that score it seems important that today discussion about the appropriate "place" of women is common among both women and men,
and between the sexes as well. The very stereotypes that gave rise to
laws "protecting" women by barring them from various activities are
under daily and publicized attack, and are the subject of equally
spirited defense. (That the common stereotypes are so openly described and debated, as they are not in the case of racial minorities,
is itself some evidence of the comparatively free and nonthreatening
nature of the interchange.) Given such open discussion of the traditional stereotypes, the claim that the numerical majority is being
"dominated," that women are in effect "slaves" who have no realistic choice but to assimilate the stereotypes, is one it has become impossible to maintain except at the most inflated rhetorical level. It
also renders the broader argument self-contradictory, since to make
such a claim in the context of the current debate one must at least
implicitly grant the validity of the stereotype, that women are in
effect mental infants who will believe anything men tell them to be-

lieve. Many women do seem to prefer the old stereotype to the new liberation. You and I may think that's a mistaken choice. But once we begin regarding serious disagreement with a choice as proof that those who made it aren't in control of their minds, we've torn up the rulebook and made substantive wrongheadedness the test of unconstitutionality.

However, most laws classifying by sex weren't passed this morning or even the day before yesterday: in fact it is rare to see a gender-based classification enacted since the New Deal. In general women couldn't even *vote* until the Nineteenth Amendment was ratified in 1920, and most of these laws probably predate even that: they should be invalidated. Throughout this discussion, however, I have been concerned with factors more subtle than the lack of a vote, and it can at least be argued that until quite recently there persisted throughout America's female population a *"Castaneda*-like" acceptance of the prejudices of males, unventilated by more than token airing of their validity. Given what appropriately makes a classification suspicious, it is not necessarily a unitary question whether discrimination against a certain group should be so regarded, and the case of women seems one where the date of enactment should be important. It surely seems more helpful than anything the Court has come up with on the question of whether those who passed the law in issue were proceeding on the basis of an "archaic and overbroad generalization"[98] or whether, say, they were genuinely trying to protect women from certain physical risks to which in statistical terms they are unusually subject, realized there were counterexamples and estimated their incidence about right, but nonetheless felt the costs of identifying the exceptions were simply too high. I noted above how dangerously subjective direct attempts to judge whether a given law was generated by an overdrawn stereotype can be, since the face of the statute will inevitably be consistent with either of these descriptions of the decision process, and the legislative history will inevitably be partial and subject to manipulation. The date of passage seems a somewhat 'more solid datum, one that can at least begin to anchor the judicial inquiry. That's an aside, however, since the date of passage seems unquestionably relevant to what our analysis has suggested is a more promising approach to the question of suspiciousness—one geared to the existence of official or unofficial blocks on the opportunities of those the law disadvantages to counter by argument or example the overdrawn stereotypes we might, from the demography of the decision-making body, otherwise suspect were operative.

The case of women can be further put in perspective by exploring what should follow from a judicial determination that the suspiciousness of a given classification has not been allayed and that it therefore is unconstitutional. Here too the answer is not unitary: we have looked at several indicia of suspiciousness, and their remedial implications differ. Where a law is suspect because of what I have been calling first-degree prejudice, or indeed where it has been infected by a subtler form of stereotyping under conditions where the negatively affected group was barred from effective access at the time of passage *and still is*, the only appropriate remedy is to void the classification and insist — if the legislature wishes to continue to classify — on a different, generally more finely tuned, test of qualification. The obvious alternative to this is to have the judiciary restrike the substantive balance, attempting not to let the prejudices that apparently influenced the legislature play a part, and invalidate the classification only if in some sense it still ends up unacceptable on its merits. You will not be surprised to learn that I regard that approach as quite inappropriate. We can cite occasions on which our judiciary has displayed a lesser susceptibility to bareknuckled first-degree prejudice than our elected officials, but we also can cite some where it hasn't. Moreover, instances of such prejudice, for reasons it is not necessary to review, are almost invariably instances of self-serving comparison as well. Judges tend to belong to the same broad categories as legislators — most of them, for example, are white heterosexual males comfortably above the poverty line — and there isn't any reason to suppose that they are immune to the usual temptations to self-aggrandizing generalization. When in a given situation you can't be trusted to generalize and I can't be trusted to generalize, the answer, if possible, is not to generalize, which suggests that the Supreme Court has chosen wisely in insisting generally that a classification whose suspiciousness has not been allayed simply cannot be employed. Where in fact it was largely the product of a simple desire to disadvantage those disqualified, it probably will just be abandoned, which seems a desirable outcome. Where, however, a classification of some sort does seem necessary (though the one the legislature employed was constitutionally unacceptable), the remedy of flat-out disallowance will impose costs in both time and money, as it will generally necessitate a somewhat more individualized test of qualification. However, legislatures often incur those costs voluntarily, and courts on other occasions have forced them to do so where constitutionally protected interests will be threatened by an imperfectly fitting classification.[99] The unusual dangers of distortion in situations of self-aggrandizing generalization seem also to demand that we bear the increased costs of more individualized justice.

A case like that of women, where access was blocked in the past but can't responsibly be said to be so any longer, seems different in a way that suggests that a less drastic remedy may be appropriate. In cases of first-degree prejudice, or self-serving stereotyping where the access of the disadvantaged group remains blocked, the alternative of "remanding" the question to the political processes for a "second look"[100] would not be acceptable: we don't give a case back to a rigged jury. Here, however, such a "second look" approach seems to make sense. Technically the Court's judgment would be the same in all situations of unallayed suspiciousness: "due process of lawmaking" having been denied, the law that emerged would have to be declared unconstitutional. The difference would emerge in the event — unlikely, precisely because access is no longer blocked — that the legislature after such a declaration of unconstitutionality reconsidered and repassed the same or a similar law. The fact that due process of lawmaking was denied in 1908 or even in 1939 needn't imply that it was in 1982 as well, and consequently the new law should be upheld as constitutional.* In fact I may be wrong in supposing that because women now are in a position to protect themselves they will, that we are thus unlikely to see in the future the sort of official gender discrimination that has marked our past.[101] But if women don't protect themselves from sex discrimination in the future, it won't be because they can't. It will rather be because for one reason or another — substantive disagreement or more likely the assignment of a low priority to the issue — they don't choose to.

---

*To put on the group affected the burden of using its recently unblocked access to get the offending laws repealed would be to place in their path an additional hurdle that the rest of us do not have to contend with in order to protect ourselves — hardly an appropriate response to the realization that they have been unfairly blocked in the past.

Many of us may condemn such a choice as benighted on the merits, but that is not a constitutional argument.

An Aside on Affirmative Action

"Reverse discrimination" in favor of racial or other minorities poses a vexing ethical issue. If, on the one hand, we are to have even a chance of curing our society of the sickness of racism, we will need a good many more minority-group members in the professions and elsewhere in society's upper strata. And whatever the complex of reasons, it seems we are not likely to get them in the foreseeable future unless we take minority status into account and weigh it positively when we allocate opportunities. But no matter what we call it — a preference, a quota, a quest for diversity — weighing, say, blackness affirmatively necessarily means that others are going to be denied the opportunities in question because they were not born black.[102] I confess, therefore, that I have trouble understanding the place of righteous indignation on either side of this wrenching moral issue.

The 1978 decision in *Regents of the University of California v. Bakke* left the *constitutional* status of such programs also somewhat unclear.[103] But a difficult moral question does not necessarily generate a difficult constitutional question, and now that we understand the factors that appropriately render a classification suspect, we can further understand that each is a one-way ratchet.[104] There is no danger that the coalition that makes up the white majority in our society is going to deny to whites generally their right to equal concern and respect. Whites are not going to discriminate against all whites for reasons of racial prejudice, and neither will they be tempted generally to underestimate the needs and deserts of whites relative to those, say, of blacks or to overestimate the costs of devising a more finely tuned classification system that would extend to certain whites the advantages they are extending to blacks.[105] The function of the Equal Protection Clause, we have seen, is largely to protect against substantive outrages by requiring that those who would harm others must at the same time harm themselves — or at least widespread elements of the constituency on which they depend for reelection.[106] The argument does not work the other way around, however: similar reasoning supports no insistence that our representatives cannot hurt themselves, or the majority on whose support they depend, without at the same time hurting others as well. Whether or not it is more blessed to give than to receive, it is surely less suspicious.[107]

I do not intend to pursue the subject in a chapter on the judicial protection of minorities — I have written about it elsewhere[108] — but it may be helpful explicitly to confront a fear that apparently has prompted certain Jewish groups to oppose preferential admissions for blacks. Somehow, the concern seems to run, most of those "black places" will be taken from Jews. I do not for a moment discount the reality of anti-Semitism in our society, nor can we dismiss the feared scenario as "just one of the costs" of pursuing racial equality. It is an unacceptable scenario, and an unconstitutional one as well. An American state legislature, unlike perhaps, the Israeli Parliament, cannot legitimately pursue the goal of reducing the percentage of doctors who are Jewish. Whites generally, not Jews in particular, are a majority in our society, and consequently racial discrimination is unsuspicious only when it runs against whites in general.[109] It is hard to see, however, how this danger can form the basis for a constitutional argument against preferences for blacks or other racial minorities. A "discretionary" system of selection already leaves room for various sorts of indefensible prejudice to operate: no matter how one might feel about the comparative merits and dangers of such a system — my own feeling has never been very positive — a decision to extend preferences to blacks does not significantly alter the problem. Administrators who incline toward anti-Semitism in the one situation will very likely incline toward it in the other, and the chances of catching them — of demonstrating the illegality of what they are doing — don't seem to be greater one way than the other. Should a preferential admissions program for blacks be accompanied by an unexplained disproportionate drop in the percentage of Jews, or even by a shift to a selection system that left more room for anti-Semitism — a more discretionary system or a ceiling on the number of students from New York City — the appropriate judicial response would be clear. There would then be reason to suspect that the idea was to prefer one minority at the disproportionate expense of another for reasons of ethnic prejudice, and the scheme should be invalidated.[110] Anti-Semitism is a danger — one that should, in any event, be combated by every available tool, including constitutional litigation—but the danger is independent of a decision to extend preferences to blacks.* There is thus nothing constitutionally suspicious about a majority's discriminating against itself, but we must never relent in our vigilance lest something masquerading as that should in fact be something else.

"Process Rights," Minority Style

We saw, in Chapter 5, how various rights not mentioned in the Constitution should nonetheless receive constitutional protection because of their role in keeping open the channels of political change. A similar analysis seems applicable to the present area of concern, assuring the protection of minorities. Indeed, as mentioned earlier, the Bill of Rights itself protects some rights whose selection may be most comfortably explainable in terms of a prophylactic concern for what we later came to call equal protection. The Fourth Amendment, I suggested, can at least be viewed through this prism. Of course, at least now, proof of an invidious motive in singling a person out for arrest or search would be enough to invalidate it. But such proof will almost never be available. There won't be a contemporaneous record of the reasons an arrest or search is made (unless we require one), and patterns of selection, given the multiplicity of factors that bear on such decisions and the likely lack of a record of decisions *not* to act, will be difficult to discern. Thus indirect controls, prophylactic measures, are needed to minimize arbitrariness and invidiousness in the making of such decisions. The Fourth Amendment approaches this goal in two ways—by requiring a warrant (unless there is a good excuse for not getting one[111]) and by requiring probable cause. The warrant requirement injects the judgment of a "neutral and detached" magistrate and also has what may be the more important effect of compelling a contemporaneous

---

*I wouldn't be at all surprised by a showing that certain geographical or alumni preference programs had been substantially motivated by anti-Semitism. What is difficult to make sense of is the thought that one would be motivated by anti-Semitism in adding an affirmative action program for racial minorities. See generally note 109 to this chapter. This is not to say that it would not be fortunate were the attention focused by affirmative action programs to result in the abolition of geographical and alumni preference programs, only that the issues are not constitutionally interconnected.

recordation of the factors on whose basis the action is being taken. The probable cause requirement obviously can't guarantee a lack of arbitrariness: invidious choices among those respecting whom there is probable cause are possible. By setting a substantive parameter at one end of the decision, however, it at least requires that persons not be singled out for arrest or search in the absence of strong indication of guilt, that is, on the basis of constitutionally irrelevant factors alone.

It is apparently a similar concern that accounts for the word "unusual" in the Eighth Amendment.[112] A severe (or "cruel") punishment to which any of us who transgresses is realistically subject is one thing: assuming an impartial enforcement regime, the political processes can be counted on to block beheading as the penalty for tax fraud. If, however, there are buffers, if the system is constructed so that "people like us" run no realistic risk of such punishment, some nonpolitical check on excessive severity is needed. In 1972 in *Furman v. Georgia*, the Supreme Court, at least a plurality of it, took this underlying theory of the amendment very seriously indeed. By a vote of five to four, it ruled the death penalty, as then administered, unconstitutional. As I noted earlier, two of the five, Justices Brennan and Marshall, based their votes largely on the claim that capital punishment was out of accord with current community values. Such claims always have a good chance of being nonsense, and this one was, as the post-*Furman* spate of reenactments tragically testified. On or around a better track were the plurality—Justices Douglas, Stewart, and White—who with varying degrees of clarity focused their arguments on the fact that all the states whose systems were before the Court (and for that matter all others) left "to the uncontrolled discretion of judges or juries the determination whether defendants . . . should die or be imprisoned."[113] The point was not so much that racial or other invidious discrimination in sentencing could actually be shown. (In fact the showings to this effect were quite convincing in some states,[114] but what would such a showing as to, say, Arkansas have to do with the constitutionality of the death penalty in, say, Montana?[115]) It was rather that such discrimination is difficult to prove and that these were systems that "left room for the play of" racial, religious, wealth, social class, and similar prejudice in the decision who is to live and who to die. "Thus, these discretionary statutes are . . . pregnant with discrimination and discrimination is an ingredient not compatible with the idea of equal protection of the laws that is implicit in the ban on cruel and unusual punishment."[116]

The most obvious legislative response to *Furman* was a system of mandatory death sentences for particularly heinous categories of murders, and a number of states so responded. In a cluster of cases decided in 1976, however, the Court declared mandatory death penalties unconstitutional, upholding at the same time certain statutory schemes that purported to channel discretion by listing a number of factors the jury was to take into account.[117] In 1978 the U-turn was completed, when in *Lockett v. Ohio*[118] the Court seemed to opt for *maximum* discretion by holding it unconstitutional to exclude from the consideration of the jury anything that might plausibly be thought to bear on whether the defendant should be executed. Opponents of capital punishment can find some solace in this game of hide-and-seek, since in operation it has meant the reversal of a good many death sentences imposed under systems modeled on what the Court had previously seemed to indicate it wanted. The theoretical trend has been in exactly the wrong direction, however. It is by *reducing*, hardly by increasing, the discretion of juries, and thus to some extent removing the buffers that ensure that people like us will never be executed, that we move to protect those who are not so insulated from the sort of "unusual" enforcement regime it is the point of the Eighth Amendment to preclude (and in the process to provide political safeguards against excessive penalties).

Unfortunately it is not obvious exactly what the Court should do thus to restrict discretion. On the surface a system of mandatory death penalties for certain categories of killings may seem a sensible answer, but on deeper analysis it collapses. The convincing point on this score is not the one stressed by the Court in its 1976 decisions, that mandatory penalties don't leave juries enough discretion. It is rather one the Court made more softly — which, being the contradiction of the first, is exactly right — that because experience shows that juries rarely convict of first-degree murder when that carries a mandatory death sentence, there is reason to suppose that such a system yields more, not less, effective discretion. "Instead of rationalizing the sentencing process, a mandatory scheme may well exacerbate the problem identified in *Furman* by resting the penalty determination on the particular jury's willingness to act lawlessly."[119] The sorts of answer the Court in the 1976 cases proved ready to accept, however, were even worse. To take just one example,[120] the Georgia scheme upheld by the Court "instructs" the jury to impose the death sentence if it finds any of ten statutorily defined "aggravating circumstances." That sounds as if it might be a sensible approach until you begin to read the standards. Here's one: was the murder "outrageously or wantonly vile, horrible or inhuman" in that it involved "depravity of the mind"? Nor is that the end of it: even if the jury does find the presence of one or more of the aggravating circumstances, it is empowered to spare the defendant's life if it finds them outweighed by mitigating circumstances (not enumerated) "which, in fairness and mercy, may be considered as extenuating or reducing the degree" of moral culpability or appropriate punishment.[121] "In this way the jury's discretion is channeled," Justice Stewart wrote for the plurality. "No longer can a jury wantonly and freakishly impose the death sentence; it is always circumscribed by the legislative guidelines."[122] In less serious circumstances this would be amusing.

Is the answer, then, that the 1976 Court had discovered the right principle but just hadn't developed the knack of applying it? Rather clearly not. I'm sure we could do a better job of channeling jury discretion than the legislatures whose "systems" the Court upheld in 1976 had done, but I'm also sure we couldn't do a very good one. So long as the jury is entrusted with the job of deciding whether the defendant acted with "malice aforethought" (which typically makes a killing murder rather than manslaughter) and "premeditation" (which makes it first degree) — and it is difficult to imagine a decision compelling the elimination of those time-honored terms from the definition — there will inevitably be a substantial amount of play in the joints. And even if we *could* succeed in channeling the jury, there are, as Charles Black has demonstrated, opportunities for discretionary selection all along the process — from the pretrial decision of what charge to bring (or accept a plea to) to the posttrial decision on clemency.[123]

I expect like many readers of this book, I got my first notion of what it might be to be a lawyer when I was a teenager, arguing to or with anyone who would listen the immorality of capital punishment. I don't suppose I've ever held a nontrivial moral position with greater certainty. Well, I'm not a teenager anymore, and along with other changes I confess my resolution on this issue has softened. When I read about someone soaking a hapless wino in gasoline and setting fire to him, or some "religious" leader inducing his flock to serve their babies Kool-Aid laced with cyanide, I'm tempted to respond that the swine deserves to die. But then I reflect on the simply inescapable equal protection problem. People like us don't commit murder very often, I know, but we do sometimes. Yet "[o]ne searches our chronicles in vain for the execution of any member of the affluent strata of this society."[124] Obviously there is a very effective series of buffers at work here, protecting those who make the laws and others like them from the harshness of their application. And even assuming what we plainly should not, that those who manage the system will ever gather the incentive to try to remove those buffers, the task does not seem even theoretically possible. Death being the ultimate and irreversible penalty,[125] one can at least strongly argue that a "prophylactic equal protection" holding that capital punishment violates the Eighth Amendment is appropriate. It is so cruel we know its imposition will be unusual.*

*This hardly falls into the category of arguments with which it is impossible responsibly to disagree, chiefly because it seems to apply, though in watered-down form, to any criminal penalty. There are three distinctions that set capital punishment apart, however. The first is that the language that defines the crime of first degree murder is a good deal vaguer than that used in defining most other crimes (and inevitably so, I should think, given our unwillingness so to classify all intentional killings). That increases the discretion existing all along the process. Second, because capital punishment is perceived as our most serious penalty, it is least likely to be susceptible to effective mandatory prescription. Of course there is always the possibility that a jury will acquit to avoid a mandatory sentence it thinks is too harsh, but there's a difference in kind as well as degree here: a prison sentence leaves the perpetual possibility of reduction, and juries know that. Once the switch is thrown, a death sentence does not. The final point comes into sharper focus when we recognize that the constitutional argument against capital punishment is expressible not simply in equal protection terms but in due process terms as well. It is boilerplate and unavoidable due process doctrine that the more serious the consequences, the more scrupulous we should become about procedural requirements. Death being our supreme punishment, it is there we should be supremely scrupulous, even to the point of taking seriously the realization that no procedural system can wholly eliminate the potential for invidious choice. See generally C. Black, *Capital Punishment: The Inevitability of Caprice and Mistake* (1974).

The obvious alternative is to follow the course the Court in large measure has followed over the years, one of insisting in capital cases that the procedures below have been picture perfect. Human beings are rarely if ever capable of perfection, however, which means it's the rarest of death sentences that will stand under such an approach (a fact that only further exacerbates the equal protection problem).

Whether or not one is prepared to go so far as to void the death penalty altogether, the sort of prophylactic concern with uncontrollable discretion in the visiting of important consequences that moved the Court in *Furman* is one of our Constitution's important themes, one whose potential application to other areas has not been fully explored. It surely is evident in other work of the Court, notably its (sometime) concern that criminal statutes not get too vague —"fair warning" is surely implicated there, but so is the threat of invidious discrimination in application—and its close review of discretionary licensing or other permission-granting systems in the First Amendment area. These are admirable campaigns, but one sometimes gets the impression that the Court may be missing their unity, seeing them instead as isolated pockets of concern—the "void for vagueness doctrine," the ban on "prior restraints," and so forth. Some notice of the gravity of the consequences at issue must always play a role, but a discretionary system of selection *always* carries the potential for invidious discrimination, not simply when the case fits into one of the familiar pigeonholes. Such systems amount to failures of representation, in that those who make the laws (by refusing effectively to make the laws) have provided a buffer to ensure that they and theirs will not effectively be subjected to them. Thus the nondelegation doctrine—you will have noticed that that essentially is what we're talking about, albeit from another angle—is one that serves not simply to ensure that decisions are being made democratically but also to reduce the likelihood that a different set of rules is effectively being applied to the comparatively powerless.

The "right to travel" from state to state has been a favorite of both the Warren and Burger Courts. The Constitution makes no mention of any such right. By now we know that cannot be determinative, but we are entitled to some sort of explanation of why the right is appropriately attributable. In recent years the Court has been almost smug in its refusal to provide one.[126] Back in 1868,

---

Perhaps the theoretical existence and rare imposition of the death penalty do have some deterrent effect, but such a system is very costly in monetary as well as human terms, hardly one supporters of the death penalty can be overjoyed about. Yet an insistence on the utmost procedural regularity in the imposition of the death penalty, unlike its complete constitutional invalidation, *is* something respecting which I have trouble envisioning responsible disagreement.

however, in *Crandall v. Nevada*, an explanation was attempted, and in fact it was along the constitutionally appropriate ("Chapter 5") line that the right to travel freely through the various states is critical to the exercise of our more obviously political rights:

> [T]he citizen . . . has the right to come to the seat of government to assert any claim he may have upon that government, or to transact any business he may have with it. To seek its protection, to share its offices, to engage in administering its functions. He has a right to free access to its sea-ports, . . . to the sub-treasuries, the land offices, the revenue offices, and the courts of justice in the several States, and this right is in its nature independent of the will of any State over whose soil he must pass in the exercise of it.[127]

That makes some sense, though I suppose on this theory the right might appropriately be limited to travel for political purposes. But if this defense makes sense in a case like *Crandall*, which involved a tax on the privilege of passing through the state, it has little or nothing to do with the modern cases, which have involved and frequently invalidated durational residency requirements that states have attached to various rights and services. The right at issue in the modern cases thus is not simply a right to travel to or through a state but rather a right to move there—the right, if you will, to relocate.

Now that we have begun to explore the possibility that rights can legitimately be inferred that relate not simply to one's ability to participate in the democratic decision process but also to the plight of the dissenting or "different" individual resident in a society, however, we are in a position to construct a different and more relevant rationale for the right to relocate. In fact it is in these terms that the right to personal mobility has been seen as important throughout our history. To a large extent America was founded by persons escaping from environments they found oppressive.[128] Mobility was quite free during the colonial period, and "[a]s a result, most colonials who dissented from their own community's conception of right and justice could move without great difficulty to a more congenial community."[129] And of course the symbolism, and indeed the reality, of "the frontier" took much of its sustenance from the notion that a person should have the option of pulling up stakes and starting over elsewhere.[130] Obviously I am not suggesting that this tradition is enough to make what Albert Hirschman has called the "exit" option a constitutional right.[131] I cite it rather because I think it points us in the right direction, one that associates the right to relocate not with the idea that it is some kind of handmaiden of majoritarian democracy but, quite to the contrary, with the notion that one should have an option of escaping an incompatible majority. Thus viewed, the right is one that fits quite snugly into the constitutional theory of this book. Precisely *because* the choosing of values is a prerogative appropriately left to the majority (so long as it doesn't by law or administration provide different rules for others than it does for itself), a dissenting member for whom the "voice" option seems unavailing should have the option of exiting and relocating in a community whose values he or she finds more compatible. I am aware that increased communication, to say nothing of the homogenizing pressure of vastly increased federal regulation, has diminished the differences among the states, but some differences remain — relating perhaps most pertinently to the extent to which deviance of various sorts is tolerated or repressed by law or enforcement policy, and indeed to the scope of such government services as education and welfare.[132] As I say, it's an old idea, dating back at least as far as Rousseau's "droit d'émigration": it's just that the Court hasn't fixed on it. That is unfortunate, since it provides something the Court hasn't, a rationale for the right to travel it in fact has established.

Conclusion

THE elaboration of a representation-reinforcing theory of judicial review could go many ways, and Chapters 5 and 6 are obviously just one version. But however elaborated, the general theory is one that bounds judicial review under the Constitution's open-ended provisions by insisting that it can appropriately concern itself only with questions of participation, and not with the substantive merits of the political choice under attack.

In saying that so clearly I have set myself up for a familiar form of attack: "You'd limit courts to the correction of failures of representation and wouldn't let them second-guess the substantive merits? Why, that means you'd have to uphold a law that provided for _____!" There are two ways of filling in the blank. The first is exemplified by Michael Perry's recent observation that "the skeptical view that the process of policymaking is a higher value than the content of policymaking is a difficult position to defend in this post-Holocaustal age."[1] I doubt there are many who would argue that process is of "higher value" than substance, though some of us would say that substantive decisions are generally to be made democratically in our society and constitutional decisions are generally to be limited to policing the mechanisms of decision and distribution. Perry's adjectival reference is the most powerful of our age: "You wouldn't let courts second-guess the substantive merits? Why, that means you'd have to uphold the constitutionality of the Holocaust!" It's not good enough to answer that the Holocaust couldn't happen here. We can pray it couldn't, I believe it couldn't, but nonetheless we should plan our institutions on the assumption that it could (for whatever barrier *anyone's* constitutional theory is likely to pose in such a situation). But the reason the example cannot responsibly be dismissed on this ground is precisely the reason it is covered by the

181

constitutional theory of this book. A regime this horrible is imaginable in a democracy only because it so quintessentially involved the victimization of a discrete and insular minority.

Thus examples like Perry's are important to keep in mind, but they serve only to buttress the approach for which I have been arguing. The other way to fill in the blank is with a law, passed pursuant to a free and open democratic process, that does something frightful to all of us and thus does not single out a powerless minority for victimization. Harry Wellington suggests an example, "a statute making it a crime for any person to remove another person's gall bladder, except to save that person's life." Surely, he says, *that* has to be unconstitutional.[2] Now Wellington has me (sort of): I don't think that law is unconstitutional. Curtains for my theory? I've led you along all this way only to confess error at the very end? Well, no, since that law couldn't conceivably pass.

"But suppose it did."

"Come on, it wouldn't. We've got problems enough without hypothesizing absurdities."

"Suppose it did."

"Okay, I'll play your game. If it passed, I think we could get it repealed pretty quick."

"What if we couldn't?"

"Then I'd suppose my elected representatives had found out something about gall bladders that you and I are unaware of."

"Suppose they hadn't. Suppose they were just acting crazy."

"Vote them out. Impeach them. Repeal the law."

"Can't. Most people believe they're doing the right thing."

"And they're just acting crazy too?"

"Right."

"I don't suppose we can reason with them."

"Nope."

"You know what you're telling me? That you don't believe in democracy. With neuroses like yours, I sure as hell would be worrying about problems a lot less rarified than substantive versus participational review. Like whether I'm going to read in tomorrow's paper that my dog is under consideration for Secretary of Agriculture."

"Let's leave your dog (and my psychological state) out of this. They pass it. What do you do?"

"Find out more about gall bladders. If this law is really dangerous, I suppose I don't obey it. I doubt that this is an example, but everyone has a breaking point. Sit in at the Capitol, I suppose, if people are actually getting seriously ill because the legislature and the electorate have simultaneously gone mad."

"And if you're a judge? Surely it's better to declare the law unconsistutional than to occupy the Capitol."

"That's an old debate the abolitionists had: should a judge distort the (pre-Civil War) Constitution by pretending it doesn't support slavery, or resign from the bench and fight his battles elsewhere? There were good people on both sides, but I guess I'd have been with those who said that given what you regard as a massive enough moral evil—especially one actually written into the Constitution and thus immune to legislative repeal—you fight it as effectively as you can, even if that means staying on the bench and engaging in a little judicial civil disobedience. At that point you'd hardly be acting like a judge, any more than you would in occupying the Capitol, but maybe it's what you should do anyhow. I'm not sure."

I'm not either, but that's not our issue. It is an entirely legitimate response to the gall bladder law to note that it couldn't pass and refuse to play any further. In fact it can only deform our constitutional jurisprudence to tailor it to laws that couldn't be enacted, since constitutional law appropriately exists for those situations where representative government cannot be trusted, not those where we know it can.

Notes

1. The Allure of Interpretivism

1. See Grey, "Do We Have an Unwritten Constitution?" 27 *Stan. L. Rev.* 703 (1975). These specific terms may be new, but the issue has been with us throughout our history. See, e.g., T. Cooley, *A Treatise on the Constitutional Limitations* *164, 168 (2d ed. 1871).

2. But see R. Berger, *Government by Judiciary* (1977).

3. Compare also Shapiro v. Thompson, 394 U.S. 618, 662 (1969) (Harlan, J., dissenting) (for purposes of equal protection review, fundamental interests must find basis in Constitution), with Poe v. Ullman, 367 U.S. 497, 542-43 (1961) (Harlan, J., dissenting) (for purposes of substantive due process review, such interests to be derived from nation's traditions; mistake to suppose must be indicated elsewhere in Constitution). I do not believe Justice Harlan ever attempted to reconcile these positions. They seem flagrantly inconsistent.

4. 381 U.S. 479, 507 (1965).

5. Some things *did* happen to Black as he stayed too long on the bench. His ability to reason by analogy, to sense the relevance of constitutionally stated principles in unfamiliar settings, did atrophy somewhat. E.g., Cohen v. California, 403 U.S. 15, 27 (1971) (Blackmun, J., joined by Black, J., dissenting); Wyman v. James, 400 U.S. 309 (1971); Katz v. United States, 389 U.S. 347, 364 (1967) (Black, J., dissenting). And the old judge who had spent so many years widening and paving the avenues of legal redress displayed a sense of betrayal that distorted analysis when someone would shun those avenues and resort to civil disobedience. E.g., Brown v. Louisiana, 383 U.S. 131, 167-68 (1966) (Black, J., dissenting). The interpretivism, however, was there all along. See also, e.g., Freund, "Mr. Justice Black and the Judicial Function," 14 *U.C.L.A. L. Rev.* 467 (1967).

6. See Adamson v. California, 332 U.S. 46, 89-92 (1947) (Black, J., dissenting); Duncan v. Louisiana, 391 U.S. 145 (1968) (Black, J., concurring).

7. See Grey, "Origins of the Unwritten Constitution: Fundamental

Law in American Revolutionary Thought," 30 *Stan. L. Rev.* 843, 846 (1978).

8. 410 U.S. 113 (1973).

9. See, e.g., Bork, "Neutral Principles and Some First Amendment Problems," 47 *Ind. L. J.* 1, 3-4 (1971); Grey, supra note 1, at 706: "[I]f judges resort to bad interpretation in preference to honest exposition of deeply held but unwritten ideals, it must be because they perceive the latter mode of decisionmaking to be of suspect legitimacy."

10. It is also tempting to suppose that an interpretivist approach will generate a more predictable, less episodic set of decisions. This seems false in one sense but true in another. Once a dispute has been identified as appropriately constitutional, I doubt that the acceptance of an "interpretivist" philosophy by the decision-maker will render the outcome any more predictable, since constitutional language is characteristically delphic, its accompanying legislative history partial and inconsistent. (This is by no means interpretivism's problem alone. *Any* constitutional theory—aside, I suppose, from a total renunciation of review—will repeatedly generate debatable questions. My point is simply that interpretivism cannot convincingly claim any significant competitive edge in this regard.) What interpretivism *does* render more predictable are the occasions of constitutional intervention: one can be quite certain, for example, that Justice Black would not have agreed that *Roe v. Wade* was appropriately treated as a constitutional dispute, whereas there must exist substantial doubt about how Justice Harlan would have voted in that case. To note that, however, is simply to note that the interpretivist will not intervene without a warrant in the Constitution. That is the defining characteristic of an interpretivist approach, but to identify its comparative attractions we must turn to the factors discussed in the text.

11. Of course the key question, and it is a question at the heart of this book, is whether the Constitution is different in this respect. That it is not seems rather clearly to have been the assumption underlying Chief Justice Marshall's opinion for the Court in Marbury v. Madison, 1 Cranch 137 (1803), which established the power of judicial review. Marshall's inference, which depends heavily on the assumption that constitutional review involves merely the traditional judicial function of comparing one legally prescribed mandate with another to see if they conflict, is one that flows much more comfortably if one assumes an interpretivist approach to construing the Constitution. It is no accident that Alexander Bickel, the preeminent noninterpretivist theorist of our age, was also preeminent in his criticism of the logic of Marshall's opinion. See A. Bickel, *The Least Dangerous Branch* 1-14 (1962).

12. Id. at 19. See also Chapter 3.

13. In a few unusual situations, as where the Court is enforcing the Commerce Clause against state legislation, its decisions are subject to over-rule by the Congress. This thus approaches a "common law" jurisdiction, and the problems of democracy adverted to in the text are substantially attenuated.

14. I have suggested that the appeal of democracy can best be understood in terms of its connections with the philosophical tradition of utilitarianism. Ely, "Constitutional Interpretivism: Its Allure and Impossibility," 53 *Ind. L. J.* 399, 405-08 (1978). Since nothing in the ensuing analysis depends on this claim, it is omitted here.

15. *The Federalist* no. 40, at 292 (B. Wright ed. 1961) (Madison) (emphasis omitted).

16. G. Wood, *The Creation of the American Republic, 1776-1787,* at 379 (1969).

17. See also, e.g., id., chs. 7 and 8 and pp. 532-33; R. Palmer, *The Age of the Democratic Revolution,* vol. 1, *The Challenge* 214-15 (1959); Morgan, "The American Revolution Considered As an Intellectual Movement," in *The Reinterpretation of the American Revolution, 1763-1789,* at 574-75 (J. Greene ed. 1968).

18. E.g., E. Morgan, *The Birth of the Republic, 1763-1789,* at 138 (1956); Kenyon, "Republicanism and Radicalism in the American Revolution: An Old-Fashioned Interpretation," 19 *Wm and M. Q.* 153 (1962).

19. *The Federalist* no. 39, at 280 (B. Wright ed. 1961) (Madison).

20. Id. at 280-81. Hamilton, on the other hand, tended to stress more the negative side of republicanism, that it excluded monarchical governments. Of course the two are compatible, but Hamilton's is obviously less restrictive. See generally G. Stourzh, *Alexander Hamilton and the Idea of Republican Government* (1970). But see 2 *The Works of Alexander Hamilton* 92 (H. Lodge ed. 1904).

21. *The Federalist* no. 57, at 384 (B. Wright ed. 1961) (Madison).

22. E.g., R. Palmer, *The Age of the Democratic Revolution,* vol. 2, *The Struggle* 525-26 (1964); R. Cover, *Justice Accused* 132 (1975); Elkins and McKitrick, "The Founding Fathers: Young Men of the Revolution," 76 *Pol. S. Q.* 181 (1961).

23. See also J. Story, *Commentaries on the Constitution of the United States* §§327-30 (3d ed. 1858); G. Wills, *Inventing America* 355-57 (1978).

24. Of course we didn't live happily ever after. And though the Civil War was surely in part about slavery and in part about local control, it can also be said to have been in part about democracy, about whether a national majority could control the conduct of a group that in national terms constituted a minority. The South's willingness to resist to the point of

bloody rebellion proves what can hardly surprise, that there will be issues about which minorities can feel so strongly that they are unwilling to recognize the legitimacy of majority control. But to the extent that it is fair to view the war's causes through this prism, it must be just as fair to focus on the final outcome and insist that the North's unwillingness to recognize the secession demonstrates the strength of the majority's resolve that this nation remain controllable by majority will.

25. E.g., M. Parenti, *Democracy for the Few* 57 (2d ed. 1977).

26. In fact the role the Senate was envisioned as playing evolved considerably during the very course of the Convention: the original concept, that the "upper House" would represent the propertied classes, came under early and understandable attack and was soon displaced by the now commonplace idea that the Senate represents the states while the House represents the people. See, e.g., J. Pole, *Foundations of American Independence: 1763-1815*, at 192 (1972); Diamond, "Democracy and 'The Federalist': A Reconsideration of the Framers' Intent," 53 *Am. Pol. Sci. Rev.* 52 (1959).

27. R. Dahl, *Democracy in the United States* 137 (3d ed. 1976).

28. A. de Tocqueville, *Democracy in America* 59 (Anchor ed. 1959). See also, e.g., C. Becker, *The Declaration of Independence* 233 (Vintage ed. 1958); A. Schlesinger, Jr., *The Age of Jackson* 14 (1945); H. Hyman, *A More Perfect Union* 4 (1973). Cf. W. Brock, *Conflict and Transformation* 27 (1973).

29. R. Dahl, supra note 27, at 493.

30. See generally E. Purcell, *The Crisis of Democratic Theory* (1973).

31. E.g., Berger, "Government by Judiciary: John Hart Ely's 'Invitation,' " 54 *Ind. L. J.* 277, 281-82 (1979); Strong, "Bicentennial Benchmark: Two Centuries of Evolution of Constitutional Processes," 55 *N. C. L. Rev.* 1, 114 (1976); Wright, "Professor Bickel, the Scholarly Tradition, and the Supreme Court," 84 *Harv. L. Rev.* 769, 788 (1971).

32. Grey, supra note 1, at 705. See also, e.g., Heymann and Barzelay, "The Forest and the Trees: *Roe v. Wade* and Its Critics," 53 *B. U. L. Rev.* 765, 781 (1973); Sandalow, "Judicial Protection of Minorities," 75 *Mich. L. Rev.* 1162, 1173 (1977); Holland, "American Liberals and Judicial Activism: Alexander Bickel's Appeal from the New to the Old," 51 *Ind. L. J.* 1025, 1042 (1976); cf. L. Tribe, *American Constitutional Law* 10, 48 (1978).

2. The Impossibility of a Clause-Bound Interpretivism

1. Even this is not necessarily so. It is theoretically possible that the thirty-eight states ratifying an amendment will contain only 40 percent of

the nation's population — recall that over half of it is concentrated in nine states — and of course there is nothing to guarantee anything approaching unanimity of opinion within the ratifying states.

2. Pollsters never tire of reminding us that most Americans would reject many provisions of the Bill of Rights. E.g., CBS News Poll, ser. 70, rpt. 2, March 20, 1970.

3. G. Wood, *The Creation of the American Republic, 1776-1787*, at 379 (1969) (emphasis omitted).

4. 5 *The Writings of Thomas Jefferson* 116, 121 (P. Ford ed. 1895) (emphasis omitted).

5. E.g., *The Federalist* no. 50 (B. Wright ed. 1961) (Madison).

6. But cf. Chapter 4. Bishin, "Judicial Review in Democratic Theory," 50 *S. Cal. L. Rev.* 1099 (1977), though purporting to establish the democratic character of judicial review, in fact establishes only this. See id. at 1112: "In sum, if we accept the thesis that the government created by the Constitution is a democracy, it follows that it is consistent with democracy, and is therefore 'democratic,' to confine and supervise the exercise of majority rule." Cf. E. Rostow, *The Sovereign Prerogative* ch. 5 (1962). The inference is solid enough; it's the premise that's problematic.

7. E.g., Linde, "Judges, Critics, and the Realist Tradition," 82 *Yale L. J.* 227, 254 (1972); Winter, "Poverty, Economic Equality, and the Equal Protection Clause," 1972 *Sup. Ct. Rev.* 41, 86-89; R. Berger, *Government by Judiciary* (1977). Compare Bork, "Neutral Principles and Some First Amendment Problems," 47 *Ind. L. J.* 1, 8 (1971), with id. at 17.

8. See W. Shakespeare, *Macbeth*, act IV, scene I.

9. Linde, supra note 7, at 254.

10. 198 U.S. 45 (1905). See also, e.g., Coppage v. Kansas, 236 U.S. 1 (1915); Adkins v. Children's Hospital, 261 U.S. 525 (1923).

11. 410 U.S. 113 (1973).

12. A. Cox, *The Role of the Supreme Court in American Government* 113 (1976). Compare Frankfurter, "The Red Terror of Judicial Reform," 40 *New Republic* 110, 113 (1924) ("the due process clause ought to go") with Malinski v. New York, 324 U.S. 401, 414 (1945) (Frankfurter, J., concurring): "Here we are concerned with the requirement of 'due process of law' . . . Experience has confirmed the wisdom of our predecessors in refusing to give a rigid scope to this phrase. It expresses a demand for civilized standards of law." Part of the intervening "experience," of course, involved the elevation of Professor Frankfurter to the bench. But cf. p. 39.

13. This much is admitted even by commentators who find elsewhere in the Constitution or its informing traditions authorization for textually untethered substantive review. See, e.g., Kelly, "The Fourteenth Amendment Reconsidered," 54 *Mich. L. Rev.* 1049, 1052 (1956); Curtis, "Review and Majority Rule," in *Supreme Court and Supreme Law* 177 (E.

Cahn ed. 1954); Corwin, "The Doctrine of Due Process of Law Before the Civil War," 24 *Harv. L. Rev.* 366, 368, 372-73 (1911).

Certain historical antecedents of the phrase suggest an additional and somewhat distinct meaning. To the extent that its roots are in the French term *process de ley*, see Dunham, "Magna Carta and British Constitutionalism," in *The Great Charter* 26 (1965), the phrase would seem to convey the requirement that serious injury be inflicted only in accord with (a process of) law, as opposed, presumably, to a process of anarchy or unbridled discretion. Cf. E. Coke, *Second Part of the Institutes of the Laws of England* 46, 50 (1671); Dartmouth College v. Woodward, 4 Wheat. 518, 581 (1819) (argument of Daniel Webster). At one point, indeed, Justice Black expressed a willingness to add this sort of requirement to his incorporationist interpretation: "For me the only correct meaning of [due process of law] is that our Government must proceed according to the 'law of the land' — that is, according to written constitutional and statutory provisions as interpreted by court decisions." In re Winship, 397 U.S. 358, 382 (1970) (Black, J., dissenting). (It's difficult to believe he was serious about this, since it would make every question of state law a federal question.) The propriety of equating this "law of the land" concept with due process is far from clear. See, e.g., Jurow, "Untimely Thoughts: A Reconsideration of the Origins of Due Process of Law," 19 *Am. J. Leg. Hist.* 265 (1975). In any event, this possible additional historical meaning, whose adoption seems unthinkable in the context of the Fourteenth Amendment and unnecessary in the context of the Fifth, does not authorize courts to evaluate the substantive merits of duly enacted statutes. Cf. Chapter 6.

14. Frank and Munro, "The Original Understanding of 'Equal Protection of the Laws,' "50 *Colum. L. Rev.* 131, 132 n.6 (1950). But cf. note 79 infra.

15. Morrison, "Does the Fourteenth Amendment Incorporate the Bill of Rights? The Judicial Interpretation," 2 *Stan. L. Rev.* 140, 166 (1949). See also, e.g., R. Berger, supra note 7, at 193-214; 2 L. Boudin, *Government by Judiciary* 385-86 (1932); Linde, "Due Process of Lawmaking," 55 *Neb. L. Rev.* 197, 237-38 (1976); Crosskey, "Charles Fairman, 'Legislative History,' and the Constitutional Limitations on State Authority," 22 *U. Chi. L. Rev.* 1, 6 (1954); 2 J. Story, *Commentaries on the Constitution of the United States* §§ 1941, 1944 (T. Cooley ed. 1873).

16. 13 N.Y. 378 (1856).

17. 19 How. 393, 450 (1857). See D. Fehrenbacher, *The Dred Scott Case* 381-84, 403-04 (1978).

18. See, e.g., State v. Paul, 5 R.I. 185 (1858); State v. Keeran, 5 R.I. 497 (1858). See generally Corwin, supra note 13, at 474-75; Warren, "The New Liberty under the Fourteenth Amendment," 39 *Harv. L. Rev.* 431, 442 (1926).

19. Part of the Fourteenth Amendment's point was to overrule *Dred Scott*'s holding that blacks could not be citizens, but that doesn't tell us anything about its framers' views on the decision's invocation (as opposed to its application) of the concept of substantive due process. Raoul Berger's dismissal of the relevance of *Dred Scott* on the grounds that it was "universally execrated by the abolitionists, and also decried by Lincoln," R. Berger, supra note 7, at 204 n.36, thus seems somewhat brisk.

20. Abolitionist rhetoric also sometimes mentioned due process in arguing the unconstitutionality or injustice of slavery. See generally J. tenBroeck, *The Antislavery Origins of the Fourteenth Amendment* (1951). On examination, however, and tenBroeck is quite objective in representing the matter thus, the references turn out to be casual and only obliquely to the point. Due process generally was invoked only in the context of a quiverful of arguments against slavery, see id. at 66; seldom if ever was it the main one, id. at 25-26, 96-100; and indeed it seems most often to have been invoked as a "same goes for you" sort of answer to the claim that freeing the slaves would "retroactively" deprive their owners of property without due process. Id. at 23. Thus "the abolitionist due process argument was rebuttal in character and altogether negative in function." Id. at 26. Probably the best-known due process argument against slavery, that of Alvan Stewart, was one that used the provision's procedural meaning, focusing on the fact that the slaves had been placed in that status (and often returned to it after capture) without a jury trial or other requisites of fair procedure. Id. at 44. See also W. Wiecek, *The Guarantee Clause of the U.S. Constitution* 155 (1972). The oft-relied-on Republican Platforms of 1856 and 1860 — see, e.g., Kelly, supra note 13, at 1053 — are ambiguous but susceptible to this construction. See J. tenBroeck, supra, at 120-21 nn.5 and 6. But cf. id. at 119-20 and nn.3 and 4 (Free Soil Platforms of 1848 and 1852). This is not to say that due process was not mentioned by some abolitionists in an apparently substantive way — it was — but only that such invocations tended to be haphazard. Moreover, recent scholarship has tended to minimize the contribution of such exaggerated argumentation to the thinking behind the Fourteenth Amendment. See R. Cover, *Justice Accused* ch. 9 (1975).

21. See also Chapter 6.

22. See, e.g., Frank and Munro, supra note 14, at 133; Miller, "The Forest of Due Process of Law: The American Constitutional Tradition," in *Nomos XVIII: Due Process* 16 (J. Pennock and J. Chapman eds. 1977).

23. See Oregon v. Mitchell, 400 U.S. 112, 195 (1970) (Harlan, J., concurring in part and dissenting in part).

24. T. Cooley, *A Treatise on the Constitutional Limitations* *66-67 (2d ed. 1871).

25. E.g., R. Berger, supra note 7.

26. Linde, supra note 15, at 237.

27. See also H. Graham, *Everyman's Constitution* 446-47, 487 (1968) (noting, albeit for a different purpose, the general failure after ratification of framers and others to rely on a substantive reading of either Due Process Clause in legal contexts where such a reading would have helped their cause).

28. Here as elsewhere primary stress should be laid on the constitutional language actually employed. No clear answer to the present question will be found there, however, because "liberty" is a term that can be used, and was at the time of the Fourteenth Amendment, both narrowly (to refer only to freedom from restraints on locomotion) and broadly (to mean freedom from virtually any sort of inhibition). Compare Shattuck, "The True Meaning of the Term 'Liberty' in Those Clauses in the Federal and State Constitutions Which Protect 'Life, Liberty, and Property,' " 4 *Harv. L. Rev.* 365 (1891) (narrow reading), with, e.g., 2 J. Story, supra note 15, §1950 (broad reading). See also H. Hyman, *A More Perfect Union* 447 (1973): "[B]y the mid-1860's some Americans were accepting views of liberty derived from Adam Smith, Bentham and Mill as something more than the absence of restraints on an individual's physical freedom. Republicans asserted that liberty also involved civil rights; i.e., the absence of inequitable governmental interferences with private pursuits." Those seeking to minimize the range of the Due Process Clauses stress Blackstone's narrow definition of "liberty." E.g., Shattuck, supra, at 377; R. Berger, supra note 7, at 270. What they fail to mention is that his adjacent definition of "life" referred to "the right of personal security [which] consists in a person's legal and uninterrupted enjoyment of his life, his limbs, his body, his health, and his reputation." Miller, supra note 22, at 7. Since the constitutional language (considered in light of its contemporary usage) does not generate a clear answer, responsible recourse must be to the overall policy informing the Due Process Clauses, that the government should not be able to injure you, at least not seriously, without employing fair procedures. At all events, the in-between position of the current Court (even assuming an informing princple could be identified) cannot find support in the history.

29. E.g., Bell v. Burson, 402 U.S. 535 (1971); Hannah v. Larche, 363 U.S. 420, 442 (1960); Joint Anti-Fascist Refugee Committee v. McGrath, 341 U.S. 123, 168 (1951) (Frankfurter, J., concurring). See also J. Story, supra note 15, §1945.

30. See Board of Regents v. Roth, 408 U.S. 564 (1972); Perry v. Sindermann, 408 U.S. 593 (1972); Meachum v. Fano, 427 U.S. 215, 224-25 (1976).

31. Compare Paul v. Davis, 424 U.S. 693 (1976), with Wisconsin v. Constantineau, 400 U.S. 433 (1971).

32. See Board of Regents v. Roth, 408 U.S. 564, 577 (1972): "To

have a property interest in a benefit, a person clearly must have more than an abstract need or desire for it. He must have more than a unilateral expectation of it. He must, instead, have a legitimate claim of entitlement to it."

33. The proposition that due process invariably requires a full hearing may sound nice and liberal, but it doesn't take much reflection to realize that it can lead only to a contraction of the set of occasions on which any process at all will be constitutionally required. See generally Eisenberg, "Participation, Responsiveness, and the Consultative Process: An Essay for Lon Fuller," 92 *Harv. L. Rev.* 410, 419-23 (1978); cf. Goss v. Lopez, 419 U.S. 565, 580, 583-84 (1975).

34. In re Winship, 397 U.S. 358, 377-78 (1970) (Black, J., dissenting). See also Goldberg v. Kelly, 397 U.S. 254, 271 (1970) (Black, J., dissenting); Stovall v. Denno, 388 U.S. 293, 304-05 (1967) (Black, J., dissenting).

35. Leland v. Oregon, 343 U.S. 790, 803 (1952) (Frankfurter, J., joined by Black, J., dissenting). See also Edelman v. California, 344 U.S. 357, 362 (1953) (Black, J., dissenting); Thompson v. Louisville, 362 U.S. 199 (1960); Pyle v. Kansas, 317 U.S. 213 (1942); Miller v. Pate, 386 U.S. 1 (1967). See also H. Black, *A Constitutional Faith* 33-34 (1968).

36. Yarbrough, "Justice Black, the Fourteenth Amendment, and Incorporation," 30 *U. Miami L. Rev.* 231, 253-54 (1976).

37. 16 Wall. 36 (1873).

38. But see note 59 infra.

39. 16 Wall. at 96 (Field, J., dissenting).

40. L. Lusky, *By What Right?* 199 (1975). See also Benedict, "Preserving Federalism: Reconstruction and the Waite Court," 1978 *Sup. Ct. Rev.* 39, 59.

41. But cf. Colgate v. Harvey, 296 U.S. 404 (1935), overruled by Madden v. Kentucky, 309 U.S. 83 (1940).

42. Cf. Colgate v. Harvey, 296 U.S. 404, 445 (1935) (Stone, J., dissenting).

43. 16 Wall. at 100-01.

44. E.g., E. Foner, *Free Soil, Free Labor, Free Men* 102, 122-23 (1970); Graham, "The Early Antislavery Backgrounds of the Fourteenth Amendment," 1950 *Wisc. L. Rev.* 479, 491, 636-41; J. tenBroeck, supra note 20, at 13-14, 104-05.

45. But see pp. 24-25. Article IV, Section 2 is hardly a model of precision drafting, but by entitling the "citizens of each State" to "all Privileges and Immunities of Citizens in the several States," it will bear an equality construction, to the effect that when a citizen of one state travels to another, he or she gets whatever legal prerogatives are enjoyed by the

locals. The syntax of the Privileges or Immunities Clause of the Fourteenth Amendment seems inescapably that of substantive entitlement.

46. 16 Wall. at 104-05.

47. Adamson v. California, 332 U.S. 46, 71, 74 (1947) (Black, J., dissenting).

48. E.g., Graham, "Our 'Declaratory' Fourteenth Amendment," 7 *Stan. L. Rev.* 3, 23 (1954); L. Lusky, supra note 40, at 202; A. Bickel, *The Morality of Consent* 40-43 (1975).

49. E.g., Karst, "Foreword: Equal Citizenship under the Fourteenth Amendment," 91 *Harv. L. Rev.* 1, 44 (1977). Cf. Wechsler, "Equal Protection Is a Double-Edged Sword," in *One Hundred Years of the Fourteenth Amendment* 44-45 (J. Gerard ed. 1973); Freund, "The Supreme Court and Fundamental Freedoms," in *Judicial Review and the Supreme Court* 128-29 (3d ed. L. Levy 1976).

50. This formulation is derived from Green, "The Bill of Rights, the Fourteenth Amendment, and the Supreme Court," 46 *Mich. L. Rev.* 869, 904 (1948).

51. The received reading of the Privileges or Immunities Clause, as limiting its protection to citizens, seems particularly difficult to reconcile with the widely accepted view that its companion Equal Protection Clause is properly read to extend unusually strenuous protection to aliens. Surely one ought to think carefully about at least one of these positions. But cf., e.g., Karst, supra note 49, at 44.

52. The Due Process Clause can be seen as an apt vehicle for incorporating those provisions of the Bill of Rights that relate to "process." The fact that there is an identical clause in the Fifth Amendment (save that it applies to the federal government) certainly seems troublesome to such a notion, but on historical reexamination it turns out to be less than overwhelmingly so. In 1855, in Murray's Lessee v. Hoboken Land and Improvement Co., 18 How. 272, a unanimous Supreme Court had indicated very clearly—though the remark was unnecessary and somewhat bizarre—that the Fifth Amendment's Due Process Clause incorporated the "process" commands of the Fourth, Fifth, Sixth, Seventh, and Eighth Amendments, and had independent procedural content as well. Id. at 276-77. See also Slaughter-House Cases, 16 Wall. 36, 118 (1873) (Bradley, J., dissenting), referring to the Fifth Amendment's Due Process Clause as "including almost all the rest" of the Bill of Rights. The insertion in the Fourteenth Amendment of an identical clause applicable to the states thus *might* have been calculated to apply those provisions to them. Neither is it bizarre to conclude that the process "due" from the states includes—though here as elsewhere the inference that it is *all* that is due is more tenuous—the process that had for a century been constitutionally required of the federal

government. It is, moreover, the "process" provisions of the Bill of Rights that have caused most of the shouting, the incorporation of the First Amendment having been accomplished largely without incident, and the Second and Third Amendments, rightly or wrongly, having turned out to have little relevant content.

53. Duncan v. Louisiana, 391 U.S. 145, 166 (1968) (Black, J., concurring).

54. 332 U.S. 46, 92-123.

55. Fairman, "Does the Fourteenth Amendment Incorporate the Bill of Rights? The Original Understanding," 2 *Stan. L. Rev.* 5 (1949).

56. See, e.g., Kelly, "Clio and the Court: An Illicit Love Affair," 1965 *Sup. Ct. Rev.* 119, 132-34; Graham, supra note 48, at 19-20 n.80. Actually, Fairman's own verdict on Black's thesis does not seem to have been a good deal stronger than "not proven." The claim that he had proved its contrary is one that has been added by more enthusiastic advocates. E.g., R. Berger, supra note 7, at 137. But see A. Bickel, *The Least Dangerous Branch* 102-03 (1962): "[W]hat we have is an assertion of an exact original intention, followed by its refutation. But the refutations disprove the assertion, they do not prove its opposite."

57. *Cong. Globe*, 39th Cong., 1st Sess. 2765-66 (1866). "[N]o member of the Committee gave a different interpretation or questioned his statements in any particular." H. Flack, *The Adoption of the Fourteenth Amendment* 87 (1908).

58. Fairman also argued that even clear statements that "the bill of rights" was to be incorporated wouldn't have meant in the mid-nineteenth century what they would mean today, since the term "bill of rights" was then sometimes used, specifically by Congressman Bingham, to signal not the first eight or nine amendments but rather only the Due Process Clause of the Fifth Amendment and Article IV's Privileges and Immunities Clause. Fairman, supra note 55, at 26. This does appear to have been the usage sometimes, though I think not most often. See, e.g., *Cong. Globe*, 39th Cong., 1st Sess. 1089-90 (1866) (remarks of Congressman Bingham, referring to "the bill of rights under the articles of amendment to the Constitution" in the course of a criticism of Barron v. Baltimore, 7 Pet. 243 (1833), which had refused to apply what we would call the Bill of Rights to the states). You will also have noticed that Howard's statement is clear to the same effect.

Assume for the sake of argument, however, that Fairman was right that "bill of rights" often meant only the Fifth Amendment's Due Process Clause and the Privileges and Immunities Clause. But now factor in the additional datum that it was at least a sometime part of the rhetoric of abolitionism that the Fifth Amendment's Due Process Clause already incorporated most of the rest of what we would call the Bill of Rights. Recent scholarship tends to downplay the influence of such seemingly eccentric pre-War constitutional views. This particular view, however, had been adopted by the Supreme Court in 1855. See note 52 supra. One who held it, of course, need only have thought he was incorporating the Fifth Amendment's Due Process Clause to believe that most of what we would call the Bill of Rights was being incorporated. And we shall see that assumptions concerning the sweeping coverage of Article IV's Privileges and Immunities Clause were even more widespread.

It was also part of antislavery rhetoric that *Barron v. Baltimore* had been wrongly decided and was therefore a nullity. See sources cited Fairman, supra, at 26-36, 118-20. Again we must be careful not to attribute too much influence to such views, but it is at least worthy of note that this one appears to have been held by Bingham himself. See *Cong. Globe*, 39th Cong., 1st Sess. 2542-44 (1866). In terms of the original understanding, *Barron* was almost certainly decided correctly. But if you were committed to the proposition that the Bill of Rights already applied to the States, your silence on the subject of whether the Fourteenth Amendment would apply the Bill of Rights to the states wouldn't mean much, would it?

59. It is generally assumed that "[a]mong the broad interpretations of the 14th Amendment implicitly rejected by the Slaughter-House Cases was the position that all the Bill of Rights guarantees had been made applicable to the states as a result of the post-Civil War constitutional changes." G. Gunther, *Cases and Materials on Constitutional Law* 505 (9th ed. 1975). However, a close reading of the various opinions in that case suggests at least the possibility that all nine justices meant to take exactly that position! The most explicit statement to this effect appears in Justice Bradley's dissent, 16 Wall. at 118-19, but it seems he was not alone. The majority indicated that "lest it should be said that no such privileges and immunities are to be found if those we have been considering are excluded, we venture to suggest some which owe their existence to the Federal government, its National character, its Constitution, or its laws." Id. at 79. The reference to rights that owe their existence to the federal Constitution has to be tantalizing in the present context, and indeed in the course of the ensuing list the Court says, "The right to peaceably assemble and petition for redress of grievances, the privilege of the writ of *habeas corpus*, are rights of the citizen guaranteed by the Federal Constitution." Id. No other provision of the Bill of Rights is mentioned, but the import of this sentence seems unmistakable: if it's a right guaranteed elsewhere in the Constitution —if, in particular, it's a right previously guaranteed only against the federal government—then it belongs on the list of privileges and immunities protected against state denial by the Fourteenth Amendment. (That the

introductory reference to rights that owe their existence to the Constitution was not simply a reference to rights the Fourteenth Amendment itself guarantees is underscored by the Court's subsequent observation that another privilege, that of attaining state citizenship, "is conferred," obviously unlike the others, "by the very article under consideration." Id. at 80.)

We have already seen Justice Field's complaint (joined by the other three dissenters) that the majority's was a trivial construction, that it should have gone further. "If this inhibition . . . only refers, as held by the majority . . . to such privileges and immunities as were before its adoption specially designated in the Constitution or necessarily implied as belonging to citizens of the United States, it was a vain and idle enactment . . . " Id. at 96. Taken at face value, this seems to imply an understanding that the majority had not meant to incorporate the Bill of Rights. We all know enough about dissents, though, to know we shouldn't necessarily take it at face value. Field thought the plaintiffs challenging the monopoly should win; the incorporation of the Bill of Rights—which the majority's reference to First Amendment rights had at least strongly suggested—wouldn't help the plaintiffs; from Field's perspective, therefore, the majority's construction was trivial. (Field's characterization, of course, is technically accurate: even on the reading I am suggesting, the majority *had* included only those prerogatives that were obviously implicit in one's citizenship or already "specially designated in the Constitution." But the rights mentioned had been "specially designated" as good against only the federal government. Including them as privileges or immunities protected against *state* action by the Fourteenth Amendment was a far from trivial step.)

Thanks in part to Field's trivializing characterization, the majority's hint was soon forgotten. But it does seem a relevant piece of evidence respecting the original understanding. Early in the Court's opinion Justice Miller had observed that "fortunately" the history of the framing and ratification of the Reconstruction Amendments "is fresh within the memory of us all, and its leading features, as they bear upon the matter before us, free from doubt." Id. at 68. As regards the issues on which the case turned, that was polished brass: the Court split 5-4, thereby suggesting something short of freshness of memory and freedom from doubt. But as regards a proposition all nine appear with varying degrees of clarity to have endorsed—that whatever else it did, the Privileges or Immunities Clause at least applied to the states the constitutionally stated prohibitions that had previously applied only to the federal government—there may be something in the point.

60. Duncan v. Louisiana, 391 U.S. 145, 166 (1968) (Black, J., concurring).

61. A. Bickel, supra note 56, at 102-03.

62. 6 F. Cas. 546 (C.C.E.D. Pa. 1823). See, e.g., Slaughter-House Cases, 16 Wall. 36, 97-98 (1873) (Field, J., dissenting); Fairman, supra note 55, at 12; Graham, supra note 48, at 12.

63. 6 F. Cas. at 551-52 (emphasis added).

64. Raoul Berger, arguing for an extremely narrow interpretation of the Fourteenth Amendment's Privileges or Immunities Clause, repeatedly characterizes *Corfield*, on which he places great reliance in his book, as having construed the Article IV provision narrowly. E.g., R. Berger, supra note 7, at 22, 31-32, 38, 43, 103, 211. That is a reading of *Corfield* its language will not bear. See also, e.g., Kelly, supra note 13, at 1059, 1072. Berger surely must be congratulated for some valiant attempts, though. He relies on Washington's indication that he wasn't prepared to include as privileges and immunities "all the rights" protected by state law. R. Berger, supra, at 32. He emphasizes the word "confining" that appears in the second sentence of the quotation, id. at 22, 31, apparently without noticing that read in context what Washington says, in essence, is that he feels "no hesitation in confining" privileges and immunities to everything but the kitchen sink. He explains away Washington's fatal reference to the right "to pursue and obtain happiness and safety" in two ways: (1) by noting that it followed references to life and liberty and inferring that it must therefore have been intended as a synonym for property, and (2) by observing that in the Due Process [*sic*] Clause the framers had opted for the term "property" rather than the phrase "pursuit of happiness and safety." Id. at 33. (Berger has more recently muted his reliance on the *Corfield* discussion, dismissing it as a "rambling dictum." Berger, "Government by Judiciary: John Hart Ely's 'Invitation,' " 54 *Ind. L. J.* 277, 292 (1979).)

65. Until recently the Supreme Court had quite consistently rejected this limiting aspect of Washington's interpretation. See, e.g., L. Tribe, *American Constitutional Law* 404-12 (1978). But compare Baldwin v. Fish and Game Commission, 436 U.S. 371 (1978), with Hicklin v. Orbeck, 437 U.S. 518 (1978).

66. In arguing that the specific conceptions of the framers should take precedence over the apparent thrust of the constitutional language, Raoul Berger notes that we would misunderstand—though not very seriously in this case, he might have added—Hamlet's claim that he could tell a hawk from a handsaw were we to stick with the contemporary meaning of "handsaw" rather than troubling to find out that in Shakespeare's time it referred to a heron. R. Berger, supra note 7, at 370. That's so, but although Berger himself apparently can tell a handsaw from a handsaw, the argument suggests that he can't tell ambiguity from vagueness. Where a word or phrase might have been intended to convey either of two (or more) distinct meanings, a reference to the legislative debates, or other contem-

porary sources, is certainly in order to discern which of the meanings was intended. Hamlet's case is that. It by no means follows, however, that a vague term, which does not stand for two or more distinct concepts but whose application to a number of marginal cases is problematic, should be limited to those instances that are known to have been specifically cited by its users. (An example of this might be limiting Hamlet's claim, unhappily unrecorded, that he could distinguish "the species of birds of the air" to hawks and handsaws, since those are all he mentioned.) Quite the contrary: the choice of a vague or open-ended term should, in the absence of contrary evidence, be assumed to have been conscious.

In any event, the assumption that makes Berger's error even relevant at this stage, that the framers of the Fourteenth Amendment specifically conceptualized "privileges or immunities" exclusively in terms of the rights listed in the 1866 Civil Rights Act, is one that seems unjustified. Berger repeatedly quotes statements about the coverage of the Act as if they applied equally to the amendment. E.g., id. at 27, 30, 33, 35, 36, 118-19, 165, 170-71, 175, 241. He does not do so inadvertently, but justifies it with the claim that the coverage of the two was meant to be identical. E.g., id. at 22-23, 110-11. But equivalence in coverage is not established either by the undeniable premise that the two "bore an extremely close relationship" to one another, id. at 23 n.10, quoting Kelly, supra note 13, at 1057, or by the equally undeniable fact that part of the purpose of the amendment was to provide an impeccable constitutional basis for the Act. E.g., id. at 149, 23 n.12. (The shorthand that the amendment "embodied" the Act is used by Berger in an accordion fashion. Introduced to mean that the amendment was intended to "remove doubt as to [the Act's] constitutionality and to place it beyond the power of a later Congress to repeal," id. at 23, at other points it is invoked to suggest equivalence of coverage. E.g., id. at 102-03, 108. This sort of elision permeates Berger's argument. That Senator X said he was interested in protecting rights "such as" A, B and C ends up meaning he meant to protect only A, B and C, e.g., id. at 29, 35, 42, 103; that the Black Codes were a target of the amendment ends up meaning they are all it intended to outlaw. E.g., id. at 48, 175, 208-09.) In fact there were some actual statements of equivalence, though generally couched in terms that made clear the speaker's understandable desire to minimize the potentially radical sweep of the constitutional language. Most important, however—here as elsewhere—is the fact that the two documents, even leaving aside the observation that one of them was a statute and the other a constitutional provision, *say very different things*. See also, e.g., Kelly, supra, at 1071; Bickel, "The Original Understanding and the Segregation Decision," 69 *Harv. L. Rev.* 1 (1955); note 69 infra.

Berger's claim that "privileges or immunities" was a term of art, with a specific shadow meaning the framers understood, is one of a family of such claims. (Incredibly, he makes the same claim for the phrase "natural right." R. Berger, supra, at 35, 102, 174, 211, 213.) We have examined Justice Black's claim that "privileges or immunities" was a term of art referring to the first eight or nine amendments. (Professor Crosskey agrees, adding that "[t]he clause seems about as clear as a clause could be." Crosskey, supra note 15, at 5-6.) Yet a third view of this ilk is that of Professors tenBroeck and Graham, that "privileges or immunities," like the other phrases employed in the amendment, was a term of art with roots in the abolitionist movement that conveyed a message of racial equality. "Their antislavery, antirace-discrimination backgrounds people understood, or thought they understood; and the framers in turn believed that the people knew and understood what this language meant." Graham, supra note 48, at 22. See also J. tenBroeck, supra note 20, at 3. You will not be surprised to learn that it turns out there was no general understanding that "privileges or immunities" meant this either. R. Cover, supra note 20, ch. 9. You'd think by now we'd have gotten the message, if only by witnessing so many "clearly understood" meanings running off in so many different directions. "Privileges or immunities" had no generally understood shadow meaning of any sort: it simply was not a term of art.

67. Bickel, supra note 66, at 61.

68. Id. at 59.

69. Id. at 63. See also, e.g., National Mut. Ins. Co. v. Tidewater Transfer Co., Inc., 337 U.S. 582, 646 (1949) (Frankfurter, J., dissenting) (vague clauses "purposely left to gather meaning from experience"); W. Wiecek, supra note 20, at 13: "An attempt to find conceptual precision in a document whose most important immediate virtue had to be its acceptability may be misleading." Raoul Berger characterizes this view of the Fourteenth Amendment as "an elegant reformulation of conspiratorial purpose," R. Berger, supra note 7, at 105, "playing a trick upon an unsuspecting people." Id. at 107. See also id. at 57, 112. That puts the matter upside down, however. Obtaining ratification of open-ended language in the expectation that it will be given an open-ended interpretation is not playing a trick. Trickery would inhere in gaining ratification of *facially specific language* and then giving it a latitudinarian construction, or equally — and this is the methodology favored by Berger — in gaining ratification of open-ended language and then forever limiting its reach to the particular recorded exemplifications of the Congress that proposed it to the states.

70. Raoul Berger asserts that "[t]he key to an understanding of the Fourteenth Amendment is that the North was shot through with Negrophobia, that the Republicans, except for a minority of extremists, were

swayed by the racism that gripped their constituents . . ." R. Berger, supra note 7, at 10. But see, e.g., W. Brock, *Conflict and Transformation* 293-94 (1972); M. Benedict, *A Compromise of Principle* 325-27 (1974); E. Foner, supra note 44, at 263-64, 281, 284-85; Benedict, "Racism and Equality in America," 6 *Revs. in Am. Hist.* 13 (1978). Perhaps the most insisted-upon implication of this "key" is found in Berger's repeated assertion that given their racism the Fourteenth Amendment's framers could not conceivably have intended to draft a provision capable of one day supporting the inference that blacks were entitled to vote. E.g., R. Berger, supra, at 55-60, 91. Curiously lacking is any attempt whatever to account for the fact that the Fifteenth Amendment, explicitly granting blacks the vote, was proposed and ratified *only two years later*. Recent studies indicate what can come as no surprise, that by and large the two amendments were supported by the same people. G. Linden, *Politics or Principle: Congressional Voting on the Civil War Amendments and Pro-Negro Measures, 1838-69* (1976). Of course this suggests that the framers didn't think Section 1 of the Fourteenth Amendment had had that effect, and thus supports Berger on that specific issue. But see pp. 118-19. It is extremely damaging, however, and on precisely the ground on which he chose to argue the point, to Berger's general claim of the dominance of "Negrophobia." Obviously there was racism in the Thirty-Ninth Congress—though recognizing racism in one's constituents and being racist oneself are not equivalent. See, e.g., K. Stampp, *The Era of Reconstruction 1854-1877*, at 141 (1965); E. Foner, supra, at 108, 263, 279-80. But cf., e.g., R. Berger, supra, at 13. The recognition that there was racism in society doubtless was one reason the framers chose open-ended language capable of development over time. But cf. note 69 supra. In any event the claim that race prejudice is "the key" to interpreting the Fourteenth Amendment is one that borders on perversity: it is roughly akin to a claim that censorship is the key to understanding the First Amendment.

71. See Bickel, supra note 66, at 44-45, 60.

72. See Williamson v. Lee Optical Co., 348 U.S. 483 (1955); see generally Chapter 6.

73. But see note 69 to Chapter 6.

74. A. Cox, supra note 12, at 60.

75. See also Posner, "The *Bakke* Case and the Future of 'Affirmative Action,' " 67 *Calif. L. Rev.* 171, 173 (1979): "[S]ince blacks are disproportionately responsible for crimes of violence, it might be rational—in the generous sense of the term that the Court uses in economic cases—to require blacks, but not whites, to carry identification."

76. See also Trimble v. Gordon, 430 U.S. 762, 779-80 (1977) (Rehnquist, J., dissenting).

77. 347 U.S. 497, 500 (1954).

78. O. Holmes, *Collected Legal Papers* 295-96 (1920).

79. Congressman Bingham appears at least initially to have thought that an equal protection concept was part of the Fifth Amendment's Due Process Clause. See *Cong. Globe*, 35th Cong., 2d Sess. 983-84 (1859); *Cong. Globe*, 39th Cong., 1st Sess. 1033-34 (1866). That he came during the debates to recognize that his understanding was unusual is suggested by the fact that in redrafting the Fourteenth Amendment he added an Equal Protection Clause to the Due Process Clause that had appeared in his first draft. But cf. Chapter 4.

80. Linde, supra note 7, at 234.

81. Recall as well that the historical record of a purely procedural intendment for "due process" itself is even clearer respecting the Fifth Amendment than it is respecting the Fourteenth.

82. See generally Chapter 4.

83. Griswold v. Connecticut, 381 U.S. 479, 520 (1965) (Black, J., dissenting). See also, e.g., R. Berger, supra note 7, at 390; E. Dumbauld, *The Bill of Rights* 63-65 (1957).

84. 5 *Writings of James Madison* 271-72 (Hunt ed. 1904).

85. 1 *Annals of Cong.* 439 (1789). See also 3 J. Story, *Commentaries on the Constitution of the United States* §1861 (1833); 1 *Annals of Cong.* 435 (1789) (version originally submitted by Madison): "The exceptions here or elsewhere in the Constitution, made in favor of particular rights, shall not be so construed as to diminish the just importance of other rights retained by the people, or as to enlarge the powers delegated by the Constitution; but either as actual limitations of such powers, or as inserted merely for greater caution."

86. E.g., 5 *Writings of James Madison* 431-32 (Hunt ed. 1904). This is not to say that the proper relation between the two concepts was never apprehended. See, e.g., *The Federalist* no. 84, at 535 n.* (B. Wright ed. 1961) (Hamilton): "To show that there is a power in the Constitution by which the liberty of the press may be affected, recourse has been had to the power of taxation." Hamilton went on to argue that the example is faulty because taxes on newspapers cannot violate freedom of the press—but see Grosjean v. American Press Co., 297 U.S. 233 (1936)—but the structure of the discussion nonetheless demonstrates that the possibility of a governmental act's being supported by one of the enumerated powers and at the same time violating one of the enumerated rights is one our forebears were capable of contemplating. That is also demonstrated by the inclusion in the body of the original Constitution of the prohibitions against federal bills of attainder and ex post facto laws despite the fact that no affirmative power to pass such offending laws had anywhere been granted in terms.

87. All this encounters an argument first made by Alfred Kelly, that "if the Ninth Amendment were concerned primarily with safeguarding individual liberties, one might expect to find similar provisions in some of the bills of rights of contemporary state constitutions; but the Ninth Amendment is unique." P. Brest, *Processes of Constitutional Decision-making* 708 (1975), relying on Kelly, supra note 56, at 154. The word "contemporary" makes the claim technically accurate: no such provision appears in any eighteenth-century state bill of rights. But that interpretation, which is the only one that can preserve the claim's accuracy, makes the entire argument somewhat misleading, since there weren't many state bills of rights of any sort — or for that matter many states — back then. And when one reviews the period when most state bills of rights in fact were drafted, the nineteenth century, one discovers that no fewer than twenty-six of them contained provisions indicating that the enumeration of certain rights was not to be taken to disparage others retained by the people, and indeed several of them were quite clear about distinguishing this caveat from another we have seen, namely that unenumerated powers are not to be inferred. (Alabama 1819; Arkansas 1836; California 1849; Colorado 1876; Florida 1885; Georgia 1865; Iowa 1846; Kansas 1855; Louisana 1868; Maine 1819; Maryland 1851; Minnesota 1857; Mississippi 1868; Missouri 1875; Montana 1889; Nebraska 1866-67; Nevada 1864; New Jersey 1844; North Carolina 1868; Ohio 1851; Oregon 1857; Rhode Island 1842; South Carolina 1868; Virginia 1870; Washington 1889; Wyoming 1889. All will be found in the seven volumes of *The Federal and State Constitutions*, F. Thorpe ed. 1909. Those distinguishing the two caveats include the Kansas, Nebraska, North Carolina, Ohio, and South Carolina constitutions mentioned.) Indeed, the presence of such "little Ninth Amendments" in state constitutions was so common that in 1911 Professor Corwin referred to "*the usual caveat* that enumeration of certain rights should not be construed to disparage other rights not so enumerated." Corwin, supra note 13, at 384 (emphasis added). I haven't the slightest doubt that many of the provisions, though there are a number of minor variations in language, were inspired by the Ninth Amendment: a good deal of imitation is evident throughout the state constitutions. But that doesn't reduce their relevance a whit. The framers of the various state constitutions did not, for reasons that are entirely obvious, copy or paraphrase Article I, Section 8 or other provisions of the federal Constitution that related to the bounds of federal power. They *did* copy or paraphrase the Ninth Amendment.

It is therefore true that no eighteenth-century state bill of rights included a provision analogous to the Ninth Amendment, and that fact merits mention. But the nineteenth-century provisions do as well, in a way that tends not simply to neutralize Kelly's argument, but indeed to turn it around. The fact that the constitution-makers in, say, Maine and Alabama in 1819 saw fit to include in their bills of rights provisions that were essentially identical to the Ninth Amendment is virtually conclusive evidence that they understood it to mean what it said and not simply to relate to the limits of federal power.

88. Wellington, "Common Law Rules and Constitutional Double Standards: Some Notes on Adjudication," 83 *Yale L. J.* 221, 274 (1973).

89. See also p. 34. It appears that he went along with the Court's active use of the Equal Protection Clause up until the point at which it became impossible not to recognize that the power to review classifications is an authority as broad and powerful as straight-out can-they-do-it substantive review. Compare, e.g., Griffin v. Illinois, 351 U.S. 12 (1956) (Black, J., for the plurality), with Harper v. Virginia Board of Elections, 383 U.S. 663, 670 (1966) (Black, J., dissenting).

90. Griswold v. Connecticut, 381 U.S. 479, 511 (1965) (Black, J., dissenting).

91. R. Cover, supra note 20, at 27. See also Chapter 3.

92. See Purcell, "Alexander M. Bickel and the Post-Realist Constitution," 11 *Harv. C.R.-C.L. L. Rev.* 521, 533 (1976).

93. E.g., Dr. Bonham's Case, 8 Coke Rep. 107, 118a (1610).

94. Monroe, "The Supreme Court and the Constitution," 18 *Am. Pol. Sci. Rev.* 737, 740 (1924).

95. 7 Pet. 243 (1833). See note 58 supra.

96. Cf. H. Graham, supra note 27, at 447-48.

97. See also Strong, "Bicentennial Benchmark: Two Centuries of Evolution of Constitutional Processes," 55 *N.C. L. Rev.* 1, 42-43 (1976).

3. Discovering Fundamental Values

1. A. Bickel, *The Least Dangerous Branch* 55 (1962).

2. Id. at 103.

3. L. Tribe, *American Constitutional Law* 452 (1978).

4. Sandalow, "Judicial Protection of Minorities," 75 *Mich. L. Rev.* 1162, 1184 (1977).

5. A. Bickel, supra note 1, at 109, 68. See also, e.g., id. at 39, 79; Miller and Howell, "The Myth of Neutrality in Constitutional Adjudication," 27 *U. Chi. L. Rev.* 661, 664 (1960). This view is so predominant that even commentators generally favorable to the work of the Warren Court tend to defend in value-imposition terms decisions of that Court that are more comfortably rationalized in terms of the approach developed in the ensuing chapters. See, e.g., Cox, "Foreword: Constitutional Adjudication

and the Promotion of Human Rights," 80 *Harv. L. Rev.* 91, 98-99 (1966); Karst, "Invidious Discrimination: Justice Douglas and the Return of the 'Natural-Law-Due-Process Formula,' " 16 *U.C.L.A. L. Rev.* 716, 720 (1969).

6. Wright, "Professor Bickel, the Scholarly Tradition, and the Supreme Court," 84 *Harv. L. Rev.* 769, 797 (1971). But cf. id. at 785.

7. Discussions that come close include Arnold, "Professor Hart's Theology," 73 *Harv. L. Rev.* 1298 (1960); Forrester, "Are We Ready for Truth in Judging?" 63 *A.B.A.J.* 1212 (1977); Craven, "Paean to Pragmatism," 50 *N.C. L. Rev.* 977 (1972); L. Tribe, supra note 3, at 453-54, 574, 896. The position seems inherent as well in discussions that press the position that the Court is "just another political actor," e.g., Dahl, "Decision-Making in a Democracy: The Supreme Court as a National Policy-Maker," 6 *J. Pub. L.* 279 (1957); J. Peltason, *Federal Courts in the Political Process* (1955), or assert, without further attention to sources, that the Court should act "when the legislature won't," see M. Shapiro, *Law and Politics in the Supreme Court* 240-41 (1964).

8. Linde, "Judges, Critics, and the Realist Tradition," 82 *Yale L. J.* 227, 252 (1972).

9. See, e.g., Braden, "The Search for Objectivity in Constitutional Law," 57 *Yale L. J.* 571, 588-89 (1948): "[T]entatively, it can be argued that [Frankfurter's] objective standard is a way of expressing two things: his own set of values for his society and his own conception of the safe limits of his function. Some things he believes in strongly enough to use his power to protect them. Others he may believe in but not strongly enough to risk the charge of abuse of office."

This approach is often yoked with a claim that the "democratic" branches aren't all that democratic. However, the leading works here preceded the Court-induced rash of legislative reapportionments, the recent reforms of the Presidential nominating processes, and the perhaps less significant internal congressional reform, e.g., M. Shapiro, *Freedom of Speech: The Supreme Court and Judicial Review* 17-21, 32 (1966), and more recent commentators tend simply to rely on the earlier ones without noticing the intervening developments. E.g., Perry, "Substantive Due Process Revisited: Reflections on (and Beyond) Recent Cases," 71 *Nw. U. L. Rev.* 417, 467-68 and n.308 (1977). See also McCleskey, "Judicial Review in a Democracy: A Dissenting Opinion," 3 *Hous. L. Rev.* 354, 361-62 (1966) (emphasis added): "[Charles] Black's analogy with officials of independent agencies . . . is more difficult. One would do well to begin by recalling that the status of such officials has not escaped criticism . . . More significantly, . . . Congress can define their powers, limit their policy discretion, *overcome their decisions and actions by ordinary legislation*, and speed their removal from office by granting dismissal authority to the President or to its own officers. When one adds to these considerations the much shorter terms of office . . . and the President's informal power over them, it seems that the popular controls are sufficiently strong to warrant covering them with the democratic label."

In any event the appropriate perspective here is a comparative one, and there can be no doubt that the judicial branch, at least at the federal level, is significantly less democratic than the legislative and executive. Finally, "impurities and imperfections, if such they be, in one part of the system are no argument for total departure from the desired norm in another part." A. Bickel, supra note 1, at 18. See also R. Dworkin, *Taking Rights Seriously* 141 (1977): "The argument assumes . . . that state legislatures are in fact responsible to the people in the way that democratic theory assumes . . . In some states [that] is very far from the case. I want to pass that point, however, because it does not so much undermine the argument from democracy as call for more democracy . . . "

10. *The Federalist* no. 78, at 490 (B. Wright ed. 1961) (Hamilton).

11. E.g., L. Tribe, supra note 3, at 47-52; Dahl, supra note 7; M. Shapiro, supra note 7; Forrester, supra note 7. But see Casper, "The Supreme Court and National Policy Making," 70 *Am. Pol. Sci. Rev.* 50 (1976).

12. See Dahl, supra note 7. Even this limited claim overlooks the extent to which court decisions themselves help shape the majority will. See p. 70.

13. See R. Dahl, *Democracy in the United States* 233-34 (3d ed. 1976); P. Brest, *Processes of Constitutional Decisionmaking* 962 (1975).

14. See Ely, "Legislative and Administrative Motivation in Constitutional Law," 79 *Yale L. J.* 1205, 1306-08 (1970).

15. Choper, "The Supreme Court and the Political Branches: Democratic Theory and Practice," 122 *U. Pa. L. Rev.* 810, 852-54 (1974). The record is not so unblemished regarding the lower federal courts, but even there denial of jurisdiction is extremely rare. Cf. Ely, supra note 14, at 1306-08.

16. Compare Choper, supra note 15, at 851, with C. Fairman, *Reconstruction and Reunion 1864-88*, pt. 1, vol. 6 of *History of the Supreme Court of the United States* 716-38 (P. Freund ed. 1971).

17. The Eleventh Amendment overruled Chisholm v. Georgia, 2 Dall. 419 (1793); the Fourteenth, Scott v. Sandford, 19 How. 393 (1857); the Sixteenth, Pollak v. Farmers' Loan & Trust Co., 157 U.S. 429 (1895); and the Twenty-Sixth, Oregon v. Mitchell, 400 U.S. 112 (1970).

18. M. Miller, *Plain Speaking* 225-26 (1973); J. Weaver, *Warren: The Man, the Court, the Era* 342-43 (1967). See also W. Douglas, *Go East,*

Young Man 320 (1974); Mavrinac, "From *Lochner* to *Brown v. Topeka:* The Court and Conflicting Concepts of the Political Process," 52 *Am. Pol. Sci. Rev.* 641, 653 (1958). At least with the benefit of hindsight, it seems in general the "fault" has lain in the limited sophistication of the appointive authority's predictive apparatus rather than in any drastic change in the appointee.

19. Kurland, "Toward a Political Supreme Court," 37 *U. Chi. L. Rev.* 19, 20 (1969).

20. Monaghan, "Constitutional Adjudication: The Who and When," 82 *Yale L. J.* 1363, 1366 (1973).

21. E.g., Dennis v. United States, 341 U.S. 494, 525 (1951) (Frankfurter, J., concurring); A. Bickel, *Politics and the Warren Court* 198 (1965); Hart, "Foreword: The Time Chart of the Justices," 73 *Harv. L. Rev.* 84, 100-01 (1959); cf. L. Lusky, *By What Right?* 20-22 (1975).

22. See generally 1 C. Warren, *The Supreme Court in United States History* (1922); W. Murphy, *Congress and the Court* (1962).

23. E. Rostow, *The Sovereign Prerogative* 165 (1962).

24. I shall be suggesting in Chapter 4 that the Warren Court did not see its role as importantly involving the imposition of fundamental values. I would like to be able to suggest further that that is why the Court's prestige has not materially suffered, in fact has increased, in recent decades, but that might be cheating. The Warren Court was an activist Court, perceived as such, and that perception does not seem significantly to have diminished its strength.

Writing in 1964, Professor Philip Kurland acknowledged quite candidly that "those who have feared that the Court, by asserting its powers too frequently and too vehemently, would risk its own destruction have been wrong." Kurland, "Foreword: Equal in Origin and Equal in Title to the Legislative and Executive Branches of the Government," 78 *Harv. L. Rev.* 143, 175 (1964). But the decisions of the Warren Court really upset him, see, e.g., Kurland, "Earl Warren, the 'Warren Court,' and the Warren Myths," 67 *Mich. L. Rev.* 353 (1968), and by 1969 he too was telling us, though nothing had happened in the preceding five years to make it any truer, that the Court's "essentially anti-democratic character keeps it constantly in jeopardy of destruction." Kurland, supra note 19, at 20. See also A. Bickel, *The Supreme Court and the Idea of Progress* 32 (1970), approving the Warren Court's activism in the criminal procedure area, even though those decisions were among the Court's most controversial.

25. See also, e.g., Cox, "The New Dimensions of Constitutional Adjudication," 51 *Wash. L. Rev.* 791, 826-27 (1976); *Washington Post*, July 10, 1978, at A4, col. 1 (reporting Harris survey).

26. Karst and Horowitz, "*Reitman v. Mulkey:* A Telophase of Sub-

stantive Equal Protection," 1967 *Sup. Ct. Rev.* 39, 79. See also M. Shapiro, supra note 9, at 38-39.

27. It would obviously be an overstatement to assert that the Court need not take public opinion into account. But that proves little: "the absolute ruler—a Hitler, a Stalin, a Peron—. . . however despotic, must sometimes take popular sentiment into account . . . " H. Mayo, *An Introduction to Democratic Theory* 60 (1960).

28. P. Roth, *The Great American Novel* 19 (1973).

29. See generally C. Mullett, *Fundamental Law and the American Revolution, 1760-1776* (1933); C. Rossiter, *Seedtime of the Republic* (1953); C. Becker, *The Declaration of Independence* ch. 2 and 240-48 (1922); H. Graham, *Everyman's Constitution* (1968); Grey, "Origins of the Unwritten Constitution: Fundamental Law in American Revolutionary Thought," 30 *Stan. L. Rev.* 843 (1978).

30. W. Blackstone, *Commentaries*, quoted in J. Stone, *The Province and Function of Law* 227 (1946). See also, e.g., Corwin, "The 'Higher Law' Background of American Constitutional Law," 42 *Harv. L. Rev.* 149, 152 (1928). In fact there was no single understanding of the meaning, let alone the content, of the concept during either of the periods in question; "natural law" has always conveyed quite different meanings to different people. See B. Wright, *American Interpretations of Natural Law* 333-45 (1931); C. Rossiter, supra note 29, at 366-67. Cf. A. d'Entrèves, *Natural Law* 13-17 (2d ed. 1970).

31. R. Cover, *Justice Accused* 27 (1975), quoted more fully at p. 39. See also, e.g., B. Bailyn, *The Ideological Origins of the American Revolution* 198-229 (1967); G. Wood, *The Creation of the American Republic, 1776-1787*, at 259-60, 267-68, 290-95, 552 (1969); J. Goebel, *Antecedents and Beginnings to 1801*, vol. 1 of *History of the Supreme Court of the United States* 95 (P. Freund ed. 1971). Nor would any discussion of the thinking of the time be complete without the mandatory (though often misquoted) passage from Bentham: "Natural rights is simple nonsense; natural and imprescriptable rights, rhetorical nonsense,—nonsense upon stilts." Bentham, "Anarchical Fallacies," in 2 *Works of Jeremy Bentham* 501 (J. Bowring ed. 1962) (emphasis omitted).

32. See generally G. Wood, supra note 31; C. Becker, supra note 29, at 233-34. Cf. Horwitz, "The Emergence of an Instrumental Conception of American Law, 1780-1820," in 5 *Perspectives in American History* 287 (D. Fleming and B. Bailyn eds. 1971).

33. See, e.g., G. Wills, *Inventing America* 60 and ch. 24 (1978); J. Goebel, supra note 31, at 89; R. Palmer, *The Age of Democratic Revolution*, vol. 1, *The Challenge* 181, 234-35 (1959); C. Rossiter, supra note 29, at 142-43, 319-20, 367, 376-77, 437-39; 1 *Journals of the Continental*

Congress 67 (1774) (preamble basing Declaration of Rights on "the immutable laws of nature, the principles of the English constitution, and the several charters or compacts" of the colonies); Vanhorne v. Dorrance, 28 F. Cas. 1012, 1014-16 (C.C.D. Pa. 1795) (no. 16,857).

34. J. Pole, *The Pursuit of Equality in American History* 11 (1978). See also id. at 46.

35. The fact that many persons at the time—following a version of natural rights theory deriving largely from Hobbes and Locke—would have held that our natural rights had been "merged in," and therefore superceded by, the written guarantees of the Bill of Rights, see, e.g., Corwin, supra note 30, at 409; see also note 41 infra, seems in one sense irrelevant to the present discussion. The task before us is the location of a source of values with which to give content to such open-ended provisions as the Ninth Amendment, whose clear implication seems to be that the class of protected rights is *not* exhausted by those which are explicitly set down in the document. See Chapter 2. It does remain true, however, that the adoption of a written bill of rights constitutes some evidence of a less than wholehearted commitment to a natural rights philosophy.

36. See, e.g., H. Graham, supra note 29, chs. 4 and 7; C. Fairman, supra note 16, at 1128-34.

37. See also Chapter 4. Salmon P. Chase's argument, adopted in the Republican platforms of 1856 and 1860, that slavery was a creature of local law and Congress lacked constitutional authority to sanction it anywhere within federal jurisdiction, was considerably more plausible but went to a different point. See generally E. Foner, *Free Soil, Free Labor, Free Men* 73-74, 83 (1970).

38. B. Wright, supra note 30, at 332-33.

39. R. Cover, supra note 31. There are other legal historians writing today who might seek to contain the implications of Cover's analysis by noting that at least the early part of the period about which he was writing differed from those that preceded and succeeded it in its relative minimization of higher-law thinking. See, e.g., Nelson, "The Impact of the Anti-slavery Movement upon Styles of Judicial Reasoning in Nineteenth Century America," 87 *Harv. L. Rev.* 513 (1974); cf. Horwitz, supra note 32. Surely there is something in such a claim, but it cannot be regarded as dispositive: ideas do not pop in and out of history like so many Vonnegut characters. Cover shows that higher-law thinking was very much a part of the abolitionists' repertoire from the beginning, but he goes on to demonstrate just what that did and did not mean to contemporary observers.

40. R. Cover, supra note 31, at 29. See also id. at 16-17, 150. Cf. A. d'Entrèves, supra note 30, at 86-87, 91, 93-95.

41. E.g., R. Cover, supra note 31, at 16-18, 25-26, 34, 169, 172; W.

Brock, *Conflict and Transformation* 111, 391 (1973). Calder v. Bull, 3 Dall. 386 (1798), is generally cited as the "least equivocal" Supreme Court reference to the possibility that a statute could be held unconstitutional because it violated natural law. See P. Brest, supra note 13, at 709-10; G. Gunther, *Cases and Materials on Constitutional Law* 550-52 (9th ed. 1975). It could stand rereading. All the justices agreed as to the result, but there was no Court opinion, each of the four sitting delivering an opinion for himself alone. Justice Iredell's contains a strong denunciation of the concept of natural law. Justice Cushing's says nothing relevant to the issue, so the reliance has to be, and is, on Justice Chase's opinion and, to an extent, on Justice Paterson's. Chase's does contain a speech that seems to sound in natural law: "An act of the Legislature (for I cannot call it a law) contrary to the great first principles of the social compact, cannot be considered a rightful exercise of legislative authority." 3 Dall. at 388 (emphasis omitted). But he went on to join the others in upholding the law at issue (a Connecticut statute setting aside a judicial decree and granting a new trial!). Why was that? Well, according to Chase, "The sole enquiry is, whether this resolution or law of Connecticut, having such operation, is an ex post facto law, within the prohibition of the Federal Constitution?" Id. at 387 (emphasis omitted). And with regard to that "sole enquiry" Chase took a fiercely positivistic, even literalistic, stand: "The expressions 'ex post facto laws,' are *technical*, they had been in use long before the Revolution, and had acquired an appropriate meaning, by Legislators, Lawyers, and Authors." Id. at 391 (emphasis omitted). See also id. at 390. In particular it was held that the prohibition of ex post facto laws did not extend to civil cases. (In fact a strong case can be made that this was a historical misinterpretation. See Ely, supra note 14, at 1312 n.324 and sources cited.) What happened to the natural law reference for which the opinion is remembered? Why this slavish adherance to the terms of the document and what Chase took to be the narrow intent of its framers? The answer does not seem to be the obvious one, that the law at issue satisfied Chase's broader sense of justice as well. In fact it appears it didn't: "Every law that takes away, or impairs, rights vested, agreeably to existing laws, is retrospective, and is generally unjust . . . " 3 Dall. at 391 (emphasis omitted). Rather, the point seems to have been that in the American context, there is no judicially enforceable notion of natural law other than what the terms of the Constitution provide.

This is said rather explicitly in Paterson's opinion: "I had an ardent desire to have extended the provision in the Constitution to retrospective laws in general. There is neither policy nor safety in such laws; and, therefore, I have always had a strong aversion against them. It may, in general, be truly observed of retrospective laws of every description, that they neither accord with sound legislation, nor the fundamental principles of the social compact. But on full consideration, I am convinced, that ex post facto laws must be limited in the manner already expressed; they must be taken in their technical, which is also their common and general acceptation, and are not to be understood in their literal sense." Id. at 397 (emphasis omitted). A close reading of Chase's opinion yields the same view. Laws "contrary to the great first principles of the social compact" are indeed void, but that social compact is embodied in our Constitution. Chase allowed that he could not "subscribe to the omnipotence of a state Legislature, or that it is absolute and without control; although its authority should not be expressly restrained by the Constitution, or fundamental law, of the state." Id. at 387-88 (emphasis omitted). But note carefully the last three words. (The context makes fairly clear that by "state" he meant one of the political units that make up the union; he used "government" to refer to "the state" in its more abstract sense.) Thus all he seems to have been saying here, and the rest of the opinion and especially his vote are consistent with no other view, is that the United States Constitution, in particular the Ex Post Facto Clause, controls state action. He didn't like the law in issue, he made that clear, but in our system the only "natural law" enforceable by courts is that set down in the document: that is why the "sole enquiry" is the meaning of the prohibition of ex post facto laws. To the same effect, see Ogden v. Saunders, 12 Wheat. 213, 347-48, 351, 353-54 (1827) (Marshall, C.J., dissenting). Thus Chase's argument with Iredell seems to have been entirely a philosophical one. With regard to the appropriate sources of constitutional doctrine they were as one, and *Calder*, far from being authority for the view that natural law is enforceable in the name of the Constitution, appears on close reading as strong authority against it. But see Fletcher v. Peck, 6 Cranch. 87, 143 (1810) (Johnson, J., concurring).

42. C. Haines, *The Revival of Natural Law Concepts* vii-viii (1930).

43. 16 Wall. 130, 141 (1872) (Bradley, J., concurring). Reliance on "the nature of things" recurs in Plessy v. Ferguson, 163 U.S. 537, 544 (1896).

44. B. Wright, supra note 30, at 339-40. See also C. Rossiter, supra note 29, at 366, 375.

45. Cf. H. Mayo, supra note 27, at 181-82 (natural law historically invoked both for and against democracy); E. Warren, *The Memoirs of Earl Warren* 302-03 (1977) (split in "religiously inspired" reaction to *Brown v. Board of Education*); Katz, "Republicanism and the Law of Inheritance in the American Revolutionary Era," 76 *Mich. L. Rev.* 1, 8-9 (1977): "[N]atural rights thinking might have led in either of two directions with regard to the law of inheritance. On the one hand, it could simply have

reinforced the right of inheritance and stood as an ultimate, constitutional guarantee against the legislative abolition of that right . . . On the other, the natural rights philosophy of the Declaration might have stimulated a radical egalitarianism . . . condemning the traditional law of inheritance . . ."

46. See C. Becker, supra note 29, at 249-55.

47. R. Cover, supra note 31, at 152.

48. See, e.g., C. S. Lewis, *The Abolition of Man* 51-61 (1947); Calder v. Bull, 3 Dall. 386, 388 (1798) (Chase, J.). Cf. *The Federalist* no. 31, at 236-37 (B. Wright ed. 1961) (Hamilton).

49. R. Unger, *Knowledge and Politics* 241 (1975).

50. See also E. Purcell, *The Crisis of Democratic Theory* 235 (1973); R. Dahl, *A Preface to Democratic Theory* 45 (1956); cf. C. Rossiter, supra note 29, at 437-38.

51. B. Wright, supra note 30, at 330-31.

52. But see Meachum v. Fano, 427 U.S. 215, 230 (1976) (Stevens, J., dissenting).

53. Cf. Ely, supra note 14, at 1243, 1246-47 n.130.

54. See, e.g., R. Dworkin, supra note 9, at 155-56; Smart, "An Outline of a System of Utilitarian Ethics," in J. Smart and B. Williams, *Utilitarianism: For and Against* 8 (1973); C. Fried, *An Anatomy of Values* 26-27 (1970); J. Rawls, *A Theory of Justice* 46-53 (1971); Thomson, "A Defense of Abortion," 1 *Phil. and Pub. Aff.* 47 (1971).

55. 73 *Harv. L. Rev.* 1 (1959).

56. See, e.g., Amsterdam, "Perspectives on the Fourth Amendment," 58 *Minn. L. Rev.* 349, 351-52 (1974). Cf. Holmes, "Codes and the Arrangement of the Law," 44 *Harv. L. Rev.* 725 (1931); Arnold, supra note 7, at 1311-12.

57. See, e.g., A. Cox, *The Role of the Supreme Court in American Government* 113 (1976): "My criticism of *Roe* v. *Wade* is that the Court failed to establish the legitimacy of the decision by not articulating a precept of sufficient abstractness to lift the ruling above the level of a political judgment based upon the evidence currently available from the medical, physical, and social sciences." The ensuing discussion makes clear that there is, as indeed there must be, a further source informing the content of the principle proclaimed, in Cox's case that it be capable of developing "roots throughout the community and continuity over significant periods of time." Id. at 114. But see pp. 63-69.

58. See also Bork, "Neutral Principles and Some First Amendment Problems," 47 *Ind. L. J.* 1, 7-8 (1971); Deutsch, "Neutrality, Legitimacy, and the Supreme Court: Some Intersections between Law and Political Science," 20 *Stan. L. Rev.* 169, 187-97 (1968); A. Bickel, supra note 1, at 55.

59. Compare, e.g., Nixon v. Administrator of General Services, 433 U.S. 425 (1977), with United States v. Brown, 381 U.S. 437 (1965).

60. See also Wright, supra note 6, at 776-77; Note, "Civil Disabilities and the First Amendment," 78 *Yale L. J.* 842, 851 n.39 (1969).

61. Wellington, "Common Law Rules and Constitutional Double Standards: Some Notes on Adjudication," 83 *Yale L. J.* 221, 246-47 (1973).

62. A. Bickel, supra note 24, at 87.

63. A. Bickel, supra note 1, at 25-26. See also, e.g., Wellington, supra note 61, at 246: "This task may be called the *method of philosophy.*"

64. Id. at 249.

65. A. Bickel, supra note 1, at 267. Cf. Purcell, "Alexander M. Bickel and the Post-Realist Constitution," 11 *Harv. C.R.-C.L. L. Rev.* 521, 554 (1976): "In *The Least Dangerous Branch*, Bickel had seen the courts as the special voice of reason, uniquely suited to elaborate proper principles; the political process had appeared erratic and given to excess. When principles became 'ideological' in the late sixties and Bickel's primary goal shifted from achieving moral reform to ensuring social tranquility, the judgment had to be reversed. The judiciary became erratic, the political system rational."

66. McCleskey, supra note 9, at 360. Indeed, a case can be made that the closer the Court has come to overt fundamental-values reasoning the less impressively it has performed. See, e.g., pp. 50-51; Scott v. Sandford, 19 How. 393 (1857); Lochner v. New York, 198 U.S. 45 (1905); Roe v. Wade, 410 U.S. 113 (1973). Reasons for expecting improvement are not apparent.

67. Arnold, supra note 7, at 1311.

68. J. Rawls, supra note 54; R. Nozick, *Anarchy, State, and Utopia* (1974).

69. Dworkin, "The Jurisprudence of Richard Nixon," *New York Rev. Books*, May 4, 1972, at 27, 35 (1972), reprinted in R. Dworkin, supra note 9, at 149.

70. See B. Ackerman, *Private Property and the Constitution* 284 n.47 (1977).

71. See Tushnet, " '. . . And Only Wealth Will Buy You Justice'— Some Notes on the Supreme Court. 1972 Term," 1974 *Wisc. L. Rev.* 177, 181: "The women's movement is commonly considered a middle class movement . . . [T]he reality is unimportant. What counts is how people like the Justices see things, and given the media's presentation of the women's movement, it should not be surprising if they saw it as something that particularly concerned their wives and friends." It does not seem entirely coincidental that it was the 95th Congress that extended the time for ratifying the Equal Rights Amendment. See generally Kaiser and Rus-

sell, "A Middle Class Congress—Haves over Have-Nots," *Washington Post*, Oct. 15, 1978, at 1, col. 3. See also Chapman, "The Rich Get Rich, and the Poor Get Lawyers," *New Republic*, Sept. 24, 1977, at 9 (one of the few goods society provides in kind to the poor is lawyers, since the lawyers who run the show have decided lawyers are a truly important good).

72. E.g., San Antonio Indep. School Dist. v. Rodriguez, 411 U.S. 1, 37 (1973); id. at 115 n.74 (Marshall, J., dissenting). But cf. Dandridge v. Williams, 397 U.S. 471, 508 (1970) (Marshall, J., dissenting). Cf. Fiss, "Groups and the Equal Protection Clause," 5 *Phil. and Pub. Aff.* 107, 144 (1976); Tushnet, supra note 71, at 190.

73. McCloskey, "Economic Due Process and the Supreme Court: An Exhumation and Reburial," 1962 *Sup. Ct. Rev.* 34, 46.

74. Hart, supra note 21, at 101. See also, e.g., Tushnet, "The Newer Property: Suggestion for the Revival of Substantive Due Process," 1975 *Sup. Ct. Rev.* 261, 279: "[A] substantive due process right should be established only to the extent supported by the settled weight of responsible opinion. The Court should look to sources like the American Law Institute . . ."

75. R. Dahl, supra note 13, at 24.

76. G. Wills, supra note 33, at xiii (paraphrasing Willmoore Kendall).

77. See, e.g., Moore v. City of East Cleveland, 431 U.S. 494, 503 (1977) (Powell, J., for plurality); Duncan v. Louisiana, 391 U.S. 145, 176-77 (1968) (Harlan, J., dissenting); cf. A. Bickel, supra note 1, at 236.

78. See generally Kadish, "Methodology and Criteria in Due Process Adjudication—A Survey and Criticism," 66 *Yale L. J.* 319, 327-33 (1957). See also Moore v. City of East Cleveland, 431 U.S. 494, 549-50 (1977) (White, J., dissenting).

79. E.g., Wolf v. Colorado, 338 U.S. 25, 28-30 (1949). But cf. United States ex rel. Toth v. Quarles, 350 U.S. 11, 29-31 n.11 (1955) (Reed, J., not joined by Frankfurter, J., dissenting).

80. Thus, for example, in Betts v. Brady, 316 U.S. 455 (1942), the majority and dissenting opinions reached diametrically opposed conclusions on whether American traditions required the appointment of counsel for those who could not afford it.

81. 438 U.S. 265 (1978).

82. But cf. Ely, "Foreword: On Discovering Fundamental Values," 92 *Harv. L. Rev.* 5, 9-10 n.33 (1978).

83. 438 U.S. at 291 (Powell, J.). See also id. at 290 (quoting Hirabayashi v. United States, 320 U.S. 81, 100 (1943)): "Distinctions between citizens solely because of their ancestry are by their very nature odious to a free people . . ."; 438 U.S. at 361 (Brennan, White, Marshall and Black-

mun, JJ., concurring in the judgment in part and dissenting in part): "[T]his principle is . . . deeply rooted . . ." This reference was virtually unavoidable, since the conclusion is one that cannot be sustained in *Carolene Products* terms, see Chapter 6, and no other source of values seems of even colorable assistance. There is not, for example, anything even approaching a consensus among contemporary philosophers or laypersons to the effect that affirmative action programs are morally wrong.

84. Almost perversely, the featured exhibits are Hirabayashi v. United States, 320 U.S. 81 (1943), and Korematsu v. United States, 323 U.S. 214 (1944). 438 U.S. at 287-91 (Powell, J.).

85. Justice Powell rightly taxes Justice Stevens's opinion for just this sort of quoting out of context in connection with Title VI of the Civil Rights Act of 1964, 42 U.S.C. §§2000d to 2000d-4 (1976): "Although isolated statements of various legislators, taken out of context, can be marshaled in support of the proposition that §601 enacted a purely colorblind scheme, . . . these comments must be read against the background of . . . the problem that Congress was addressing." 438 U.S. at 284-85.

86. Cf., e.g., L. Tribe, supra note 3, at 944-46: "[I]t makes all the difference in the world what level of generality one employs to test the pedigree of an asserted liberty claim. Plainly, the history of homosexuality has been largely a history of disapproval and disgrace . . . It is crucial, in asking whether an alleged right forms part of a traditional liberty, to define the liberty at a high enough level of generality to permit unconventional variants to claim protection along with mainstream versions of protected conduct. The proper question, then, is whether the intimacy of private sexual acts reflects a traditionally revered liberty . . . [O]nce that tradition is recognized as the point of reference, it provides an umbrella capacious enough to subsume homosexual as well as heterosexual variants."

87. See also Christie, "A Model of Judicial Review of Legislation," 48 *S. Cal. L. Rev.* 1306, 1320 (1975).

88. Ch. 200, 14 Stat. 173; see 438 U.S. at 397-98 (Marshall, J.). Justice Marshall's description may not adequately stress the fact that many of the Act's benefits were quite explicitly reserved for "colored" persons or those of "African" descent. See provisions quoted in Brief of the NAACP Legal Defense and Educational Fund, Inc., as Amicus Curiae at 11-12. See also, e.g., id. at 45-48 (describing Colored Servicemen's Claim Act of 1867, J. Res. 30, 15 Stat. 26). There was, I am sure, nothing resembling affirmative action for racial minorities before the Civil War, but it would take a rare courage to draw on the racial traditions of that period as a relevant source of principle.

89. See Chapter 6.

90. In fact the framers quite wisely seldom chose to freeze their value

judgments in the Constitution, concentrating instead on the processes by which such judgments are to be made. See Chapter 4.

91. "The Supreme Court, 1976 Term," 91 *Harv. L. Rev.* 70, 136 (1977).

92. E.g., Duncan v. Louisiana, 391 U.S. 145, 176-77 (1968) (Harlan, J., dissenting); Poe v. Ullman, 367 U.S. 497, 542 (1961) (Harlan, J., dissenting); A. Bickel, supra note 1, at 236; F. Hayek, *The Constitution of Liberty* 106-07 (1960).

93. Young v. American Mini Theatres, 427 U.S. 50, 70 (1976) (Stevens, J., for plurality).

94. Sandalow, supra note 4, at 1193.

95. E.g., A. Bickel, supra note 1, at 43, 238; Grey, "Do We Have an Unwritten Constitution?" 27 *Stan. L. Rev.* 703, 709 (1975); Karst and Horowitz, supra note 26, at 57-58; Michelman, "In Pursuit of Constitutional Welfare Rights: One View of Rawls' Theory of Justice," 121 *U. Pa. L. Rev.* 962, 1001-18 (1973); Tribe, "Structural Due Process," 10 *Harv. C.R.-C.L. L. Rev.* 269, 304, 311-12 (1975). Compare R. Dworkin, supra note 9, at 126, with id. at 185. Cf. M. Walzer, *Just and Unjust Wars: A Moral Argument with Historical Illustrations* 107 (1977).

96. See also, e.g., A. Cox, supra note 57, at 113-14, 117; Deutsch, supra note 58, at 196-97; Greenawalt, "The Enduring Significance of Neutral Principles," 78 *Colum. L. Rev.* 982, 1015-16 (1978).

97. Wellington, supra note 61, at 284. See also, e.g., Perry, supra note 9, at 421 (emphasis added): "[T]o say that the right of privacy protects a woman's decision to have an abortion is *necessarily* to say that the objective of prohibiting such decisions lacks support in conventional morality."

98. Wellington, supra note 61, at 299. He also claims his approach is "one derived from the nature of American democracy." Id. at 285.

99. F. Hayek, supra note 92, at 181.

100. Levinson, "The Specious Morality of the Law," *Harper's*, May 1977, at 35, 40. See also 3 J. Story, *Commentaries on the Constitution of the United States* §1289, at 167-68 n.2 (1833): "It is one thing to believe a doctrine universally admitted, because we ourselves think it clear; and quite another thing to establish the fact . . . If public opinion is to decide constitutional questions, instead of the public functionaries of the government in their deliberate discussions and judgments, (a course quite novel in the annals of jurisprudence,) it would be desirable to have some mode of ascertaining it in a satisfactory, and conclusive form; and some uniform test of it, independent of mere private conjectures. No such mode has, as yet, been provided in the constitution. And, perhaps, it will be found upon due inquiry, that different opinions prevail at the same time on the same subject, in the North, the South, the East, and the West . . . Human na-

ture never yet presented the extraordinary spectacle of all minds, agreeing in all things; nay not in all truths, moral, political, civil, or religious."

101. Jaffe, "Was Brandeis an Activist? The Search for Intermediate Premises," 80 *Harv. L. Rev.* 986, 994 (1967). But cf. id. at 998. See also Braden, supra note 9, at 584-85.

102. R. Unger, supra note 49, at 78.

103. Breithaupt v. Abram, 352 U.S. 432, 436 (1957). But cf. Schmerber v. California, 384 U.S. 767 (1966), taking what seems a more sensible approach to such issues. (If the seizure in question is lawful under the Fourth Amendment, the fact that official force was used to overcome forceful resistance should be irrelevant.)

104. Furman v. Georgia, 408 U.S. 238, 299-300 (1972) (Brennan, J., concurring); id. at 360-69 (Marshall, J., concurring).

105. See Roberts v. Louisiana, 428 U.S. 325, 353-55 (1976) (White, J., dissenting). Compare Wright, "The Role of the Judiciary: From *Marbury* to *Anderson*," 60 *Calif. L. Rev.* 1262, 1273 (1972), in which the state Chief Justice, defending judicial review against the charge that it is anti-democratic, cited his court's invalidation of the death penalty as one properly rooted in contemporary community standards, with *Cal. Const.* art. I, §27, subsequently overruling the court. On the constitutionality of capital punishment, see also Chapter 6.

106. A. Bickel, supra note 1, at 237-38.

107. See G. Allport, *The Nature of Prejudice* 76 (1954).

108. Cf. Purcell, supra note 65, at 539: "[I]n spite of his relativistic conception of value, Bickel could not resist placing the ideal of racial equality on an absolute basis. He . . . insisted that *Plessy* had been morally wrong. But on his own pragmatic criteria, one could readily argue that *Plessy* had been morally proper. In reason, *Plessy* met the conventional wisdom standard: it had been based presumably on the shared moral values of a large majority; it had won the approval both of its time and of a half-century of the future. One could also readily argue that the separate but equal doctrine was itself a neutral principle."

109. See, e.g., C. Curtis, *Lions Under the Throne* 332 (1947); R. Hofstadter, *Social Darwinism in American Thought* ch. 2 (rev. ed. 1955). Cf. R. Billington, *American History after 1865*, at 86-98, 161-78 (1950); G. Kolko, *The Triumph of Conservatism* (1963).

110. Wellington, supra note 61, at 285. See also Perry, "The Abortion Funding Cases: A Comment on the Supreme Court's Role in American Government," 66 *Geo. L. J.* 1191, 1217 (1978); A. Cox, supra note 57, at 88.

111. Wellington, supra note 61, at 311. The only footnotes omitted are citations to the American Law Institute sections mentioned. Professor

Perry has a different technique: in support of the claim that one or another proposition does or does not reflect conventional morality he is inclined to cite Supreme Court decisions. E.g., Perry, supra note 9, at 432 and n.95.

112. Even Professor Perry parts company with Wellington here. See Perry, "Abortion, the Public Morals, and the Police Power: The Ethical Function of Substantive Due Process," 23 *U.C.L.A. L. Rev.* 689, 733-34 (1976). Compare also Wellington, supra note 61, at 292-97, with Gerety, "Redefining Privacy," 12 *Harv. C.R.-C.L. L. Rev.* 233, 279-80 (1977).

Wellington describes his technique as one of "noticing commonly held attitudes and reasoning from them." Wellington, supra, at 310. However, the best evidence of commonly held attitudes (as they bear on this issue) that we have—aside, of course, from the legislation Wellington would test by his technique—seems to undercut him. According to the most recent Gallup poll on the subject, a majority of the American people do indeed favor legalized abortion during the first trimester in cases of pregnancy caused by rape and threat to the mother's life (though a majority oppose such a right during the second and third trimesters in the rape situation). However, a majority, albeit a more modest one, also favors legalized abortion in the first trimester in the situation Wellington distinguishes as insufficiently supported in conventional morality, one where the mother's physical health is in danger. (Legal abortion during the first trimester in cases of threat to the mother's *mental* health garners only 42 percent support.) The fact that overall there is more popular support for the right to an abortion in cases where the mother's physical health is endangered (by trimester: 54 percent, 46 percent, 34 percent) than there is for such a right in cases of pregnancy caused by rape (65 percent, 38 percent, 24 percent) probably does not prove much, since the low percentages in the second and third trimesters in the rape case may stem from a feeling the abortion should have been performed earlier. But no such explanation can cope with the fact that for every trimester there is more popular support for legal abortion cases of threat to the mother's physical health (54 percent, 46 percent, 34 percent) than there is for such a right in cases where "there is a chance the baby will be deformed" (45 percent, 39 percent, 24 percent). See Gallup Opinion Index, Report no. 153 (April 1978). Indeed, you can see there is not even a majority supporting the right in any trimester in the deformity case. What Wellington has given us, therefore, is an assurance that "commonly held attitudes" support (to the point of justifying the constitutional invalidation of legislation) a right that in fact a majority has been measured as opposing, along with a report that such attitudes fail to support a right a majority has in fact been measured as favoring. Obviously I do not suggest that these poll results should be used to "correct" Wellington's assurances before we impose them as constitutional law: that is not the way we make law in a representative democracy. I invoke them only to buttress the conclusion that when judges get the notion that they have a better handle on "commonly held attitudes" than their elected representatives, they are almost certainly deluding themselves. Wellington's an awfully smart fellow, and when his readings of commonly held attitudes turn out to be questionable, there's a message for his method.

113. E.g., Perry, supra note 110, at 1234.

114. E.g., Perry, supra note 9, at 447 n.189.

115. See note 9 supra.

116. See id. I shall argue in Chapters 4 and 5 that this is an important component of the Court's proper function.

117. Choper, supra note 15, at 830-32.

118. There may of course exist situations in which a majority cannot pass a law repealing old legislation because of minority resistance. But surely antiquity alone does not suggest the existence of a disapproving majority, and the point persists that courts are not well situated to judge such allegations. Furthermore, the requirement is theoretically one of a consensus against, not simply a bare majority. If that exists, the statute likely will be repealable, since unlike constitutional provisions, statutes typically can be removed by majority vote. Griswold v. Connecticut, 381 U.S. 479 (1965), is probably the case people would be most likely to cite in an antiquity-signals-contrary-consensus connection, cf. A. Bickel, supra note 1, at 148-56, yet in fact frequent attempts to repeal the Connecticut birth control statute had been made and had failed.

119. There is a possible variation on the consensus theme that seems at least initially attractive. The idea would be to impose a Rawlsian "veil of ignorance" and ask whether people would still favor the legislation in issue if they didn't know what position they held in society. Cf. R. Dworkin, supra note 9, at 181: "The original position is well designed to enforce the abstract right to equal concern and respect . . ." (Justice Marshall's concurrence in Furman v. Georgia, 408 U.S. 238, 314 (1972), seems a plausible candidate for rephrasing in these terms.) Typically, however, it is entirely consistent with democratic theory that people know who they are when they vote. The trick is to sort out the occasions when, in a sense, it isn't, the occasions on which their perspectives will influence the classifications drawn in ways we would agree are illegitimate. See generally Chapter 6.

120. E.g., Wellington, supra note 61; R. Dworkin, supra note 9, at 123-30.

121. Recall, and often the same commentator will invoke both images, that we are speaking here of the selfsame Court that has the "isolation" to pursue "the method of moral philosophy." There is a further irony in the literature under consideration here. Frequently the same people,

and I have in mind here particularly Professor Bickel, who saw the Court's role largely as one of responding to a consensus inaccurately reflected by the legislature were highly critical of the Warren Court's efforts to render legislatures more responsive.

122. See, e.g., H. Mayo, supra note 27, at 96-97.

123. A. Bullock, *Hitler, A Study in Tyranny* 367 (1952). I cannot tell you how much willpower it took to resist making this the subsection's opening epigraph.

124. H. Mayo, supra note 27, at 217. See also id. at 97: "Lenin used to claim this god-like gift of divination of the people's 'real' interests . . ."

125. See also Young v. American Mini Theatres, 427 U.S. 50, 86 (1976) (Stewart, J., dissenting); Tribe, supra note 95, at 294 n.77. But cf. id. at 304, 311-12. Professor Dworkin also notes this fleetingly, R. Dworkin, supra note 9, at 142, but he too is unprepared to follow through on its implications.

126. A. Bickel, supra note 24.

127. E.g., Chayes, "The Role of the Judge in Public Law Litigation," 89 *Harv. L. Rev.* 1281, 1316 (1976). The call for "durable" decisions has long signaled much the same sort of criterion. See sources cited in Ely, "The Wages of Crying Wolf: A Comment on *Roe v. Wade,*" 82 *Yale L. J.* 920, 946 n.133 (1973).

128. Compare A. Bickel, supra note 24, at 116-38, with Wright, supra note 6, at 797-803.

129. See also Kennedy, "Legal Formality," 2 *J. Leg. Stud.* 351, 385 (1973); Jaffe, supra note 101, at 994-95. Cf. Karst and Horowitz, supra note 26, at 79.

130. A. Bickel, supra note 1, at 55.

131. E.g., A. Bickel, supra note 24, at 177; A. Bickel, *The Morality of Consent* 3-5 (1975).

132. E.g., A. Bickel, supra note 1, at 239.

133. A. Bickel, supra note 131. Cf. A. Bickel, supra note 1, at 239-40; A. Bickel, supra note 24, at 87.

134. But cf. Bork, supra note 58.

4. Policing the Process of Representation: The Court as Referee

1. See, e.g., L. Tribe, *American Constitutional Law* 452 (1978); Berger, "Government by Judiciary: John Hart Ely's 'Invitation,' " 54 *Ind. L. J.* 277, 287, 311-12 (1979); Wellington, "Common Law Rules and Constitutional Double Standards: Some Notes on Adjudication," 83 *Yale L. J.* 221, 305 n.280 (1973).

2. "Naming" Courts after their Chief Justices is often misleading,

and it can be so in this case. As regards the theme under discussion here, however, which I think history will record as the dominant one, it does not seem amiss. As is understandable from his earlier career, Earl Warren was a thoroughgoing democrat, who saw his role as a justice as one of ensuring that the "ins" did not freeze others out of either the processes or the bounty of representative government. See also Ely, "The Chief," 88 *Harv. L. Rev.* 11 (1974).

3. See, e.g., Loving v. Virginia, 388 U.S. 1, 12 (1967) (unnecessary addendum on "fundamental freedom" of marriage in case involving racial classification).

4. The Warren Court holding that seems the most apt prime candidate for a "fundamental values" characterization is Griswold v. Connecticut, 381 U.S. 479 (1965). On examination, however, it reveals strong interpretivist urges, struggling to relate its holding to the First, Third, Fourth, and Fifth Amendments, id. at 484, making a special effort to connect up the Fourth by speculating on the methods by which the police would likely have to enforce the law in issue. Id. at 485-86. This is quite different from the "method" employed by the Burger Court in Roe v. Wade, 410 U.S. 113 (1973). See Ely, "The Wages of Crying Wolf: A Comment on *Roe v. Wade*," 82 *Yale L. J.* 920, 928-30 (1973). Of course the Warren Court, like every other, engaged in a good bit of "interpretivist" application of the Constitution's more directive provisions. That is as it should be: the objection to interpretivism is that it is incomplete, that there are clauses it cannot rationalize. See also United States v. Carolene Products Co., 304 U.S. 144, 152-53 n.4 (1938), quoted pp. 75-76. The contrast in styles to which I refer concerns the theories by which various courts and commentators give content to the Constitution's more indeterminate phrases. On the Burger Court generally, see note 52 to Chapter 6.

5. E.g., Dahl, "Decision-Making in a Democracy: The Supreme Court as a National Policy-Maker," 6 *J. Pub. L.* 279, 283 (1957); Rossum, "Representation and Republican Government: Contemporary Court Variations on the Founders' Theme," 23 *Am. J. Jurisprudence* 88, 91 (1978).

6. The most sensitive commentator here has been Paul Freund. See Freund, "The Judicial Process in Civil Liberties Cases," 1975 *U. Ill. L. F.* 493; P. Freund, A. Sutherland, M. Howe, and E. Brown, *Constitutional Law* at xlix (4th ed. 1977). Compare R. Dahl, *A Preface To Democratic Theory* 58-59 (1956) with R. Dahl, *Democracy in the United States* 234-36 (3d ed. 1976).

7. 304 U.S. 144, 152-53 n.4 (1938) (citations omitted).

8. Reference to the "specific prohibitions" of the "first ten" amendments must have been inadvertent.

9. E.g., Braden, "The Search for Objectivity in Constitutional

Law," 57 *Yale L. J.* 571, 580 n.28 (1948).

10. L. Lusky, *By What Right?* 110-11 (1975).

11. The footnote purports to catalogue the occasions on which intensive judicial scrutiny is appropriate. It would therefore be incomplete without paragraph one.

12. E.g., *Webster's New World Dictionary of the American Language* 375 (2d college ed. 1976). See generally Choper, "The Supreme Court and the Political Branches: Democratic Theory and Practice," 122 *U. Pa. L. Rev.* 810, 812 (1974).

13. Freund, supra note 6, at 494.

14. Steele v. Louisville & Nashville R. Co., 323 U.S. 192, 202 (1944).

15. See, e.g., G. Wood, *The Creation of the American Republic, 1776-1787*, at 18, 57-63, 447 (1969); Buel, "Democracy and the American Revolution: A Frame of Reference," 21 *Wm and M. Q.* 165, 168-76 (1964). Cf. Nelson, "Changing Conceptions of Judicial Review: The Evolution of Constitutional Theory in the States, 1790-1860," 120 *U. Pa. L. Rev.* 1166, 1172, 1177 (1972).

16. See, e.g., *The Federalist* no. 57, at 385 (B. Wright ed. 1961) (Madison); G. Wood, supra note 15, at 25, 28, 56, 231, 379; *Va. Bill of Rights of 1776*, §5: "That the Legislative and Executive powers of the state should be separate and distinct from the judiciary; and that the members of the two first may be restrained from oppression, by feeling and participating [in] the burthens of the people, they should, at fixed periods, be reduced to a private station, return into that body from which they were originally taken . . ."

17. Buel, supra note 15, at 184.

18. See *The Federalist* no. 57, at 383-85 (B. Wright ed. 1961) (Madison); Buel, supra note 15, at 183-85; G. Wood, supra note 15, at 447.

19. But cf. Rossum, supra note 5, at 91.

20. See *The Federalist* no. 39, at 280-81 (B. Wright ed. 1961) (Madison). Cf. *Aristotle's Politics* 139 (Modern Library ed. 1943); J. Pole, *The Pursuit of Equality in American History* 36 (1978). See also L. Lusky, supra note 10, at 109, suggesting connection between this theme and the final paragraph of the *Carolene Products* footnote.

21. See also, e.g., 2 Del. Laws, ch. 53 (S. and J. Adams 1797); 1 N.C. Public Acts, ch. 22 (J. Iredell ed., F.X. Martin rev. 1804); J. Pole, supra note 20, chs. 2 and 3; G. Wood, supra note 15, at vii, 70; Katz, "Republicanism and the Law of Inheritance in the American Revolutionary Era," 76 *Mich. L. Rev.* 1, 14-15 (1977).

22. See Katz, "Thomas Jefferson and the Right to Property in Revolutionary America," 19 *J. L. and Econ.* 467, 481-82 (1976); sources cited note 15 supra.

23. See generally J. Pole, supra note 20, at 117-29. Compare Katz, supra note 21, with Katz, supra note 22.

24. See *The Federalist* no. 10 (Madison). See also Kenyon, "Constitutionalism in Revolutionary America," in *Nomos XX: Constitutionalism* 84, 89 (J. Pennock and J. Chapman eds. 1979); G. Wood, supra note 15, at 410-11, 606-07; Katz, supra note 22, at 486-87. Cf. Kenyon, "Men of Little Faith: The Anti-Federalists on the Nature of Representative Government," 12 *Wm and M. Q.* 3 (1955).

25. See generally A. Lovejoy, *Reflections on Human Nature* 37-65 (1961); H. Arendt, *On Revolution* 148-51 (1963); G. Wood, supra note 15, at 430-67; Adair, " 'That Politics May Be Reduced to a Science': David Hume, James Madison, and the Tenth *Federalist*," 20 *Huntington Lib. Q.* 343 (1957); Diamond, "Democracy and *The Federalist:* A Reconsideration of the Framers' Intent," 53 *Am. Pol. Sci. Rev.* 52 (1959).

26. *The Federalist* no. 51, at 357-58 (B. Wright ed. 1961) (Madison).

27. R. Dahl, *A Preface to Democratic Theory* (1956).

28. *The Federalist* no. 10, at 133-36 (B. Wright ed. 1961) (Madison). See also Morgan, "The American Revolution Considered as an Intellectual Movement," in *Paths of American Thought* 11 (A. Schlesinger, Jr. and M. White eds. 1963).

29. See United States v. Brown, 381 U.S. 437, 443 (1965). See also *The Federalist* nos. 47, 48 and 51 (Madison).

30. See generally Nelson, supra note 15.

31. Ervine's Appeal, 16 Pa. 256, 268 (1851). (The court's answer to its own question was that refuge should be found "in the courts.") See also De Chastellux v. Fairchild, 15 Pa. 18, 20 (1850); pp. 85-87.

32. See W. Brock, *Conflict and Transformation* 159-60 (1973).

33. The "Roman law dictum, adopted by Bracton, that the law to bind all should be approved by all," J. Pole, *Political Representation in England and the Origins of the American Republic* 4 (1966), is obviously inapplicable in contemporary America for practical (as well, I should think, as theoretical) reasons, but those bound must nonetheless be represented in the sense that their interests are not to be left out of account or valued negatively in the lawmaking process.

34. R. Dworkin, *Taking Rights Seriously* 180 (1977). See also J. Pole, supra note 20, at 5; R. Dahl, *Democracy in the United States* 14 (3d ed. 1976).

35. See also Nelson, supra note 15, at 1180-85.

36. C. Becker, *The Declaration of Independence* 88-89 (1958). See also B. Bailyn, *The Ideological Origins of the American Revolution* 166-67 (1967).

37. Toomer v. Witsell, 334 U.S. 385, 395 (1948).

38. See Brown v. Maryland, 12 Wheat. 419 (1827).

39. See also McGoldrick v. Berwind-White Coal Mining Co., 309 U.S. 33, 45-46 n.2 (1940); Raymond Motor Transp., Inc. v. Rice, 434 U.S. 429, 444 n.18 (1978).

40. Compare South Carolina State Highway Dept. v. Barnwell Brothers, Inc., 303 U.S. 177, 184-85 n.2 (1938), with United States v. Carolene Products Co., 304 U.S. 144, 152-53 n.4 (1938).

41. A. Bickel, *The Supreme Court and the Idea of Progress* 37 (1970).

42. 4 Wheat. 316, 436 (1819).

43. See id. at 428: "In imposing a tax, the legislature acts upon its constituents. This is, in general, a sufficient security against erroneous and oppressive taxation." See also United States v. County of Fresno, 429 U.S. 452, 459-60 (1977).

44. The point of the *McCulloch* discussion seems to have been lost in National League of Cities v. Usery, 426 U.S. 833 (1976), which invalidated the extension of the Fair Labor Standards Act to state employees. Even accepting the Court's conclusion that the interests of the states qua states will not be sufficiently protected by their congressional delegations, id. at 841-42 n.12; but see Massachusetts v. United States, 435 U.S. 444, 456 (1978), it would remain true, as regards issues relating to how strenuous the demands of the Act are to be permitted to become, that the interests of states as employers would be well represented by senators and representatives responsive to the wishes of the myriad other enterprises, generally large and medium-sized corporations, covered. The FLSA did not single out state governmental entities for especially onerous regulation, and as thus configured there was no practical danger that it would politically be permitted to achieve a degree of onerousness that would seriously disable state government operations, let alone threaten the states' "separate and independent existence." 426 U.S. at 845.

45. *The Federalist* no. 57, at 385 (B. Wright ed. 1961).

46. D. Wright, "The Role of the Judiciary: From *Marbury* to *Anderson*," 60 *Calif. L. Rev.* 1262, 1268 (1972). See also, e.g., Sandalow, "Judicial Protection of Minorities," 75 *Mich. L. Rev.* 1162, 1178 (1977); J. S. Wright, "Professor Bickel, the Scholarly Tradition, and the Supreme Court," 84 *Harv. L. Rev.* 769, 784 (1971); Murphy, "Constitutional Interpretation: The Art of the Historian, Magician, or Statesman?" 87 *Yale L. J.* 1752, 1764 (1978).

47. I suppose one might argue that the reason so few values are singled out by the document for special substantive protection is that the various framers and ratifiers were assuming that that was a function the Supreme Court could be counted on to perform. This argument seems plainly

fallacious. Judicial review was not even a clearly contemplated feature of the original Constitution (though it is certainly a bona fide feature of today's). Neither could anyone acquainted with the data argue that prior to Reconstruction the Court had been in the business of value definition long or clearly enough to suppose that the framers of the Fourteenth Amendment were framing against the assumption that that was its job.

48. See generally Chapter 2. Respecting the general technique of bringing the document's broader themes to bear on the resolution of specific questions, I have been importantly influenced by C. Black, *Structure and Relationship in Constitutional Law* (1969).

49. Fuller, "American Legal Philosophy at Mid-Century," 6 *J. Leg. Educ.* 457, 463-64 (1954).

50. R. Palmer, *The Age of the Democratic Revolution*, vol. 1, *The Challenge* 190-93, 235 (1959); G. Wood, supra note 15, at 3. To the extent that the colonists believed there was a "conspiracy" on the part of British officials to subvert the British constitution both in England and America and thus to reduce existing liberties, that belief was coupled with a faith in the virtue of the American experiment, and thus importantly buttressed the "jurisdictional" argument for American independence. See generally B. Bailyn, supra note 36.

51. "By 1774 the colonists, like Jefferson, were contending that Parliament's acts over America were void not because they were unjust, as Otis had argued in the 1760's, but because 'the British parliament has no right to exercise authority over us.' " G. Wood, supra note 15, at 352.

52. See J. Pole, supra note 20, at 14-15, 22-24; E. Morgan, *The Birth of the Republic, 1763-1789*, at 73 (1956).

53. H. Arendt, supra note 25, at 147.

54. See Kenyon, "Republicanism and Radicalism in the American Revolution: An Old-Fashioned Interpretation," 19 *Wm and M. Q.* 153, 168-78 (1962); J. Pole, supra note 20, at 48, 53. But cf. G. Wills, *Inventing America* (1978).

55. See also Katz, "The Origins of American Constitutional Thought," in 3 *Perspectives in American History* 474 (D. Fleming and B. Bailyn eds. 1969); Nelson, "The Eighteenth-Century Background of John Marshall's Constitutional Jurisprudence," 76 *Mich. L. Rev.* 893 (1978).

56. See 3 M. Farrand, *The Records of the Federal Convention of 1787*, at 163 (1911) (James Wilson in Pennsylvania Convention).

57. Cf. *The Federalist* no. 85, at 542 (B. Wright ed. 1961) (Hamilton).

58. See Comment, "The Bounds of Legislative Specification: A Suggested Approach to the Bill of Attainder Clause," 72 *Yale L. J.* 330 (1962).

59. See generally Home Building and Loan Ass'n v. Blaisdell, 290

U.S. 398 (1934); "The Supreme Court, 1976 Term," 91 *Harv. L. Rev.* 70, 83-84 (1977).

60. See 1 W. Crosskey, *Politics and the Constitution* 352-60 (1953); Ogden v. Saunders, 12 Wheat. 213, 332 (1827) (Marshall, C.J., dissenting).

61. Ogden v. Saunders, 12 Wheat. 213 (1827).

62. United States Trust Co. v. New Jersey, 431 U.S. 1 (1977); Allied Structural Steel Co. v. Spannaus, 438 U.S. 234 (1978).

63. See generally City of El Paso v. Simmons, 379 U.S. 497 (1965).

64. Cf. Slawson, "Constitutional and Legislative Considerations in Retroactive Lawmaking," 48 *Calif. L. Rev.* 216, 217-18 (1960), distinguishing "method retroactivity" (the attaching of detrimental consequences to activities terminated prior to passage of the law) from "vested rights retroactivity" (the disturbing of existing patterns of conduct which involve some investment) and noting that the latter concept is illimitable.

65. E.g., Ely, "Toward a Representation-Reinforcing Mode of Judicial Review," 37 *Md. L. Rev.* 451, 474 (1978). Cf. id. at 480.

66. I hesitate to give up on this entirely, since it arises from an appropriately "constitutional" concern with the fractionalization of decision-making authority. Unless it can be responsibly qualified, however, it yields a sort of anarchy that is at entire odds with our constitutional order, and all I can see as plausible limiting strategies — aside, of course, from the all-too-popular strategy of invoking the idea when one likes the substantive outcome and either neglecting it or announcing that it "goes too far" when one doesn't — are strategies geared on the one hand to "traditionally recognized" alternative decision centers, and on the other to those alternative decision centers that are mentioned in the Constitution. Since the former is notoriously susceptible to manipulation and played straight would protect precisely those who least need protection, it seems clearly unacceptable. That leaves the option of protecting those alternative power centers mentioned in the Constitution — the church, the press, arguably contract and property (though on the face of the document the special constitutional protection of at least the latter is limited substantially.)

67. See also *U.S. Const.*, art. I, §9, cl. 6. This obviously benefited the commercial interests of the North, just as the protection of slavery benefited southern interests.

68. Technically this is a federalism provision, since the states were left free to prohibit the importation of slaves. Since the authority was so pointedly excluded from what would otherwise have been the sweep of federal power, however, it seems fair to read the clause as what history teaches it was, an attempt to forestall a certain substantive result, the abolition of slavery in the South. I'm not prepared to fight very strenuously for this

point, however, since disagreement here is only further agreement with my overall thesis.

69. See also R. Cover, *Justice Accused* 151-52 (1975); P. Paludan, *A Covenant with Death* 3-4 (1975); Regents of University of California v. Bakke, 438 U.S. 265, 387-90 (1978) (Marshall, J.).

70. *The Federalist* no. 84, at 534 (B. Wright ed. 1961) (Hamilton). See also, e.g., J. Pole, *Foundations of American Independence: 1763-1815*, at 196 (1972); J. Goebel, *Antecedents and Beginnings to 1801*, vol. I of *History of the Supreme Court of the United States* 249 (P. Freund ed. 1971).

71. *The Federalist* no. 84, at 536 (B. Wright ed. 1961) (Hamilton).

72. *The Federalist* no. 85, at 542 (B. Wright ed. 1961) (Hamilton). See also id. no. 9, at 125 (Hamilton).

73. See Palko v. Connecticut, 302 U.S. 319, 326-27 (1937); Kovacs v. Cooper, 336 U.S. 77, 95 (1949) (Frankfurter, J., concurring, characterizing views of Holmes, J.); Blasi, "The Checking Value in First Amendment Theory," 1977 *Am. Bar Found. Research J.* 521.

74. Cf. note 10 to Chapter 5.

75. See also *U.S. Const.*, art. VI, cl. 3 (prohibiting religious tests for public office).

76. A motion to qualify the right with the phrase "for the common defense" was voted down. J. Goebel, supra note 70, at 450. That could have been because it was thought to be superfluous, as indeed it does seem to be in light of the amendment's introductory phrase—which *was* in place at the time, id.—but it needn't have been. (The fact that in colonial times a "militia" comprised little more than a lot of "good old boys" with rifles hanging on their walls would seem to erode the distinction the received interpretation suggests between a private right and the right of a state organization. That problem is largely alleviated, however, by the amendment's use of the qualifying phrase "well regulated.")

77. But cf. *U.S. Const.*, art. I, §8, cl. 8 (copyright clause).

78. Of course things are seldom unifunctional, and noninstrumental significance can also be attributed to many of these provisions. See, e.g., Tribe, "Trial by Mathematics: Precision and Ritual in the Legal Process," 84 *Harv. L. Rev.* 1329, 1391-92 (1971). Such additional significance should probably figure in a determination of whether one or another of these provisions should be construed to cover a given borderline case. The exercise in which we are at present engaged, however, is one of seeking generally to characterize the nature of the document our forebears thought they were writing, an attempt that should lead us to concentrate on the central thrusts where they are identifiable.

79. See Rogers v. Richmond, 365 U.S. 534 (1961).

80. Cf. Ely, "The Irrepressible Myth of Erie," 87 *Harv. L. Rev.* 693, 726 (1974).

81. See id. at 724-26, 739-40.

82. In light of the recent, though mercifully declining, vogue for using "privacy" to include personal autonomy, it may be well explicitly to note that the sort of privacy the Fourth Amendment appears in part to have been designed to protect is privacy properly so called, the ability to keep private information one would rather not disseminate.

83. Katz v. United States, 389 U.S. 347, 350 (1967). See also Griswold v. Connecticut, 381 U.S. 479, 509 (1965) (Black, J., dissenting), quoted in Katz v. United States, 389 U.S. 347, 350 n.4 (1967).

84. See Weems v. United States, 217 U.S. 349, 371-73 (1910).

85. See also Chapter 6.

86. See p. 81.

87. L. Tribe, supra note 1, at 463.

88. Sax, "Takings and the Police Power," 74 *Yale L. J.* 36, 75-76 (1964). See also id. at 64-65; Sax, "Takings, Private Property and Public Rights," 81 *Yale L. J.* 149, 169-70 (1971); B. Ackerman, *Private Property and the Constitution* 52-53, 68, 79-80 (1977). I'm particularly grateful to Paul Mishkin for pointing out that my earlier reading of the clause, Ely, supra note 65, at 480, gave too much away.

89. The Ninth Amendment is one of the open-ended provisions for which we are seeking guides to construction, at present by exploring the nature of the rest of the document. The Tenth Amendment is a federalism provision, underscoring the reservation of nonenumerated powers to the states. The Eleventh and Twelfth Amendments both are concerned with the mechanics of government. Even a decision to extend sovereign immunity to the states would obviously have been generated by a concern for the machinery of government rather than by a substantive decision to place the costs on the injured party rather than spread them among the population. In any event the better view seems to be that the Eleventh Amendment was intended merely to make clear that Article III did not by itself grant federal courts jurisdiction in cases where states were defendants, not to bar Congress from creating such jurisdiction.

90. Sections 3 and 4 of the Fourteenth Amendment contain what can be regarded as backward-looking substantive provisions, "punishing" the South by forbidding any state to pay off a Confederate debt and by denying certain political rights to Confederate leaders unless exempted by a two-thirds vote of Congress.

91. *Judicial* attempts to cement fundamental values in the Constitution have for similar reasons met similar fates. That *Dred Scott v. Sandford* did not prove durable is the grisliest of understatements. Neither, though

not so dramatically, did *Lochner v. New York*, and even as I write, the Supreme Court is backing away, in a quite discriminatory way at that, from *Roe v. Wade*. See note 38 to Chapter 6.

92. Even if the Contracts Clause was never intended to protect future contracts, its application to existing contracts has for years been virtually nonexistent as well, though in the latter regard we may be witnessing the early stages of a renaissance.

93. See also Linde, "Due Process of Lawmaking," 55 *Neb. L. Rev.* 197, 255 (1975); Kommers, "Abortion and Constitution: United States and West Germany," 25 *Am. J. Comp. L.* 255, 280 (1977). Cf. G. Almond and S. Verba, *The Civic Culture* 102 (1963): In response to the question "What are the things about this country that you are most proud of," 85 percent of American respondents mentioned "governmental and political institutions"; the "economic system" finished second with 23 percent. In none of the four other democracies polled were "governmental and political institutions" mentioned by more than half the respondents.

94. I suppose if one were pressed to identify "the American ideology," laissez-faire capitalism would have to be a candidate. But cf. note 93 supra. As we have seen, this is a value today's fundamental-values theorists shrink from recognizing, lest, inter alia, *Lochner* should turn out to have been right.

95. Linde, supra note 93, at 254.

96. See, e.g., 2 A. Kahn, *The Economics of Regulation* 114-15 (1971).

97. (1) and (2) will be elucidated, respectively, in Chapters 5 and 6.

98. A. Bickel, *The Least Dangerous Branch* 24 (1962).

5. Clearing the Channels of Political Change

1. The overbreadth doctrine also has a "standing" component, giving persons to whom the statute in question could constitutionally be applied the ability to challenge it "on its face" and thus to raise the rights of other persons, to whom the statutory language also applies but respecting whom application would be unconstitutional.

2. Typically, for reasons of administrative convenience, legislation can constitutionally inhibit the activity of persons who do not individually pose the danger with which the government is concerned. Thus, for example, persons not trained as optometrists can be forbidden to replace eyeglass lenses, even though a number of such persons, individually tested, could fully demonstrate their ability to do so. See also Chapter 6. By precluding this kind of "administrative convenience" defense in the First Amendment area, the Court is obviously forbidding "overbroad" inhibi-

tion under yet another rubric.

3. 389 U.S. 258, 268 n.20 (1967).

4. See Note, "Less Drastic Means and the First Amendment," 78 *Yale L. J.* 464, 467-68 (1969). Cf. D. Braybrooke and C. Lindblom, *A Strategy of Decision* (1963). A holistic "balance" on the propriety of an entire statutory program is likely to be virtually unintelligible. The entirety of a statute is likely to be in First Amendment issue, however, only where it seeks to restrain expressive activity because of the feared effects of the expression covered. (Laws not directed at expression do inhibit expression on some occasions, and on those occasions their application may be unconstitutional, but a plausible First Amendment attack on every application of such a law is unlikely.) The unintelligibility of holistic balances thus constitutes another argument for an "unprotected messages" approach to cases where the evil the state seeks to prevent is one that arises from the content of the message inhibited.

5. Thus in *Robel* the Court invalidated a provision of the Communist Control Act making it a crime for any member of a Communist-action organization to "engage in any employment in any defense facility." The prohibition was overbroad, the Court held, since not all members of such organizations are dangerous, and barring them all is therefore unnecessary. The decision is correct, but not for the reason the passage quoted from the Chief Justice's opinion suggests, that extension of the prohibition to all members of such organizations is entirely gratuitous. If security were our only goal and First Amendment freedoms not implicated, we might quite reasonably choose to bar all members of such organizations. What the decision thus has to mean is that the inhibition of expression that results from extending the prohibition to all members outweighs the security need for that broad a ban. That evaluation has to become thus involved is made clear by the Court's further stress on the fact that not all jobs in defense facilities are sensitive. 389 U.S. at 265-67. The point, obviously, is that if what were involved were the job of guarding the President's hot line to the Strategic Air Command, the disqualification could extend to all members of Communist-action organizations and doubtless to many others among us as well.

6. Schenck v. United States, 249 U.S. 47, 52 (1919). See also Frohwerk v. United States, 249 U.S. 204 (1919); Debs v. United States, 249 U.S. 211 (1919).

7. Subsequent renditions made clear that the "substantive evil" threatened had to be at least moderately serious.

8. 341 U.S. 494, 510 (1951) (plurality opinion).

9. Black, "Mr. Justice Black, the Supreme Court, and the Bill of Rights," *Harper's Magazine* 63, Feb. 1961.

10. One might maintain that all "political" expression should be absolutely protected. (This is to be distinguished from the view that such expression is all that should be protected at all. See, e.g., Bork, "Neutral Principles and Some First Amendment Problems," 47 *Ind. L. J.* 1 (1971). That view seems unjustified in light of the unqualified nature of the constitutional language. Cf. 1 B. Schwartz, *The Bill of Rights: A Documentary History* 223 (1971) (letter of October 1774 from First Continental Congress to inhabitants of Quebec, mentioning "the advancement of truth, science, morality, and arts in general" as among values promoted by free press). Whether the Fourteenth Amendment should have been interpreted this broadly is of course a separate question.) It's not entirely clear why some First Amendment rights should be absolutely protected and others not, but in any event this view will run into the same problems. Aside from examples such as a politically inspired firebombing of an induction center — which in fact cannot intelligibly be excluded from the category of political expression, though of course it should not be protected, see p. 113n — one need only hypothesize an intentional and massive eleventh-hour libel of one's political opponent, or alter the example in the text to a speech inciting the storming of an inadequately guarded embassy.

11. Brandenburg v. Ohio, 395 U.S. 444, 456 (1969) (Douglas, J., concurring).

12. Cohen v. California, 403 U.S. 15, 27 (1971) (Blackmun, J., joined by Black, J., dissenting).

13. See also Wellington, "On Freedom of Expression," 88 *Yale L. J.* 1105, 1136-41 (1979).

14. What's more, the analysis will necessarily be largely ad hoc. In any First Amendment situation, for that matter in any situation involving our liberties, it is desirable for courts to try to develop predictable and discretion-reining rules. They should try to do so here. It will be difficult, though, since there are likely to be so many relevant gradations of context — a loud sound-truck is different from one that isn't so loud, a sound-truck at three in the morning is different from one at noon, a hospital zone is different from a park — that any "code of conduct" we will be able to devise, and I repeat we should try, is likely to approach one rule for each envisioned situation, and still be incomplete.

15. I originally presented this theory in Ely, "Flag Desecration: A Case Study in the Roles of Categorization and Balancing in First Amendment Analysis," 88 *Harv. L. Rev.* 1482 (1975). I was helped by Scanlon, "A Theory of Freedom of Expression," 1 *Phil. and Pub. Aff.* 204 (1972). See also L. Tribe, *American Constitutional Law* 580-88 (1978).

16. Restrictions on free expression are seldom defended on the ground that the state simply didn't like what the defendant was saying: ref-

erence will generally be made to some danger beyond the message, such as a danger of riot, unlawful action, or violent overthrow of the government. The constitutional reference must therefore be not to the ultimate interest to which the state points, for that will always be unrelated to expression, but rather to the causal connection the state asserts. If, for example, the state asserts an interest in discouraging riots, the Court should ask why that interest is implicated in the case at bar. If the answer is, as in such cases it will likely have to be, that the danger of riot was created by what the defendant was saying, the state's interest is not unrelated to the suppression of free expression, and the inhibition should be upheld only in the event the expression falls within one of the few unprotected categories. This is not a distinction the justices have always appreciated. See Feiner v. New York, 340 U.S. 315, 319-20 (1951): "Petitioner was thus neither arrested nor convicted for the making or the content of his speech. Rather, it was the reaction which it actually engendered"; Tinker v. Des Moines Indep. Community School District, 393 U.S. 503, 526 (1969) (Harlan, J., dissenting).

There may be a temptation to conclude that one has seen all this before, or at least its functional equivalent, in the shopworn distinction between "regulation of content" and "regulation of time, place, and manner." That would be a mistaken equation, however, one with serious costs for free expression. For the state obviously can move, and often does, "simply" to control the time, place, or manner of communication out of a concern for the likely effect of the message on its audience. Thus in *Tinker* the state regulated only the place and manner of expression — no armbands in school — but it did so, or at least this is the account most favorable to the school board, because it feared the way the other students would react to the message those armbands conveyed.

17. Cf. United States v. O'Brien, 391 U.S. 367, 388-89 (1968) (Harlan, J., concurring).

18. But see L. Hand, *The Bill of Rights* (1958).

19. Letter from Learned Hand to Zechariah Chafee, Jr., Jan. 2, 1921, quoted in Gunther, "Learned Hand and the Origins of Modern First Amendment Doctrine," 27 *Stan. L. Rev.* 719, 749-50 (1975). See generally id.; Masses Publishing Co. v. Patten, 244 Fed. 535 (1917); Linde, " 'Clear and Present Danger' Reexamined: Dissonance in the *Brandenburg* Concerto," 22 *Stan. L. Rev.* 1163, 1168-69 (1970).

20. 321 U.S. 158 (1944).

21. See Kovacs v. Cooper, 336 U.S. 77 (1949).

22. United States v. O'Brien, 391 U.S. 367, 377 (1968). But cf. Ely, supra note 15, at 1484-90.

23. 403 U.S. 15, 19-26 (1971).

24. The Court's test, quoted two sentences hence in the text, went on

(where I have put the elipsis) to require that the communication in fact be "likely to incite or produce" imminent lawless action. 395 U.S. 444, 447 (1969). The two elements are stated in the conjunctive; both are plainly required. (Thus the *Brandenburg* Court, having analyzed the speech and found its content not to fit within any unprotected category, did not go on to ask whether in context it was dangerous.) One could only applaud the additional safeguard of a "specific threat" requirement (on top of the requirement of an unprotected message), see Gunther, supra note 19, at 722, 754, were it not for the possibility that in a troubling case the conjunction will be forgotten, and perceived satisfaction of the "specific threat" requirement will be permitted to compensate for less than genuine satisfaction of the requirement of an unprotected message. See also Linde, supra note 19.

25. 395 U.S. at 447.

26. Any thought that the earlier cases could be distinguished as involving, as they did, somewhat different situations (Brandenburg was a Klansman giving a typical Klan speech) seems decisively to have been foreclosed not only by the Court's indication that the quoted principle covers all cases involving government attempts to proscribe advocacy of the use of force or violation of the law, but also by its reference to *Dennis* as one of the cases that had fashioned that principle. 395 U.S. at 447. Sure it was.

27. In Virginia State Board of Pharmacy v. Virginia Citizens Consumer Council, Inc., 425 U.S. 748 (1976), the Court held that advertisements are entitled to First Amendment protection. Eliminating what had previously been an unprotected category of expression, that seems on the surface a continuation of the trend I have been describing. The Court went on to suggest, however, that advertising may receive a "different degree of protection" from other protected speech. Id. at 771 and n.24. How that will be worked out is still not entirely clear, but it does suggest, contrary to the pattern the Warren Court had begun to establish, that speech that does not come within an unprotected category may nonetheless be proscribed because of fears of how people will react to it. (Of course, if "false advertising" were designated as the unprotected category, the framework could be maintained. This is a step people seem hesitant to take, however, apparently out of an epistemological "sophistication" that seems excessive.) To the same effect is Young v. American Mini Theatres, Inc., 427 U.S. 50 (1976), which involved a Detroit zoning ordinance restricting the location of theaters showing sexually explicit "adult" movies. The films involved were not alleged to be obscene, and the Court therefore assumed the case involved "communication protected by the First Amendment." Id. at 59, 62. Nonetheless it upheld the ordinance, asserting that "[e]ven within the area of protected speech, a difference in content may require a

different governmental response," id. at 66, and concluding that "there is surely a less vital interest in the uninhibited exhibition of material that is on the borderline between pornography and artistic expression than in the free dissemination of ideas of social and political significance." Id. at 61. That, of course, runs precisely counter to the point of an "unprotected messages" approach, which is that unless the expression in question falls into one of the unprotected categories, it is fully protected against content-directed regulation, irrespective of how it might measure up against other protected expression.

In Elrod v. Burns, 427 U.S. 347 (1976), and Buckley v. Valeo, 424 U.S. 1 (1976), both of which—unlike *Virginia State Board* and *Young*—involved clearly political expression, the Court gave evidence of appreciating something very like the distinction I have been making. In each it noted that the interest on which the state relied was one in "suppressing communication," 427 U.S. at 363-64 n.17 (plurality opinion); 424 U.S. at 17, and indicated that that fact triggered more stringent review. So far so good. However, the "more stringent" review in each case turned out to involve a balancing test—albeit an exacting one demanding a "compelling" state interest—not an approach that absolutely protects all expression that does not fall within some unprotected category. Where this balancing test is satisfied, the Court went on to state, the regulations will be sustained even though they constitute "encroachments of First Amendment protections." 427 U.S. at 360; 424 U.S. at 25, 66. It may be ungracious to complain when the Court has adopted a distinction very like one I had urged a year earlier, see Ely, supra note 15, but most of the point is lost when the distinction is used in conjunction with a markedly weakened substantive test. See also L. Tribe, supra note 15, at 656: "[I]t is one thing to make *eligibility* for first amendment protection turn on a different line, and quite another to use the same line for the far less momentous purpose of recognizing *shades of difference* in the application of settled principles."

28. See, e.g., Chaplinsky v. New Hampshire, 315 U.S. 568 (1942); Miller v. California, 413 U.S. 15 (1973).

29. G. Wood, *The Creation of the American Republic, 1776-1787*, at 23 (1969).

30. Assertions that the Supreme Court does not recognize a constitutional right to vote are common—see, e.g., Brest, "The Conscientious Legislator's Guide to Constitutional Interpretation," 27 *Stan. L. Rev.* 585, 595 (1975); cf. San Antonio Ind. School Dist. v. Rodriguez, 411 U.S. 1, 35 n.78 (1973)—but they are hard to make sense of. Typically, what we mean by labeling something a constitutional right is that the state cannot deny it to everyone and that when it denies it to some but not others it had better have a very good reason for doing so. That is precisely the status of the

right to vote in both federal and state elections, and it would thus seem that the Court more correctly understood the meaning of its decisions when it indicated in Reynolds v. Sims, 377 U.S. 533, 554 (1964), that "[u]ndeniably the Constitution of the United States protects the right of all qualified citizens to vote, in state as well as in federal elections."

31. But see *U.S. Const.* art. I, §2, cl. 1: "The House of Representatives shall be composed of Members chosen every second Year by the People of the several States . . ."; *U.S. Const.* amend. XVII: "The Senate of the United States shall be composed of two Senators from each State, elected by the people thereof . . ." The Twenty-fourth Amendment adverts to "[t]he right of citizens of the United States to vote . . . for President or Vice President [or] for electors for President or Vice President," but does so by way of outlawing the abridgment of such a right by reason of failure to pay a poll tax. Several amendments analogously provide that "the right of citizens to vote" (in either federal or state elections) shall not be abridged on various grounds.

32. Compare, e.g., Poe v. Ullman, 367 U.S. 497, 522 (1961) (Harlan, J., dissenting), with Carrington v. Rash, 380 U.S. 89, 97-99 (1965) (Harlan, J., dissenting). See also R. Berger, *Government by Judiciary* 392 (1977).

33. See, e.g., H. Mayo, *An Introduction to Democratic Theory* 120 (1960): "These and other instances which could be multiplied indefinitely show that groups holding political power have normally resisted extensions of the franchise . . ." For a case study, see J. Blum, *V Was for Victory* 250-51 (1976).

34. 395 U.S. 621, 627-28 (1969). See also Reynolds v. Sims, 377 U.S. 533, 555 (1964): "The right to vote freely for the candidate of one's choice is of the essence of a democratic society, and any restrictions on that right strike at the heart of representative government." An argument can be made that the results in these two cases would have been more convincingly supported had their rationales been exchanged. Cf. Lee, "Mr. Herbert Spencer and the Bachelor Stockbroker: *Kramer v. Union Free School District No. 15*," 15 *Ariz. L. Rev.* 457, 463 (1973).

35. See Reynolds v. Sims, 377 U.S. 533, 595-602 (1964) (Harlan, J., dissenting); Oregon v. Mitchell, 400 U.S. 112, 154-200 (1970) (Harlan, J., concurring in part and dissenting in part).

36. See generally Van Alstyne, "The Fourteenth Amendment, the 'Right' to Vote, and the Understanding of the Thirty-Ninth Congress," 1965 *Sup. Ct. Rev.* 33; Oregon v. Mitchell, 400 U.S. 112, 250-78 (1970) (opinion of Brennan, White, and Marshall, JJ.). Harlan's claim that §2, which provides for reduction of a state's basis of representation for certain denials of voting rights, was understood to preempt any possible applica-

tion of §1 to voting rights seems shaky in light of the separate development of the two sections and the statements of some proponents that no preemption of other remedies was intended. See also p. 119n. That essentially reduces Harlan's evidence to certain statements that §1 was not intended to cover voting, but such statements are few and far between, a fact that seems devastating in light of the facial breadth of the provision. Paradoxically, the strongest evidence on Harlan's side are statements of Congressman Bingham and Senator Howard. See 377 U.S. at 598-600. This is an arrangement we have seen before, in connection with the "incorporation" dispute. See Chapter 2. The reason it is paradoxical is that in this case, unlike the other, the statements of those two men are arrayable on the conservative or "strict construction" side. But see p. 119n. Commentaries that accept their rendition of the amendment here but reject it there — that accept Justice Harlan's argument on voting rights but reject Justice Black's similarly contoured argument on incorporation — do not pause to explain the methodological discrepancy. E.g., R. Berger, supra note 32. Here as there principal recourse should be to the language actually proposed and ratified.

37. The principal evidence for this limited claim, beside which all else pales to the point of not meriting mention, is the fact that the Fifteenth Amendment, ratified two years later, explicitly forbids states to deny the franchise on account of race. (On the other hand, the ratification of the Fifteenth Amendment so soon after the Fourteenth is one reason, though the reach of the constitutional language is the main one, that the lack of any specific expectation that the earlier provision would apply to voting should not mean it shouldn't be interpreted to do so. See pp. 119-20n.)

38. See Poe v. Ullman, 367 U.S. 497, 540 (1961) (Harlan, J., dissenting): "[T]he basis of judgment as to the Constitutionality of state action must be a rational one, approaching the text . . . not in a literalistic way, as if we had a tax statute before us, but as the basic charter of our society, setting out in spare but meaningful terms the principles of government." See also, e.g., Holmes v. City of Atlanta, 350 U.S. 879 (1955) (no racial segregation on public golf courses), and Mayor of Baltimore v. Dawson, 350 U.S. 877 (1955) (beaches), both joined by Justice Harlan.

39. See also R. Dworkin, *Taking Rights Seriously* 134-36 (1977).

40. 347 U.S. 483, 489 (1954). See also Bickel, "The Original Understanding and the Segregation Decision," 69 *Harv. L. Rev.* 1 (1955).

41. 380 U.S. 89 (1965).

42. 383 U.S. 663 (1966).

43. Indeed, one of Texas's justifications was not simply weak, it itself violated the Constitution — namely the argument that if military personnel were given the vote, they might start influencing elections. Throughout

most of our history, in most states, persons under age 21 were denied the franchise on the theory that those too young to understand the issues or their interests should grow up a little before they vote. Of course, 21 was an arbitrary cut-off, but not more arbitrary than any fixed age would have been. *No* fixed age, then? That seems much worse: any scheme that tried to test maturity of political outlook case by case would be of dubious constitutionality and in any event undesirable. It plainly shouldn't have required a constitutional amendment to extend the vote to women, and today it wouldn't, but in 1920 the Equal Protection Clause had scarcely been discovered, let alone applied to voting.

44. See also, e.g., Baker v. Carr, 369 U.S. 186, 259 (1962) (Clark, J., concurring); J. Locke, *Two Treatises on Government* 391 (2d ed., P. Laslett ed. 1967); R. Dahl, *Democracy in the United States* 195 (3d ed. 1976).

45. See, e.g., Auerbach, "The Reapportionment Cases: One Person, One Vote—One Vote, One Value," 1964 *Sup. Ct. Rev.* 1, 2: "No cases in modern times have more sharply provoked such disagreement [about the propriety of judicial review] than the congressional districting and state legislative reapportionment cases."

46. E.g., Colegrove v. Green, 328 U.S. 549, 556 (1946).

47. E.g., Baker v. Carr, 369 U.S. 186, 268 (1962) (Frankfurter, J., dissenting); Reynolds v. Sims, 377 U.S. 533, 621 (1964) (Harlan, J., dissenting).

48. 377 U.S. 533 (1964).

49. E.g., Baker v. Carr, 369 U.S. 186, 267 (1962) (Frankfurter, J., dissenting); id. at 340 (Harlan, J., dissenting).

50. C. Miller, *The Supreme Court and the Uses of History* 119 (1969): " 'One person, one vote,' the popular simplication of the Court's holding, has come to sound almost as indigenous as one of its ancestors, 'No taxation without representation.' " In part, of course, this is because of the influence Supreme Court pronouncements inevitably have on public opinion.

51. Jaffe, "Was Brandeis an Activist? The Search for Intermediate Premises," 80 *Harv. L. Rev.* 986, 991 (1967).

52. See, e.g., Tigner v. Texas, 310 U.S. 141 (1940). See generally Baker v. Carr, 369 U.S. 186, 336 (1962) (Harlan, J., dissenting).

53. Lucas v. Colorado Gen. Assembly, 377 U.S. 713, 753-54 (1964) (Stewart, J., dissenting).

54. See M. Shapiro, *Law and Politics in the Supreme Court* 219 (1964): "Government by the people therefore becomes, for nearly all democratic theorists, equal opportunity for every individual to participate in governing." See also, e.g., H. Mayo, supra note 33, at 62-64, 70, 126; Ranney and Kendall, "Democracy: Confusion and Agreement," 4 *West.*

Pol. Q. 430, 438-39 (1951); H. Dean, *Judicial Review and Democracy* 37-38 (1960). Cf. R. Dahl, supra note 44, at 13. Insofar as democracy is understood as a sort of applied utilitarianism, see note 14 to Chapter 1, this component — "each to count for one and none for more than one" — would seem to follow, though of course it has also been embraced by many who would not describe themselves as utilitarians.

55. See, e.g., G. Wood, supra note 29, at 170-71 (John Adams); J. Pole, *Foundations of American Independence: 1763-1815,* at 87 (1972) (Thomas Jefferson); J. Pole, *The Pursuit of Equality in American History* 124 (1978) (John Taylor of Caroline County); id. at 281 (James Wilson); 2 M. Farrand, *The Records of the Federal Convention of 1787,* at 241 (1911) (James Madison). But cf. J. Pole, *The Pursuit of Equality in American History* 282 (1978) (Madison). See also J. Locke, supra note 44, at 390-92; Baker v. Carr, 369 U.S. 186, 307 (1962) (Frankfurter, J., dissenting): "For the guiding political theorists of the Revolutionary generation, the English system of representation, in its most salient aspects of numerical inequality, was a model to be avoided, not followed"; Wesberry v. Sanders, 376 U.S. 1, 27 (1964) (Harlan, J., dissenting); A. Bickel, *The Least Dangerous Branch* 192 (1962). The original constitutions of thirty-six of the states provided that both houses of their legislatures were to be based completely or predominantly on population. Reynolds v. Sims, 377 U.S. 533, 573 (1964). See also G. Wood, supra, at 172. Despite all this, malapportionment was quite common throughout our later history prior to *Reynolds.*

56. See generally Bonfield, "The Guarantee Clause of Article IV, Section 4: A Study in Constitutional Desuetude," 46 *Minn. L. Rev.* 513, 520-26 (1962); W. Wiecek, *The Guarantee Clause of the U.S. Constitution* chs. 1 and 2 (1972).

57. In political debate, where the clause has been invoked throughout our history, the propriety of a line of growth has been quite consistently assumed. See generally id. See also *Memoir and Letters of Charles Sumner* vol. 4: 1860-1874, at 258-59 (E. Pierce ed. 1893): "Words receive expansion and elevation with time. Our fathers builded wiser than they knew. Did they simply mean a guarantee against a king? Something more, I believe, — all of which was not fully revealed to themselves, but which we must now declare in the light of our institutions."

58. See, e.g., Comment, *"Baker v. Carr* and Legislative Apportionments: A Problem of Standards," 72 *Yale L. J.* 968 (1963); Baker v. Carr, 369 U.S. 186, 323 (1962) (Frankfurter, J., dissenting); id. at 346-47 (Harlan, J., dissenting).

59. Deutsch, "Neutrality, Legitimacy, and the Supreme Court: Some Intersections between Law and Political Science," 20 *Stan. L. Rev.* 169, 247 (1968).

60. It has sometimes been asserted that one of *Reynolds*'s companion cases, Lucas v. Colorado Gen. Assembly, 377 U.S. 713 (1964), was especially wrong because the malapportionment had been approved "by a substantial majority of the voters" in a popular referendum. E.g., A. Bickel, *The Supreme Court and the Idea of Progress* 110 (1970). The argument sounds plausible at first, but is off the mark. The reasons for judicial intervention are just as compelling when, say, 65 percent of the voters vote themselves 80 percent of the effective legislative power as when the representatives of 40 percent of the voters secure for themselves 55 percent of the effective power.

61. Here too the Burger Court has backed away somewhat, indicating in Gaffney v. Cummings, 412 U.S. 735 (1973), that population deviations of less than 10 percent are acceptable. This too avoids the unadministrability thicket: it is just as mechanical as one person, one vote. "One person, one vote, give or take 10 percent," somehow doesn't *sound* like a constitutional principle, though.

62. 372 U.S. 335 (1963).

63. See A. Lewis, *Gideon's Trumpet* 123-24, 126-27 (1964).

64. 384 U.S. 436 (1966).

65. See also Monaghan, "Foreword: Constitutional Common Law," 89 *Harv. L. Rev.* 1, 20-23 (1975).

66. See generally G. Gunther, *Cases and Materials on Constitutional Law* 671-78 (9th ed. 1975).

67. Gunther, "Foreword: In Search of Evolving Doctrine on a Changing Court: A Model for a Newer Equal Protection," 86 *Harv. L. Rev.* 1 (1972).

68. E.g., Weinberger v. Wiesenfeld, 420 U.S. 636, 650 (1975); McGinnis v. Royster, 410 U.S. 263, 270 (1973); Massachusetts Bd. of Retirement v. Murgia, 427 U.S. 307, 314 (1976).

69. See, e.g., New Orleans v. Dukes, 427 U.S. 297, 304 (1976); Weinberger v. Wiesenfeld, 420 U.S. 636, 648 (1975); Trimble v. Gordon, 430 U.S. 762, 767-68 (1977); Gunther, supra note 67, at 46-47.

70. See generally 1978 *Supplement* to G. Gunther, supra note 66, at 97, 216-17.

71. The notion that the state's lawyer will hesitate to cite a purpose he or she finds embarrassingly political or archaic, see L. Tribe, supra note 15, at 1083-88, seems susceptible to the same set of objections—plus the question why the state should be penalized for entertaining a permissible but embarrassing purpose. See Linde, "Due Process of Lawmaking," 55 *Neb. L. Rev.* 197, 221 (1976).

72. If on the other hand the state attorney general is at odds with the dominant legislative majority, he or she might for that reason *refrain* from

citing a purpose that could save the legislation.

73. Compare Sturgis v. Attorney General, 358 Mass. 37 (1970), with Eisenstadt v. Baird, 405 U.S. 438 (1972). The word "usually" qualifies the claim in the text to exclude the case of the unconstitutional purpose. The purpose that fits the classification best almost always will be the one that actually inspired it. When that purpose is unconstitutional, however, far from saving the classification, it should invalidate it.

74. "Recitals of findings and purposes are the task of anonymous draftmen, committee staffs, and counsel for interested parties, not legislators. Such recitals will be an attempt to provide whatever, under prevailing case law, is expected to satisfy a court. Except for this purpose, a legislator has no reason to care about them nor to debate their truth or relevance as long as he favors the bill." Linde, supra note 71, at 231.

75. Certain requirements found in state constitutions, for instance that each statute deal with only one subject and that that subject be faithfully reflected in the statute's title, are obviously directed at least in part to the promotion of accountability. While accountability probably must in the end depend on the willingness of special interest groups and political opponents to follow the statutes closely and summarize them for the rest of us, and in that context such requirements may seem somewhat supererogatory, this may in fact represent a more helpful direction. The thought of a federal court's instituting such a requirement seems far-fetched, however.

76. See also R. Dahl, supra note 44, at 200. Although theories of democracy postulating continuous citizen participation have not recently been in vogue, but cf. C. Pateman, *Participation and Democratic Theory* (1970), there has been agreement that popular influence is felt through the periodic election of decision-makers. See, e.g., J. Schumpeter, *Capitalism, Socialism, and Democracy* 269-83 (1942).

77. The "legislative process" as used here includes the executive in his or her role as signer or vetoer of legislation.

78. The usual assumption is that whatever nondelegation doctrine is derivable from the federal Constitution is applicable only to the federal government, respecting which one can point to Article I, Section 1, which provides that "All legislative powers herein granted shall be vested in a Congress of the United States . . ." Application of the doctrine to the states would have to be textually assigned to the Republican Form of Government Clause. Insofar as the case involves a delegation to an unelected official, however, it is difficult to see why the latter clause is less germane than the former. There does not seem anything reckless in the proposition that a government is not "republican" unless the important policy issues are decided by elected officials: in fact we have seen that that is close to the term's core meaning. I am aware, however, that as a practical matter the

federal nondelegation doctrine, even assuming it were resuscitated for the federal government, is not very likely to be extended by federal courts to the states—if only because the Republican Form Clause has so long lain fallow. In fact, however, the nondelegation doctrine is significantly more alive in the states than it is at the federal level, thanks to the efforts of state courts construing provisions of the constitutions of their states.

79. M. Parenti, *Democracy for the Few* 248 (2d ed. 1977). See also, e.g., Bruff and Gellhorn, "Congressional Control of Administrative Regulation: A Study of Legislative Vetoes," 90 *Harv. L. Rev.* 1369, 1373 n.10 (1977).

80. Cutler and Johnson, "Regulation and the Political Process," 84 *Yale L. J.* 1395, 1400 (1975).

81. 122 *Cong. Rec.* H10,685 (daily ed. Sept. 21, 1976).

82. 122 *Cong. Rec.* H10,673 (daily ed. Sept. 21, 1976).

83. 293 U.S. 388 (1935).

84. 295 U.S. 495 (1935).

85. FPC v. New England Power Co., 415 U.S. 345, 352-53 (1974) (Marshall, J., concurring). But cf. National Cable Television Ass'n. v. United States, 415 U.S. 336 (1974).

86. Having the administrators issue standards to bind themselves, see, e.g., Davis, "A New Approach to Delegation," 36 *U. Chi. L. Rev.* 713 (1969), does promote regularity and fair warning, but it does little to increase the control and accountability of elected officials.

The increasingly common statutory provisions that require administrative rules to be submitted to one or both Houses of Congress (where they can be "vetoed") before taking effect obviously do increase such control and accountability. The gain, however, is hardly unalloyed. The device seems, for one thing, to be contributing still further to the inversion of the usual governmental process, in that its effect quite understandably has been to encourage still flabbier initial delegations. See, e.g., Bruff and Gellhorn, supra note 79, at 1427. More important, it provides special interest lobbies an additional confined and none-too-public arena in which to exert their force, cf. note 91 infra, by permitting them to pressure the administrators first and, if they fail there, the relevant congressional committee (and its staff) second. Thus—even leaving aside the argument that a law sufficiently directive to satisfy the nondelegation doctrine may nonetheless by its retention of a legislative veto be unconstitutional for violating the understood federal separation of powers—such laws may aggravate as much as they alleviate the problem of nondirective delegation.

87. But see T. Lowi, *The End of Liberalism* 297-98 (1969); Wright, "Beyond Discretionary Justice," 81 *Yale L. J.* 575 (1972); McGowan, "Congress, Court, and Control of Delegated Power," 77 *Colum. L. Rev.* 1119,

1127-30 (1977). That two such experienced and capable judges of the D.C. Circuit should be leading the charge — that court more than any other is involved in the review of administrative action — does much to undercut the conventional wisdom that a revival of the nondelegation ideal might be fine in theory but would be unworkable in practice.

88. E.g., Stewart, "The Reformation of American Administrative Law," 88 *Harv. L. Rev.* 1669, 1695 (1975).

89. See E. Redman, *The Dance of Legislation* 17-18 (1973).

90. Stewart, supra note 88, at 1695.

91. " '[T]aking things out of politics' [means] taking things out of popular control. This is a frequent device of special-interest groups to effect the transfer of governmental power away from the large public to the special-interest small publics." P. Appleby, *Policy and Administration* 162 (1949).

92. See also Wright, supra note 87, at 585.

93. Id.

6. Facilitating the Representation of Minorities

1. E.g., Mavrinac, "From *Lochner* to *Brown v. Topeka:* The Court and Conflicting Concepts of the Political Process," 52 *Am. Pol. Sci. Rev.* 641, 657 (1958); A. Bickel, *The Supreme Court and the Idea of Progress* 37 (1970). (Of course Professor Bickel was also critical of the Warren Court's activism in securing for minorities access to the political process.)

2. J. Pennock, *Democratic Political Theory* 8-9 (1979). See also Wellington, "On Freedom of Expression," 88 *Yale L. J.* 1105, 1137 (1979).

3. E.g., R. Dahl, *A Preface to Democratic Theory* (1956); R. Dahl, *Who Governs?* (1961). See also, e.g., A. Bickel, supra note 1, at 85.

4. See, e.g., W. Gamson, *The Strategy of Social Protest* (1975); T. Lowi, *The Politics of Disorder* (1971); P. Bachrach, *The Theory of Democratic Elitism* 83-92 (1967); E. Schattschneider, *The Semi-Sovereign People* (1960). The principal architects of the theory have begun to acknowledge its bounds, e.g., R. Dahl, *Democracy in the United States* 54 (3d ed. 1976), but much of the legal community continues to invoke it in its original unqualified form. E.g., Posner, "The *DeFunis* Case and the Constitutionality of Preferential Treatment of Racial Minorities," 1974 *Sup. Ct. Rev.* 1, 30-31; Sandalow, "Judicial Protection of Minorities," 75 *Mich. L. Rev.* 1162, 1190-91 (1977).

5. See generally Ely, "Legislative and Administrative Motivation in Constitutional Law," 79 *Yale L. J.* 1205 (1970).

6. R. Nozick, *Anarchy, State, and Utopia* 153-55 (1974).

7. Ely, supra note 5, at 1208-12.

8. Palmer v. Thompson, 403 U.S. 217, 224 (1971).

9. Village of Arlington Heights v. Metropolitan Housing Development Corp., 429 U.S. 252, 265 (1977). See also Washington v. Davis, 426 U.S. 229 (1976).

10. Such a choice violates the representative's duty to accord the entirety of his or her constituency equal concern and respect. See p. 157; Dept. of Agriculture v. Moreno, 413 U.S. 528, 534 (1973): "[A] bare congressional desire to harm a politically unpopular group cannot constitute a *legitimate* governmental interest."

11. The Court's sometime refusal to see this—while consistently (and correctly) treating explicit racial classifications that disfavor minorities as "suspect" and presumptively unconstitutional—was a case of seeing the cart and missing the horse. Racial classifications that disadvantage minorities are "suspect" because we suspect they are the product of racially prejudiced thinking of a sort we understand the Fourteenth Amendment to have been centrally concerned with eradicating. See Personnel Adm'r of Massachusetts v. Feeney, 99 S.Ct. 2282, 2292 (1979). At the same time the Court was proceeding on this theory with respect to explicit racial classifications, however, actions such as the closing of the Jackson pools, which were not racial in terms but which the complainants wanted a chance to prove to be the product of racial prejudice, were apt to be pronounced beyond constitutional condemnation.

12. Palmer v. Thompson, 403 U.S. 217, 224-25 (1971).

13. See Ely, supra note 5, at 1266-68, 1308.

14. The phrase, though not its application to this situation, is Hans Linde's. Linde, "Due Process of Lawmaking," 55 *Neb. L. Rev.* 197 (1975).

15. See generally Ely, supra note 5. Educated by a chorus of criticism, I am convinced that I overextended this point in 1970 by indicating that the possibility of alternative explanation rendered proof of illicit motivation completely irrelevant.

16. See also Christie, "A Model of Judicial Review of Legislation," 48 *S. Cal. L. Rev.* 1306, 1354 (1975). Brest, *"Palmer v. Thompson:* An Approach to the Problem of Unconstitutional Legislative Motive," 1971 *Sup. Ct. Rev.* 95, is also very helpful on this point, and in various ways has helped me correct and refine positions taken in my original article. I have also been helped by Samford, "Toward a Constitutional Definition of Racial Discrimination," 25 *Emory L. J.* 509 (1976), and Simon, "Racially Prejudiced Governmental Actions: A Motivation Theory of the Constitutional Ban against Racial Discrimination," 15 *San Diego L. Rev.* 1041 (1978).

17. The *Carolene Products* footnote's reference to "statutes directed at" religious, national, and racial minorities must have been intended to

signal motivation analysis, since it cited as examples Pierce v. Society of Sisters, 268 U.S. 510 (1925), and Meyer v. Nebraska, 262 U.S. 390 (1923), in neither of which the law in issue engaged in such classification overtly.

18. But see, e.g., Karst, "The Costs of Motive-Centered Inquiry," 15 *San Diego L. Rev.* 1163, 1165 (1978).

19. Carter v. Jury Comm'n, 396 U.S. 320, 343 (1970) (Douglas, J., dissenting in part).

20. See generally Ely, supra note 5, at 1284-89.

21. 364 U.S. 339, 347 (1960).

22. 391 U.S. 367, 384 (1968).

23. Courts have issued such orders to remedy intentional discrimination in the other direction, on the apparent theory that since race is being taken into account anyway, it should be taken into account in a way that will return the situation to what it likely would have been had race not been taken into account in the first place. See Ely, supra note 5, at 1289-91.

24. 376 U.S. 52 (1964).

25. 393 U.S. 97, 109 (1968).

26. There might be circumstances in which an unconstitutional motivation could be found to underlie the elimination of all study of human origins or even the study of biology altogether. The most obvious example would be an action taken by Arkansas authorities in response to the *Epperson* decision.

27. 393 U.S. 233, 237 (1968).

28. The effect of induction on the expression of one who opposed the war would be much the same whether he was selected at random or on the basis of some legitimate criterion on the one hand, or because of his views on the other. Of course, *announcing* that draft selections are being made on the basis of political expression would have a substantial deterrent effect on expression; such a threat (whether or not it was carried out, I should think) would violate the First Amendment by its impact alone. But we are concerned with more than this; even if the criterion is not announced, selection on the basis of political expression is obviously unconstitutional.

29. 391 U.S. at 384-85.

30. See Giragi v. Moore, 301 U.S. 670 (1937). Cf. Associated Press v. N.L.R.B., 301 U.S. 103 (1937).

31. Neither would it make sense to argue that the law's classification was irrational. It is not irrational to tax only larger businesses, and while a cutoff of 20,000 is arbitrary in a sense, any other figure would be equally so. Except maybe zero: the case might be rationalized in terms of a command that if some periodicals are taxed, all must be, presumably at a uni-

form rate geared to ability to pay. Such a broad prophylactic rule might be defended on the theory that whereas discretion to tax only those businesses whose volume exceeds a certain level is ordinarily tolerable, First Amendment freedoms are so peculiarly delicate, and the possibility of discrimination against certain ideas without effective judicial review so evident, that taxes imposed in a First Amendment area must be universal and uniform. Imposing such a rationale upon this 1936 opinion seems anachronistic, however. Its language makes clear that the Court intended to invalidate a specific tax, the Louisiana tax, and that it was doing so because of the motivation with which that tax had been enacted. It might be that Chief Justice Warren, who wrote the Court's opinion in *O'Brien*, was engaging in a bit of constructive construction, telling us that what the *Grosjean* Court *should* have meant is that the tax in question was voidable on the basis of its impact alone. But such a holding seems at least questionable: a judicial insistence that limited-circulation periodicals be taxed at the same rate as large ones seems calculated to entrench "established" ideas and viewpoints.

32. 297 U.S. 233, 250 (1936).

33. Id. at 251.

34. Record, at 43, Grosjean v. American Press Co., 297 U.S. 233 (1936).

35. Thus, for example, there must be juries, but no individual has a constitutional right to sit on one. Nor has anyone a constitutional right to have the boundaries of Tuskegee drawn to include his or her house: the point of *Gomillion* was that a nonconstitutional right had been distributed on an unconstitutional basis. No one has a substantive constitutional right to a municipal swimming pool: that is what made a reference to motivation in *Palmer* critical. Nor has anyone, to touch the other cases we have considered, a constitutional right to be taught Darwin (there may not even be a biology course), to a IV-D draft classification, or to an exemption from taxes. In each case it was the principle of selection that was constitutionally offensive.

36. Proof of an unconstitutional motivation should always suffice to invalidate a governmental action: due process of lawmaking has been denied in all such cases. What I mean by saying such proof is irrelevant in these situations is that the motivation question needn't be reached: the denial itself establishes the violation.

37. See generally Note, "Legislative Purpose, Rationality, and Equal Protection," 82 *Yale L. J.* 123 (1972).

38. Occasionally there may not be, however. Skinner v. Oklahoma, 316 U.S. 535 (1942), for one, should have been decided on this basis. Given that an admission of the real goal of the distinction in issue (a desire to punish larcenists more harshly than embezzlers) would have rendered the

law as applied to Skinner an ex post facto law (and a strongly arguable violation of the Cruel and Unusual Punishment Clause as well), the state was disabled from relying on that goal, which left the classification without another to which it related even rationally. (*Skinner* also involved a discrimination in favor of a class of criminals with whom the legislators could identify and against one with whose members they could not. The fundamental-values methodology actually employed thus seems the least desirable of several possibilities.) Considered in the context of the Court's earlier decision in Roe v. Wade, 410 U.S. 113 (1973), the case of Maher v. Roe, 432 U.S. 464 (1977), upholding the exclusion of abortions from the class of operations to which poor people are statutorily entitled to funding, is susceptible to a similar analysis. The goal in terms of which the Court upheld this legislative choice, that of discouraging abortions, is one that it had resoundingly declared unconstitutional four years earlier in *Roe*. That left only the goal of saving the taxpayers' money, to which discouraging abortions among poor people arguably does not relate even rationally. (Of course, under *Roe*, the law should have been subjected to scrutiny even stricter than this.) Cf. Linde, supra note 14, at 229 (rationality test more likely to be candidly invocable respecting acts of bodies of limited legislative jurisdiction, since many goals will be foreclosed); United States v. Brown, 381 U.S. 437 (1965) (direct or "tautological" defense uninvocable due to unconstitutionality under First Amendment; indirect or "empirical" defense to which government thus forced to resort held bill of attainder).

39. See also Simon, supra note 16.

40. On the costs of explicitness in this context, see Karst, supra note 18, at 1165.

41. Ely, "The Constitutionality of Reverse Racial Discrimination," 41 *U. Chi. L. Rev.* 723, 726 (1974).

42. Note, "Mental Illness: A Suspect Classification?" 83 *Yale L. J.* 1237, 1251 (1974).

43. P. Brest, *Processes of Constitutional Decision-Making* 489 (1975).

44. See Lee v. Washington, 390 U.S. 333, 334 (1968) (Black, Harlan, and Stewart, JJ., concurring).

45. Permanent racial segregation of the prison would not be defensible on such a theory, even though the postulated goal of maintaining racial peace would remain the same (and therefore equally weighty). But see Korematsu v. United States, 323 U.S. 214 (1944) (upholding Japanese relocation program largely by reference to undeniable importance of goal, without sufficient attention to availability of closer-fitting alternative classifications).

46. Even a law that classifies explicitly by race to the disadvantage of

a minority might on very rare occasion satisfy special scrutiny: a requirement that blacks, but not whites, contemplating marriage be tested for
sickle-cell anemia and undergo genetic counseling if they have it might be
one. See also Hamm v. Virginia Bd. of Elections, 230 F. Supp. 116 (E.D.
Va.), *aff'd per curiam sub nom* Tancil v. Woolls, 379 U.S. 19 (1964).
Where, however, the state seeks to prohibit interracial marriage and defend on the ground that it wants to contain the spread of sickle-cell anemia
—I know it sounds like something I made up, but see Brief of Appellee at
44, McLaughlin v. Florida, 379 U.S. 184 (1964)—the imposition so outweighs the harm on which the state relies that the suspicion of racially prejudiced behavior cannot be allayed. (Note also that the goal the state
argued boils down to confining the disease to the children of black cou-
ples.) A similar analysis and conclusion would be appropriate in the
hypothetical case Professor Karst raises, where the state requires a designation of race when one registers to vote and defends it on grounds of prevent-
ing fraud. Karst, " 'A Discrimination So Trivial': A Note on Law and the
Symbolism of Women's Dependency," 35 *Ohio St. L. J.* 546, 549 (1974).
(Yes, it will inevitably involve balancing, but balancing with a standard,
whether what the state is now arguing really could have been the motivation. See also Clark, "Legislative Motivation and Fundamental Rights in
Constitutional Law," 15 *San Diego L. Rev.* 953, 981 (1978).)

47. See p. 151.

48. See, e.g., Trimble v. Gordon, 430 U.S. 762, 777 (1977) (Rehnquist, J., dissenting).

49. Most dramatically, compare Boddie v. Connecticut, 401 U.S.
371 (1971), with Ortwein v. Schwab, 410 U.S. 656 (1973). But see Memorial Hosp. v. Maricopa County, 415 U.S. 250 (1974); Department of Agriculture v. Moreno, 413 U.S. 528 (1973).

50. See, e.g., James v. Valtierra, 402 U.S. 137 (1971); Dandridge v.
Williams, 397 U.S. 471 (1970). See also p. 162.

51. See Fiallo v. Bell, 430 U.S. 787 (1977); Mathews v. Lucas, 427
U.S. 495 (1976).

52. See Foley v. Connelie, 435 U.S. 291 (1978); Ambach v. Norwick,
99 S.Ct. 1589 (1979). There is a temptation to suppose that this record is
partially redeemed by the Burger Court's activity in the gender discrimination area, which has indeed been more extensive than that of any predecessor, including the Warren Court. Here too, however, the progress has been
uneven, and the fact that some of the more prominent of these cases have
invalidated laws disadvantaging *men* suggests that the Court is here animated by something other than a concern with protecting the powerless.
See Ely, "Foreword: On Discovering Fundamental Values," 92 *Harv. L.
Rev.* 5, 9 nn.29 and 30 (1978). That suspicion is underscored by the deci-

sion in *University of California Regents v. Bakke*, at least to the extent one takes seriously the indications in the various opinions that laws discriminating against whites are to be subjected, if not exactly to "special scrutiny," at least to a higher than usual standard. 438 U.S. 265, 299 (1978) (Powell, J.); id. at 361-62 (Brennan, White, Marshall and Blackmun, JJ., concurring in the judgment in part and dissenting in part).

What outlook *does* underlie the Burger Court's constitutional jurisprudence? The safest answer, and in this case probably the most accurate, is what Winston Churchill is reported to have said of a pudding someone served him: it seems to lack a theme. One can, however, identify strong elements of a value-imposition methodology. The most obvious example is the 1973 abortion decision, Roe v. Wade, 410 U.S. 113 (1973). Attempts to defend that decision in what amount to process terms have foundered, for the obvious reason that the genuine source of trouble in the abortion context is not that the issue is peculiarly unsuited to democratic decision but rather that democratic decision quite consistently generates value choices with which many of us, myself included, rather fervently disagree. See generally Ely, "The Wages of Crying Wolf: A Comment on *Roe v. Wade*," 82 *Yale L. J.* 920 (1973). This value-imposition methodology has continued as a strong element in the Burger Court's work, principally though not exclusively in the "area" of sex-marriage-childbearing-(childnonbearing)-childrearing — but see Ely, "On Discovering Fundamental Values," at 11 n.40 — complete with all the apparent inconsistency and (at least in the case of abortion) apparently political compromise to which such a "we'll protect it because it seems important" approach is unusually susceptible.

From this perspective, the current Court's activity in the area of gender discrimination becomes easier to explain. Classifications by sex seem to be treated as constitutionally suspect not on a *Carolene Products* theory, which would limit the activism to laws disadvantaging women, but rather as a perceived part of the sex-children cluster the Court has asserted as a fundamental set of values. Professor Tushnet made essentially this point in 1974 and carried it a step further, suggesting that this cluster of values, like others the Burger Court has been unusually active in protecting, is one it seems to identify with the interests of the middle class. Tushnet, " '. . . And Only Wealth Will Buy You Justice'—Some Notes on the Supreme Court. 1972 Term," 1974 *Wisc. L. Rev.* 177, 181. Surely one could cite counterexamples to the general claim, but the specific point could hardly have been more powerfully corroborated than it was by Maher v. Roe, 432 U.S. 463 (1977), holding it constitutional for states under Medicaid-type programs to pay for various operations and medical procedures, including childbirth, but refuse to pay for nontherapeutic abortions. See note 38 supra. Thus the middle class is now effectively entitled to the abortions that prior to *Roe v. Wade* only those rich enough to fly to Japan could afford, but the poor are not. No *Carolene Products* Court this.

As we have seen, the indications in *Bakke* that racial preferences disadvantaging whites are to be subjected to at least semispecial scrutiny are explicitly traceable to a value-oriented jurisprudence. Indeed there is even reason to believe that the current Court's best line of performance in *Carolene Products* terms—its protection of free expression—flows not from a *Carolene Products* perspective nor even from a Blackian respect for the document's language, but rather from a jurisprudence that defines the Court's role as one of protecting those values the Court views as truly fundamental. Speaking for a plurality and rejecting a First Amendment claim in 1976, Justice Stevens explained that "few of us would march our sons and daughters off to war to preserve the citizen's right to see 'Specified Sexual Activities' exhibited in the theaters of our choice." Young v. American Mini Theatres, Inc., 427 U.S. 50, 70 (1976). Fortunately, interests in free expression seem usually to rank more highly than this in the Court's rendition of America's constellation of values.

53. E.g., Parham v. Hughes, 99 S.Ct. 1742, 1745 (1979) (plurality opinion); Frontiero v. Richardson, 411 U.S. 677, 686 (1973) (plurality opinion).

54. See, e.g., In re Griffiths, 413 U.S. 717, 718 n.1 (1973).

55. E.g., Levy v. Louisana, 391 U.S. 68 (1968); Weber v. Aetna Casualty and Surety Co., 406 U.S. 164 (1972). It is true that in these cases the legal disability ran to the child and only the parent could remove it (by acknowledgement). However, in Glona v. American Guarantee & Liability Ins. Co., 391 U.S. 73 (1968), the disability ran to the parent (who could have removed it).

56. E.g., Frontiero v. Richardson, 411 U.S. 677, 686 (1973) (plurality opinion); Sail'er Inn, Inc. v. Kirby, 5 Cal.3d 1, 18 (1971); O'Fallon, "Adjudication and Contested Concepts: The Case of Equal Protection," 54 *N.Y. U. L. Rev.* 19, 62 (1979).

57. "Developments in the Law—Equal Protection" 82 *Harv. L. Rev.* 1065, 1127 (1969). See also, e.g., Sail'er Inn, Inc. v. Kirby, 5 Cal.3d 1, 19 (1971).

58. The reference to stigma is generally invoked as a way of distinguishing affirmative action programs from discrimination against minorities. However, such programs are distinguishable in terms of the factors that appropriately serve to make classifications suspect, without necessary reference to stigma. See pp. 170-72.

59. Graham v. Richardson, 403 U.S. 365, 372 (1971).

60. Sugarman v. Dougall, 413 U.S. 634, 657 (1973) (dissenting opinion). See also, e.g., Braden, "The Search for Objectivity in Constitu-

tional Law," 57 *Yale L. J.* 571, 581 (1948).

61. Goodman, "De Facto School Segregation: A Constitutional and Empirical Analysis," 60 *Calif. L. Rev.* 275, 313 (1972).

62. But cf. pp. 160-161.

63. Goodman, supra note 61, at 315.

64. Two factors often mentioned to account for the special scrutiny accorded racial classifications are that racial minorities have been subjected to legal disadvantage throughout our history, e.g., Frontiero v. Richardson, 411 U.S. 677, 684 (1973) (plurality opinion), and that race is "generally . . . irrelevant to any legitimate public purpose." "Developments in the Law," supra note 57, at 1108; see also Frontiero v. Richardson, 411 U.S. 677, 686 (1973) (plurality opinion). Neither factor alone can adequately account for extraordinary scrutiny. Some minorities (extortionists, for example) have been repeatedly disadvantaged by the law with good reason. And the fact that a characteristic is irrelevant in almost all legal contexts (as most characteristics are) need not imply that there is anything wrong in seizing upon it in the rare context where it does make a difference. Still, these two factors in combination can add up to something significant. The fact that a group has repeatedly been disadvantaged in ways that no one could convincingly defend should make us suspicious of any legislation that singles out that group for disadvantage. There is reason to suspect that the prejudices that generated the flagrantly hostile legislation of past eras are also largely responsible for the facially more palatable classifications of the present day.

65. At first blush a statute providing that anyone who has been convicted of burglary cannot ever be licensed to practice medicine seems to present a very different question. The fit between the classification and the goal, say, of assuring competence or trustworthiness is obviously a good deal looser than refining the classification (to exclude some burglars and include some nonburglars) could make it. The problem is that the fit, again, is very close with the goal of discouraging burglaries. (The party in question may be fully reformed, but it will help deter others to know that convicted burglars remain forever subject to this additional deprivation.) If, therefore, the additional sanction of never being able to become a licensed doctor were imposed prospectively, as part of the penalty prescribed (along with a prison term), we would rightly object on grounds of unenlightened penology, but it would be hard to make out a plausible case of unconstitutionality. Enacting such an employment bar for those convicted earlier seems different, though. For the fit is perfect, and thus "special scrutiny" is satisfied, only in terms of a goal whose invocation seems to violate the prohibition against ex post facto laws. (In fact the Court probably would not so hold, on the theory that this additional sanction does not qualify as a "penalty," but that, I would argue, is a misconstruction of the

Ex Post Facto Clause. See Ely, supra note 5, at 1312 n.324.)

66. E.g., Regents of the University of California v. Bakke, 438 U.S. 265, 404 (1978) (Blackmun, J.).

67. *Webster's New World Dictionary of the American Language* 1396-97 (2d College ed. 1976).

68. Williamson v. Lee Optical Co., 348 U.S. 483 (1955).

69. This baseline "rationality" test is one it is difficult to defend in theory—not because legislatures are inevitably irrational, e.g., Dixon, "The Supreme Court and Equality: Legislative Classifications, Desegregation, and Reverse Discrimination," 62 *Corn. L. Rev.* 494, 497, 500 (1977), but for the quite opposite reason that if all the legislative cross-purposes are sensitively taken into account the classification in issue is bound to relate at least "rationally" (in fact quite closely) to them. Legislatures do not act for no reason (though they sometimes do act for unconstitutional reasons). See generally Note, supra note 37. In addition, it has been the point of this book that unless there is special reason to distrust the democratic process in a given case, substantive review of its output, no matter how "weak," is not justified. See also Linde, "Without 'Due Process': Unconstitutional Law in Oregon," 49 *Ore. L. Rev.* 125 (1970); Loewy, "A Different and More Viable Theory of Equal Protection," 57 *N.C. L. Rev.* 1, 50-51 (1978).

We have seen, however, that like its stronger sibling "special scrutiny" (though not nearly so often), a "rationality" test can serve as an indirect way of voiding government acts for unconstitutional motivation. Note 38 supra. Where there exists no licit purpose to which the classification in issue relates even rationally, however, a direct inference of unconstitutional motivation will probably be virtually inevitable: retention of the rationality test is thus difficult to justify as an important fact-finding tool. It is arguable, however, that it should be retained for its utility in permitting courts (and complainants) to void (and attack) certain laws for unconstitutional motivation without actually having to put it in those terms—an advantage I had tended to shrug off until the appearance of Professor Karst's sensitive discussion of the costs of an overtly motivation-centered inquiry. Karst, supra note 18. This doesn't seem sufficient, however. Cases in which the rationality test is likely to provide a politic way of getting at unconstitutional motivation are also likely, though it is not inevitable, to be cases in which the classification in question is sufficiently suspicious to justify special scrutiny. The gains in terms of flushing out unconstitutional motives thus seem quite speculative, and against them must be measured the realization that to arm the judiciary with a universal warrant to review for "rationality," a term whose meaning is obviously elastic, is unavoidably to tempt judges to exercise a general and illegitimate substantive review authority.

To the extent that Professor Gunther's "articulated purpose" requirement can be made to work, it would seem that a rationality test would be that much more useful. Cf. note 38 supra. Beyond the fact that I'm not convinced the approach can work, however, it would seem that to the extent that one is serious about requiring only a rational relationship, there will very likely be one or more articulated purposes that can serve to uphold the law.

I suppose there is little chance that the rationality test in fact will be abandoned, however, so the best hope may be that courts will understand that it is defensible only as a roundabout way of getting at illicit legislative ends.

70. An approach that needn't detain us even as long as this is one geared to whether the stereotype in question is "true" or "false." E.g., Alexander, "Introduction: Motivation and Constitutionality," 15 *San Diego L. Rev.* 925, 944 (1978); Clark, supra note 46, at 967. Stereotypes are not true or false (save only, I suppose, in the unlikely event that *no* member of the class in question possesses the attributed characteristic), but rather are distinguished by their relative incidence of counterexample.

71. See also P. Brest, supra note 43, at 1010.

72. A remand for reconsideration by the same tribunal is a questionable remedy where it appears that the conditions giving rise to the original misapprehension are likely to persist. I shall give the remedies question separate attention once I have clarified the various likely sources of misapprehension.

73. A similar distinction is drawn in G. Allport, *The Nature of Prejudice* 78 (1954).

74. Mathews v. Lucas, 427 U.S. 495, 520 (1976) (Stevens, J., dissenting).

75. To the extent that the makeup of the electorate is essentially that of the legislature (as is likely save as to gender), self-flattering generalizations may generate more tangible rewards at election time.

Statutes are imaginable that appear to involve a psychic loss but a tangible gain to those making the decision. Under the analysis suggested here, either sort of gain should suffice to make the statute at least initially suspect. At that point the question becomes whether the suspicion thus generated can be allayed by a convincing benign explanation. An explanation in terms of the law's self-denigrating features will sometimes be sufficient to allay such suspicions, though sometimes it will not. A defense of a law limiting the admission of Jews to the state university, for example, should not be salvageable on the theory that it rests on the self-denigrating generalization that Jews are better students and thus if we make admissions decisions on their individual merits there will be insufficient diversity in the student body. In that case the tangible gain to the legislatively dominant group speaks much louder to the ultimate issue of motivation than this self-denigrating rationalization.

Laws of the opposite configuration are also possible. Assuming for now that discrimination against women should be treated as suspicious, cf. pp. 164-170, a law drafting men but not women for military service should be treated as initially suspicious since it incorporates the self-flattering generalization that men are physically tougher than women. However, it seems to me that the suspicion thus generated is almost immediately allayed by the fact that in tangible terms the law is one whose comparative disadvantaging of men is massive. A law exempting women from the possibility of being ordered to pay alimony seems, if anything, even more clearly constitutional. (Given the usual assumption of the literature that a law's constitutionality is inextricably bound up with its merits, an assumption I reject, it may be well to note explicitly that I'm opposed to both these distinctions. I think women should be drafted if anyone is, and I think under appropriate financial circumstances they should be as liable as men to an alimony order. I just don't think either distinction is unconstitutional.) The fact that such an alimony law, unlike the draft law and many others that comparatively disadvantage males, is one that is personally threatening to the legislators themselves powerfully underscores its nonsuspicious nature. (In addition, the generalization in which it is rooted — that our male-dominated society has made it harder for middle-aged women than for middle-aged men to make their own way financially — is hardly a generalization that is flattering to men.) The Supreme Court, of course, has gone the other way on the alimony law. Orr v. Orr, 99 S.Ct. 1102 (1979). In general I'm tempted to suppose that the tangible effects of a distinction, being the harder datum, will ordinarily "trump" any psychic effects running in the other direction. But that too may be an overgeneralization.

76. The landmark work here is William Graham Sumner's *Folkways*, originally published in 1906. See, e.g., id. at 14-15: "The Jews divided all mankind into themselves and Gentiles. They were the 'chosen people.' The Greeks and Romans called all outsiders 'barbarians.' In Euripedes' tragedy of *Iphigenia in Aulis* Iphigenia says that it is fitting that Greeks should rule over barbarians, but not contrariwise, because Greeks are free, and barbarians are slaves. The Arabs regarded themselves as the noblest nation and all others as more or less barbarous. In 1896, the Chinese minister of education and his counselors edited a manual in which this statement occurs: 'How grand and glorious is the Empire of China, the middle kingdom! She is the largest and richest in the world. The grandest men in the world have all come from the middle empire.' In all the literature of all the states equivalent statements occur, although they are not so naively expressed. In Russian books and newspapers the civilizing mission

of Russia is talked about, just as, in the books and journals of France, Germany, and the United States, the civilizing mission of those countries is assumed and referred to as well understood. Each state now regards itself as the leader of civilization, the best, the freest, and the wisest, and all others as inferior. Within a few years our own man-on-the-curbstone has learned to class all foreigners of the Latin peoples as 'dagos,' and 'dago' has become an epithet of contempt. These are all cases of ethnocentrism." Sumner has been criticized by Robert Merton for insufficient recognition of the fact that "out-groups" can sometimes be the object of positive reference. R. Merton, *Social Theory and Social Structure* 331, 352 (3d ed. 1968). That is true, but surely the less common case. Moreover, there will in such cases exist strong pressures toward explicit recognition of the fact that the superiority of the "out-group" is statistical only and a consequent tendency to eschew irrebuttable legal presumption in favor of a more individualized test. Finally, what is of greatest relevance to the subject of suspect statutory classification is the tendency of those groups which are dominant in a society to rationalize their dominance by self-flattering generalizations, a tendency I do not understand Merton to question.

77. G. Allport, supra note 73, at 372.

78. See also, e.g., id. at 42, 121, 134, 153, 319-20, 390-91; Bettelheim, "The Dynamism of Anti-Semitism in Gentile and Jew," 42 *J. Abnormal and Social Psych.* 153 (1947).

79. "Seven-year-old children in one town were asked, 'Which are better, the children in this town or in Smithfield (a neighboring town)?' Almost all replied, 'The children in this town' . . . What is alien is regarded as somehow inferior, less 'good,' but there is not necessarily hostility in it." G. Allport, supra note 73, at 42.

80. Fredrickson, "The Legacy of Malthus," *New York Times Book Review*, March 13, 1977, p. 7.

81. Should such a generalization be employed as the basis of a law *favoring* the minority in question—say, giving Jews a boost on college admissions on the theory that the best students will put their education to better use—that would not be a proper object of constitutional concern. There exist political safeguards sufficient to guard against a dominant majority's improvidently accepting an exaggeratedly self-deprecating generalization and proceeding to disadvantage itself on the basis thereof (which, I need hardly add, is precisely the reason such a law wouldn't be passed). Much more likely is an attempt to use such a generalization to rationalize a law putting a *ceiling* on the percentage of Jewish students admitted, on the theory that if we went by test scores alone the colleges would be inundated with Jews. Despite the attempt to dress it up in a self-deprecating (and therefore presumptively trustworthy) generalization, this law

would plainly be unconstitutional, imbued as it so obviously is with first-degree anti-Semitism.

The special case of the nondominant group that adopts the dominant group's self-favoring generalization is one I shall take up later.

82. See Massachusetts Bd. of Retirement v. Murgia, 427 U.S. 307, 313-14 (1976).

83. On the other hand an attitude of "I had it rough—it made me what I am—so why shouldn't you?" is one we all have seen, and people often neglect the *future* until it is upon them. This isn't likely to matter greatly on the "youth" end, since in most of the cases it will be clear that some sort of requirement of maturity is appropriate, and that seems to be something that cannot sensibly or safely be measured by anything other than an arbitrary cut-off. See note 43 to Chapter 5.

84. Recall that Justice Stone's formulation included both prejudice, and discreteness and insularity. See also Note, supra note 42, at 1254-58. I have earlier criticized this refinement, essentially on the ground that it complicates the analysis. Ely, supra note 41, at 734-35 n.45. It does, but nonetheless it seems appropriate. I hereby confess error.

85. Cf. Simon, supra note 16, at 1051 n.23; G. Allport, supra note 73, at 263.

86. See id. at 172-73, 226, ch. 16; G. Murphy, L. Murphy, and T. Newcomb, *Experimental Social Psychology* (1937).

87. E.g., G. Allport, supra note 73, at 35, 346-47; Ambach v. Norwick, 99 S.Ct. 1589, 1597 (1979) (Blackmun, J., dissenting): "These New York statutes, for the most part, have their origin in the frantic and overreactive days of the first World War when attitudes of parochialism and fear of the foreigner were the order of the day."

88. James v. Valtierra, 402 U.S. 137 (1971).

89. See also Simon, supra note 16, at 1112, 1126-27.

90. 163 U.S. 537 (1896).

91. This situation seems to be changing, precisely because gays are increasingly willing to bear the brunt of our prejudices in the short run in order to diminish them in the long run. I'll be delighted if this book remains in print long enough to render this discussion obsolete.

92. This means that laws denying homosexuals certain benefits, most likely occupational opportunities, must be defended in terms of a virtually perfect fit with a legitimate and substantial goal. This will seldom, if ever, be possible. A law making a crime of a defined homosexual act—assuming away vagueness problems, which in fact most such laws suffer from—presents a difficult question. The Supreme Court seems to disagree, Doe v. Commonwealth's Attorney, 425 U.S. 901 (1976), but certain commentators would doubtless argue that such a law violates some constitu-

tionally unstated fundamental right. My opinion of that line of argument has been rendered clear. (This does not excuse the Court's failure to attempt a reconciliation of *Doe* with its abortion decisions, though.) Neither is there anything unconstitutional about outlawing an act due to a bona fide feeling that it is immoral: most criminal statutes are that at least in part. (Attempting to preclude the entire population from acting in ways that are perceived as immoral is not assimilable to comparatively disadvantaging a given group out of simple hostility to its members. But see O'Fallon, supra note 56, at 71-75. In raising my children not to act in ways I think are immoral, even punishing them when they do, I may incur the condemnation of some, but the sin is paternalism or some such, hardly that of leaving my children's interests out of account or valuing them negatively.) This doesn't mean that simply by incanting "immorality" a state can be permitted successfully to defend a law that in fact was motivated by a desire simply to injure a disfavored group of persons. The legislature couldn't, for example, outlaw the wearing of yarmulkes or dashikis and defend on the ground that it regards such conduct as immoral. The question here thus reduces to whether the claim is credible that the prohibition in question was generated by a sincerely held moral objection to the act (or anything else that transcends a simple desire to injure the parties involved). It is tempting for those of us who oppose laws outlawing homosexual acts to try to parlay a negative answer out of the fact that, at least in the case of consenting adults, no one seems to be hurt in any tangible way, but on honest reflection that comes across as cheating.

93. Societal prejudice against "illegitimates" also acts to thwart correction by keeping the people concerned "in the closet." It can at least be argued, however, that where the legislature has extended the right at issue (to wrongful death benefits, intestate succession, or whatever) to illegitimate children whom the father has acknowledged—and surely by thus assuming a duty to support the father does signal some feeling of closeness to the child—it has made the "fit" about as close as it can. No one could say it is perfect, particularly as the scheme is applied to subcultures where going into a government building to acknowledge a child is a step not lightly undertaken, but it's at least an effort in some "objective" way to approximate the father's likely feelings of affection and responsibility—enough of an effort, I am inclined to believe, to negate whatever inference of prejudiced behavior might otherwise be suggested by the terms of the law. It is at least a coherent view of this line of cases, therefore, that prior to Trimble v. Gordon, 430 U.S. 762 (1977), the Court had things upside down, striking down various statutory schemes that left the escape hatch of acknowledgement open but—in Labine v. Vincent, 401 U.S. 532 (1971)—upholding one that didn't. Compare Parham v. Hughes, 99 S.Ct. 1742 (1979), with Caban v. Mohammed, 99 S.Ct. 1760 (1979).

94. "Some of my best friends are Negro" got to be a parody of white hypocrisy, but *the* best friend of most men really is a woman, which eliminates the real hostility and fear that persists among the races. It is also instructive to contrast white resistance, often literally murderous, to the enforcement of the Fifteenth Amendment with the uneventful enforcement of the Nineteenth Amendment, which obviously had to be fought for but once ratified was accepted with apparent good grace. See also Wasserstrom, "Racism, Sexism, and Preferential Treatment: An Approach to the Topics," 24 *U.C.L.A. L. Rev.* 581, 589 (1977).

95. See J. Pole, *The Pursuit of Equality in American History* 320, 322 (1978).

96. 430 U.S. 483, 503 (1977) (Marshall, J., concurring), citing G. Allport, supra note 73, at 150-53; A. Rose, *The Negro's Morale* 85-96 (1949); G. Simpson and J. Yinger, *Racial and Cultural Minorities* 192-95, 227, 295 (4th ed. 1972); Bettelheim, "Individual and Mass Behavior in Extreme Situations," 38 *J. Abnormal and Social Psych.* 417 (1943). See also L. Tribe, *American Constitutional Law* 1044 n.12 (1978); Simon, supra note 16, at 1079 n.87; G. Allport, supra, at 142 ("One's reputation, whether false or true, cannot be hammered, hammered, hammered, into one's head without doing something to one's character"), 159-60; Brown v. Board of Education, 347 U.S. 483, 494 (1954): "To separate them from others of similar age and qualifications solely because of their race generates a feeling of inferiority as to their status in the community that may affect their hearts and minds in a way unlikely ever to be undone."

97. See A. de Tocqueville, *Democracy in America* 319 (Anchor ed. 1959).

98. E.g., Schlesinger v. Ballard, 419 U.S. 498, 508 (1975).

99. See, e.g., pp. 105-06.

100. Cf. Bickel and Wellington, "Legislative Purpose and the Judicial Process: The Lincoln Mills Case," 71 *Harv. L. Rev.* 1 (1957).

101. Although more men than women appear to favor the Equal Rights Amendment, a majority of each appears to (albeit apparently a majority insufficient to assure ratification).

102. The frequently articulated position that "I don't mind blackness being a factor—I just don't want it to be the only factor" is gibberish. No one has ever suggested that, say, medical students be selected simply on the basis of race without considering other factors. On the other hand any affirmative action plan that counts blackness affirmatively, even in the context of numerous other factors, necessarily results in the rejection of some applicants who would not be rejected were they black, and in that sense are being turned away "only" because they are not black.

103. Ely, "Foreword: On Discovering Fundamental Values," 92 *Harv. L. Rev.* 5, 9-10 n.33 (1978).

104. Of course it is a separate question whether various affirmative action programs violate the 1964 Civil Rights Act or other legislation. Cf. United Steelworkers of America v. Weber, 99 S.Ct. 2721 (1979).

105. Justice Powell's *Bakke* opinion made a good deal of the fact that the white majority comprises a number of white ethnic groups, each by itself constituting a minority of our entire population. See, e.g., 438 U.S. at 295-97. See also Sandalow, "Racial Preferences in Higher Education: Political Responsibility and the Judicial Role," 42 *U. Chi. L. Rev.* 653, 694 (1975). That is true, but the Court historically has recognized that often these various white ethnic groups will choose to ignore their differences and act as a monolith, classifying so as to place whites on one side of a legal line and one or more nonwhite groups on the other. Most often they have chosen comparatively to *advantage* themselves (and in such situations the observation that the "white majority" is really a collection of minorities would strike us as zany, at any rate beside any pertinent point). In the *Bakke* situation, however, those of us who define ourselves as white have chosen to ignore whatever differences exist among us, and to disadvantage white persons generally in order comparatively to advantage certain nonwhite minorities we feel have been treated unjustly in the past. See also note 109 infra.

106. See generally Chapter 4. See also Railway Express Agency, Inc. v. New York, 336 U.S. 106, 112-13 (1949) (Jackson, J., concurring); F. Hayek, *The Constitution of Liberty* 210 (1960).

107. It is unlikely that the positions of the decision-makers themselves will be threatened by the affirmative action program they are enacting. See Greenawalt, "Judicial Scrutiny of 'Benign' Racial Preference in Law School Admissions," 75 *Colum. L. Rev.* 559, 573-74 (1975). But of course such persons are not characteristically threatened personally by any legislation or policy they enact. We generally treat classifications as unsuspicious unless there is reason to do otherwise, and what is critical here is that the factors that appropriately give rise to suspicion are absent. It *is* troubling, however, that decisions of this sort are often actually made by faculties, which are comparatively isolated from political pressures. See id.; Sandalow, supra note 105, at 695-96. Even assuming an unwillingness to resuscitate the nondelegation doctrine, courts should exert pressure to assure that affirmative action plans are described candidly, so that political officials at least can make an informed choice whether to intervene. Obfuscation in this area is common.

108. Ely, supra note 41. See also Ely, supra note 103, at 9-10, 12-14, 40-42.

109. Of course, if about 40 percent of the white students are Jewish it would follow (and it had *better* follow if the plan is to remain constitution-

ally unsuspicious) that about 40 percent of the white students turned away as the result of an affirmative action program would be Jewish. In such a case Jews would make up a substantially higher percentage of the group injured by the program than they do of the population in general. That's an inflammatory statistic until one realizes that the reason is that they make up a disproportionately large percentage of those admitted. White Jewish admissions may be cut from forty to thirty-six, but white "Gentile" admissions will be comparably cut from sixty to fifty-four, a pattern that disadvantages whites generally but does not in any sense I can understand disadvantage Jews relative to other whites.

If the idea is that the white Gentiles on the faculty will somehow identify more closely with blacks than with Jews and thus be acting in a sort of self-interest when they "trade in" four Jews for ten blacks ("unfortunately" sacrificing six who are even more clearly "their own" in the process), it is nonsense. Even leaving out of account the likely presence of what is often a substantial Jewish representation on university and professional school faculties, the argument plainly misdescribes the white Gentile faculty members' probable feelings of relative identification. Most white Gentile faculty members spring from upper-middle-class Protestant roots, most often Episcopalian or Calvinist (Presbyterian-Congregationalist), and thus more than the general range of Gentiles share with their Jewish colleagues a good deal by way of background and outlook. Lipset and Ladd, "The Changing Social Origins of American Academics," in *Qualitative and Quantitative Social Research* 319 (R. Merton, J. Coleman, and P. Rossi eds. 1979). (These are stereotypes, of course, but I'm answering an argument rooted in stereotypes.) And even if that connection is attenuated, as it surely is to a degree by anti-Semitism, those particular Gentile subgroups (like Jews) are likely to make up a disproportionately high percentage of the white student body and consequently will also suffer "disproportionately" by the institution of an affirmative action program. (Jews constitute about 2 percent of our population and Episcopalians about 3 percent. Roughly 59 percent of adult American Jews have attended college; for Episcopalians the figure is 58 percent. For Presbyterians, about 5 percent of the population, it is 50 percent. It is 21 percent for the largest Protestant sect, the Baptists, who also make up 21 percent of the nation's population. See generally *Public Opinion*, November/December 1978, at 33-34.) The reason no one screams about the "disproportionate" effect of affirmative action programs on Episcopalians and Calvinists is that we know those groups are well represented on faculties (and elsewhere). (Jews, Calvinists, and Episcopalians make up about a third of our faculties nationwide, although they are only about 10 percent of the nation's population. At "high prestige" universities the "overrepresentation" of all three groups is substantially more striking.

Lipset and Ladd, supra.) But given the requirement that the hurt run undifferentiatedly against the white applicant pool, upper-middle-class Protestant faculty members — assuming they are thinking in such subgroup terms, which I doubt but which the argument I am answering assumes — are necessarily providing *other* groups that will suffer disproportionately (such as Jews) with a sort of "virtual representation" (to add to whatever actual representation on the faculty they also have).

110. Justice Powell's observation that the white majority is composed of minorities may not have been relevant to the case before him, but it should have reined his effusive praise for the "Harvard plan," in particular that feature of it that proclaims: "A farm boy from Idaho can bring something to Harvard College that a Bostonian cannot offer. Similarly, a black student can usually bring something that a white person cannot offer." Quoted, 438 U.S. at 613. That one-two punch is deadly — deadly to whites from the urban northeast and thus deadly to Jews and certain other white ethnic subgroups. Whatever the origins of geographical preferences — and I doubt they're very pretty, at least at schools that need not worry about maintaining a "national" image — it seems unfortunate that Powell went out of his way to praise, and thus induce schools to move toward, a plan whose effect will be to guarantee the admission of an inordinately low percentage of white northeasterners.

111. For some reason arrests have been exempted from this requirement.

112. See Goldberg and Dershowitz, "Declaring the Death Penalty Unconstitutional," 83 *Harv. L. Rev.* 1773, 1789 (1970).

113. 408 U.S. 238, 253 (1972) (Douglas, J., concurring).

114. See sources cited Goldberg and Dershowitz, supra note 112, at 1792-93; Polsby, "The Death of Capital Punishment? *Furman v. Georgia*," 1972 *Sup. Ct. Rev.* 1, 29 n.97.

115. See id. at 29.

116. 408 U.S. at 256-57 (Douglas, J., concurring).

117. Gregg v. Georgia, 428 U.S. 153 (1976); Woodson v. North Carolina, 428 U.S. 280 (1976); Roberts v. Louisiana, 428 U.S. 325 (1976).

118. 438 U.S. 586 (1978).

119. 428 U.S. at 303 (plurality opinion).

120. See also C. Black, *Capital Punishment: The Inevitability of Caprice and Mistake* ch. 7 (1974) (analyzing Texas's statutory scheme).

121. See Gregg v. Georgia, 428 U.S. 153, 165-66 n.9 (1976); Coker v. Georgia, 433 U.S. 584, 590-91 (1977). The death sentence in *Coker* was reversed, since it was imposed for the crime of rape, but the Georgia sentencing criteria, upheld as applied to murder convictions in *Gregg*, were not disapproved in the later case.

122. 428 U.S. at 206-07.

123. C. Black, supra note 120.

124. 408 U.S. at 251-52 (Douglas, J., concurring). See also sources cited id. at 249-52.

125. In one sense a prison term, once served, is as "irreversible" as a death sentence, but at least once begun it can be reconsidered and reduced.

126. See Shapiro v. Thompson, 394 U.S. 618, 630 (1969); United States v. Guest, 383 U.S. 745, 757-58 (1966). Cf. Edwards v. California, 314 U.S. 160 (1941).

127. 6 Wall. 35, 44 (1868). The Court also noted the federal government's need to be able to move its officials and employees freely. Id. at 43-44.

128. See, e.g., L. Hartz, *The Liberal Tradition in America* 64-65 (1955).

129. Nelson, "The Eighteenth-Century Background of John Marshall's Constitutional Jurisprudence," 76 *Mich. L. Rev.* 893, 921 (1978). See also, e.g., Madison's "Memorial and Remonstrance against Religious Assessments" ¶10, quoted in Everson v. Board of Education, 330 U.S. 1, 69 (1947) (appendix to opinion of Rutledge, J., dissenting).

130. See, e.g., F. Turner, *The Frontier in American History* 38 (1920).

131. See generally A. Hirschman, *Exit, Voice and Loyalty* (1970).

132. This altered rationale obviously also supports a right to emigrate from the United States altogether.

Conclusion

1. Perry, "The Abortion Funding Cases: A Comment on the Supreme Court's Role in American Government," 66 *Geo. L. J.* 1191, 1216 (1978).

2. Wellington, "Common Law Rules and Constitutional Double Standards: Some Notes on Adjudication," 83 *Yale L. J.* 221, 304-05 (1973).

Index